AFRICAN STUDIES
HISTORY, POLITICS, ECONOMICS, AND CULTURE

Edited by
Molefi Asante
Temple University

A ROUTLEDGE SERIES

AFRICAN STUDIES
HISTORY, POLITICS, ECONOMICS, AND CULTURE
MOLEFI ASANTE, *General Editor*

A ROADMAP FOR UNDERSTANDING AFRICAN POLITICS

Leadership and Political Integration in Nigeria

Victor Oguejiofor Okafor

Routledge
New York & London

Routledge
Taylor & Francis Group
270 Madison Avenue
New York, NY 10016

Routledge
Taylor & Francis Group
2 Park Square
Milton Park, Abingdon
Oxon OX14 4RN

Transferred to Digital Printing 2008

International Standard Book Number-10: 0-415-98106-9 (Hardcover)
International Standard Book Number-13: 978-0-415-98106-4 (Hardcover)

Library of Congress Cataloging-in-Publication Data

Okafor, Victor Oguejiofor.
    A roadmap for understanding African politics : leadership and
political integration in Nigeria / by Victor Oguejiofor Okafor.
       p. cm. -- (African studies)
    Includes bibliographical references and index.
    ISBN 0-415-98106-9 (alk. paper)
    1. Nigeria--Politics and government--20th century. 2. Political
leadership--Nigeria--History--20th century. I. Title. II. Series:
African studies (Routledge (Firm))

JQ3096.O446 2006
320.9669--dc22

           2006013367

Visit the Taylor & Francis Web site at
http://www.taylorandfrancis.com

and the Routledge Web site at
http://www.routledge-ny.com

This work is dedicated to my parents, Ugochukwutubelu Chukwuma Okafor and Mrs. Grace Ifeoma Okafor (nee Okagbue).

Contents

List of Figures and Tables

FIGURES

TABLES

Preface

My book, *A Roadmap for Understanding African Politics: Leadership and Political Integration in Nigeria* examines the impact of post-colonial political leadership on political integration in Nigeria. Although the work focuses on Nigeria—a country that is regarded as a micro-cosm of Africa because of its immense size and diversity—its literature review is continental in scope, and its analysis includes a discussion of the implications of the study for leadership and political integration in Africa in general.

The book is enriched by my firsthand experience of Nigerian politics as a political reporter and editor for the Federal Radio Corporation of Nigeria (FRCN), which encompasses my coverage of a Nigerian presidential candidate and my coverage of the proceedings of Nigeria's House of Representatives during Nigeria's Second Republic.[1] This book also benefits from my several years of researching and teaching in the field of Black Studies in the United States. It's informed by my interdisciplinary education, which encompasses a Ph.d. in African American Studies (Temple University, 1994), a Master's degree in Public Affairs (Indiana University, 1988), and a Bachelor's degree in Journalism with a Minor in Business (Indiana University, 1986).

The book comes at a most auspicious time indeed—a time that the world is watching to see whether Nigeria will succeed in its current third experiment with representative democracy, which was launched in 1999. The book is set to help students, policy makers and observers of Nigerian politics and African politics in general to achieve an in-depth understanding of the historical and contemporary forces that shape the ebb and flow of Nigeria's national politics. With this book in hand, students and policy makers, as well as observers, will be equipped with a tool for making sense of the twists and turns of Nigeria's turbulent political environment.

After reviewing, briefly, Nigeria's pre-colonial and colonial political histories, the book discusses how those histories, along with contemporary external forces like neo-colonialism, as well as internal social, economic and political structures and developments, have affected emerging post-independence politics in that country. The book demonstrates how this constellation of variables influenced the course of political leadership and political integration in this most-populous African nation of more than one hundred and thirty million people.

The study climaxes with an Afrocentric/Africa-centered theory of political and integrative leadership and then uses it as a prism for analyzing six Nigerian post-independence political leaderships, encompassing Nigeria's First and Second Republics, along with their military interregna. The work concludes that, to varying degrees, those leaderships fell short of the expectations of the Afrocentric/Africa-centered theory. However, the study finds, among others, that the leadership of Murtala Muhammed (July 1975–February 1976) came closest to satisfying the constructs of the theory.

Chapter One
Introduction

Leadership takes place at various levels and units of human existence, rang-
ing from a small group of individuals like a family or a class to a nation or
even a group of sovereign nations such as the United Nations. Leadership
also occurs in various spheres of life; it could be the social, cultural, economic or political domain. Chinua Achebe observes that leaders are role
models whose behavior and mannerisms are emulated by others. This is
why, he points out, leaders must be self-disciplined, for if they are not, their
indiscipline would exert a ripple effect on their followers.[1]

Despite the significant role of political leadership in the fortunes of
human societies, students of politics have tended to de-emphasize leadership as a major focus of academic study because of the belief that leaders
are not free agents, but subject to sociopolitical and economic forces as well
as institutions that determine the political course of events.[2] Yes, political
leaders are constrained by their sociopolitical, economic forces and institutions; but the true leader is one who can adjust the course of events. Otherwise known as transforming leaders, they are visionaries who take definite
measures to implement their visions of society. Other kinds of leaders, better known as the transactional, are merely content to maintain society as
it is—to transact business as usual. They are simply determined to keep
things going.[3] "Change" is not a key concept on their agenda.

Political leadership is merely one of various kinds of leadership, and
it relates to the conduct of governmental affairs. Thus, political leadership
is broader than any other form of leadership. Political leadership is wielded
over a variety of subject-matters.[4] Jean Blondel defines national political
leadership as "the power exercised by one or a few individuals to direct
members of the nation towards action."[5] While this power can be used to
control, dominate and subjugate, it can also be used to uplift, improve and
develop.[6] Given this critical potential of political leadership, it deserves to

be treated as a vital field of academic enquiry. Blondel sheds some insight on this point: "If leadership is to be harnessed for the common good and for development, . . . then it is imperative to study leadership in its generality; and it is essential to assess how far, and under what conditions, leadership is likely to be good."[7]

Notice the reference to 'conditions' for good leadership. This is a critical point, for the environment in which a political leadership operates is a significant factor, just as the "qualities" of the leader himself or herself. Major factors that affect the ability of leaders to provide effective leadership include: (1) the personality or personal sources of the power that leaders exercise; (2) the institutional instruments that aid or restrain leaders, (3) the actions of the leaders, and (4) the environment in which these actions occur.[8] Indeed, an effective means of assessing the real strength of leaders is by studying the environment in which they operated. How did they resolve the problems that they were confronted with? Did they allow themselves to become slaves of their environment? Blondel regrets that such questions have been the least examined aspect of leadership partly because they are methodologically difficult to tackle.[9]

One of the pitfalls of most studies of political leadership is their preoccupation with classifications—with dichotomies and trichotomies which create categories such as liberal vs. authoritarian leaders, democratic vs. autocratic leaders, etc. as if to say that these boundaries do not criss-cross.[10] As Blondel observes, the realities of political leadership are much more complex, and a given political leadership can exhibit liberal and authoritarian traits.[11] Hence, he urges scholars of political leadership to move away from their pre-occupation with dichotomies and trichotomies and instead to explore and establish models and methodological techniques that could provide a more realistic picture of the contours of political leadership.[12]

This book examines post-independence political leadership in Nigeria with a focus upon six political leaders, encompassing the First Republic that took off when Nigeria became independent of British colonial rule in 1960 up to the end of the Second Republic in 1983. The leaderships include the military rulership of General Olusegun Obasanjo who, incidentally, is now the civilian president of Nigeria. (The present study does not encompass his record as an elected civilian leader.) The study is more concerned with the philosophical outlook, policies, actions and results of political leadership as well as the environment in which leadership operates than with classifications, dichotomies or trichotomies. Specifically, the study seeks to explore, explain, and comparatively analyze how the environment of political leadership, the philosophical outlook, actions and policies of political leadership furthered or negated political integration in Nigeria since the attainment of independence. Where relevant, the study includes pre-colonial and colonial political developments in its discussions and analyses. Among the questions asked are, what has been the nature of the conduct of governmental affairs in this country? To what extent has national leadership fostered political integration in Nigeria? What case studies of political leadership in Africa might be useful in throwing light on Nigeria's situation? Thus, the study also includes relevant discussions of case studies of a cross-section of other political leaderships in Africa in their historical unfolding.

Principally, the book seeks to establish the relationship of African political leadership and political integration to the Afrocentric/Africa-centered epistemological paradigm. In other words, how has political leadership in Nigeria been located or centered in the matter of political integration? The leading proponent of the Afrocentric theory and African philosopher and prolific author, Molefi Kete Asante writes that "the Afrocentric enterprise is framed by cosmological, epistemological, axiological, and aesthetic issues."[13] Asante posits that "the Afrocentric method pursues a world voice distinctly Africa-centered in relationship to external phenomena."[14]

Among the aims of this study is the determination of the African voice in political leadership in Nigeria in particular and Africa in general. In general, political leadership in Africa has been bedeviled by instability. Political or governmental instability is defined as follows: the condition under which a state is prone to abrupt, unconstitutional, arbitrary and unsystematic changes of government. Conversely, political stability means the existence of a durable, systematic and constitutional mode of governance based on effective institutions and the mandate of the citizens. This implies an institutionalized government based on legitimate rules and regulations derived from law and convention and from equitable and humane social norms. Such a political dispensation is essential for sociopolitical peace and national development.

The book is made up of eight chapters as follows:

I.   Chapter One is the introduction, including an articulation of the problem, the philosophy and significance of the study, and the research procedure and methodology.

II.   Chapter Two contains a brief discussion of the history of political leadership in Nigeria.

III.   Chapter Three contains a review of the literature on political leadership and political integration in Africa in general and Nigeria in particular.

IV.   Chapter Four, "State Creation: A Tool for Political Integration in Nigeria," discusses how Nigeria's post-independence political leadership applied the tool of state-creation in its drive for political integration.

V.   Chapter Five consists of an Afrocentric/Africa-centered theory of political and integrative leadership and an analysis of the leaderships of six governments of Nigeria with a view to ascertaining the extent to which each of those leaderships met the constructs of the theory. There are seven constructs in this theory, including four modified structural characteristics adapted from Claude Ake's theory of political integration. The analyzed leaderships are those of Abubakar Tafawa Balewa, J.T.U. Aguiyi-Ironsi, Yakubu Gowon, Murtala Muhammed, Olusegun Obasanjo (his military record of leadership) and Shehu Shagari.

VI: Chapter Six provides a comparative summary of the Afrocentric/Africa-centered analyses of the six Nigerian political leaderships; it discusses the findings and recommendations of the study.

VII: Chapter Seven discusses General Ibrahim Babandiga's scuttling of the June 12, 1993 presidential election. It reveals the extent to which the ill-fated election and the surrounding issues corroborated the findings of this book.

VIII.   Chapter Eight discusses the implications of the study's findings for African political leadership.

In terms of its research procedure and methodology, the book employs the historical method, using both inductive and deductive approaches. Using the inductive approach, a theory was derived from the study's general facts, observations and findings. On the deductive side, this theory was then applied to specific cases such as the six Nigerian political leaderships.

The study is based on my first hand experience of Nigerian politics, which encompasses my coverage (as a political reporter and editor of the Federal Radio Corporation of Nigeria) of a national presidential campaign and my coverage of the proceedings of the House of Representatives (that is, the second chamber of the National Assembly) of the Second Republic, and on documented primary and secondary studies of political leadership and political integration (and related studies and subjects) in Nigeria in particular and Africa in general. The study's philosophical orientation to data, that is, its methodology, stems from a paradigm that treats Africans as subjects of their own history. Otherwise known as the Afrocentric or Africa-centered paradigm, this is the idea that African ideals and values should be at the center of any analysis involving African culture and behavior. More specifically, "the Afrocentrist seeks to uncover and use codes, paradigms, symbols, motifs, myths, and circles of discussion that reinforce the centrality of African ideals and values as a valid frame of reference for acquiring and examining data."[15] This approach does not exclude relevant ideas and techniques from other human experiences; however, "such a method appears to go beyond Western history in order to re-valorize the African place in the interpretation of Africans, continental and diasporan."[16] C. Tsehloane Keto adds that "the Africa-centered paradigm above all represents the quest to define and affirm an African center for philosophizing, a framework for conceptualizing African reality and a paradigm for accumulating knowledge about Africans."[17]

While this book provides a focused analysis of six of the political leaderships of post-independence Nigeria, it provides, as an important background, an overview of pre-colonial political structures such as kingdoms and empires, a review and analysis of the history of the formation of the Nigerian nation state, including the impact of the Great Enslavement on African economic, social and political evolution, as well as the colonial roots of some of the problems that characterize post-colonial leadership in Nigeria in particular and Africa in general. With the exception of necessary cursory references, the book does not deal with state or local governments. (Nigeria is a federation made up of a relatively strong federal government, thirty-six state governments [see Figure 4.1 for a map depicting the thirty-six states of Nigeria] and seven hundred and seventy-four local administrations). The study's frame of reference embraces civilian and military regimes.

THE NATURE OF NIGERIA'S POLITICAL INSTITUTIONS

The nature of Nigeria's political institutions has varied from time to time. Before colonialism, African political systems and structures held sway in the Kingdoms and empires that were located within this territory. During colonialism, the British ruled through such traditional structures wherever possible (particularly in the Northern section of Nigeria) by superimposing the British style and structure of governance.

The indigenous civilian governments (at the federal and regional levels), which took over from the British in 1960 were modeled after the British-type parliamentary system of governance. The military regimes that followed governed by fusing the roles of the executive and legislative arms of government. Generally, the military governments ruled by decree.

Unlike the First Republic, which was based on the British parliamentary system, the second post-independence civilian administration, which lasted from 1979–1983, was based on a constitution (the 1979 constitution) that was modeled after the American-style presidential system of government.[18]

Currently, Nigeria is a multiparty, presidential system of democracy with as many as thirty registered political parties. But one party dominates the political scene at the federal, state and local levels. It's known as the Peoples Democratic Party (PDP). This current civilian administration in Nigeria began in 1999 and is based on the 1999 Constitution, which is a revised version of the 1979 and 1989 editions of Nigeria's supreme law.

Among other key provisions, the Constitution specifies the Fundamental Objectives and Directive Principles of state. Those objectives and principles establish the general purposes and parameters for the exercise of legislative and executive powers.[19] Generally, government is to be exercised for the security and welfare of the people.

The Constitution provides for three separate but interrelated arms of government—the executive, the legislature and the judiciary—anchored upon a set of checks and balances. The executive branch, headed by the President, who is the chief executive of the nation, implements the laws/policies of the land; the legislature, which is bicameral,[20] makes the law and carries out an "oversight" of the executive; and the judiciary interprets the law and also exercises "judicial review" of the actions of the executive and the legislature. Even though there are in-built mechanisms for one branch to "check" another, "it is an unconstitutional usurpation for one organ to exercise the functions of another organ."[21]

Under Nigeria's 1979 Constitution (as well as the now operative 1999 constitution), governmental powers were divided between the federal and state governments. Each has a will of its own and has exclusive authority to legislate over certain matters. Ben O. Nwabueze explains:

> The sharing follows upon the principle of enumerated powers and residual powers, with the federal government having enumerated powers while the residue goes to the state governments. Any exercise of power by one tier of government over a matter within the exclusive jurisdiction of the other is unconstitutional and void.[22]

Note also that the Constitution provides for a third tier of government—local governments run by elected councils. The Constitution requires every state government to ensure that local governments are established by law. Under this Constitution, a state is forbidden from appointing officers to run local government councils; the local governments must be operated by democratically elected councils, and the state governments have an obligation to safeguard their existence.[23]

The constitution guarantees fundamental rights under a Bill of Rights. These include the right to life, dignity of the human person, personal liberty, right to an impartial determination by an independent tribunal of civil rights and obligations, right to private and family life, freedom of thought, conscience and religion, freedom of expression and the press, freedom of peaceful assembly and association, freedom of movement, freedom from discrimination and the right to prompt payment of compensation for property compulsorily acquired or occupied.[24]

An issue of critical importance is whether the Constitution guarantees freedom of private enterprise. Nwabueze suggests that the Constitution does not guarantee freedom of private enterprise. This is against the backdrop of the fact that in practice Nigeria exemplifies a mixed economy boosting a fairly buoyant private sector. Nwabueze observes that what the Constitution guarantees to every person is "the right positively to engage in business or enterprise."[25] In addition, it pledges to every one "freedom to decide whether to be self-employed or to work for an employer."[26] This matter calls for clarification, and for this, I will turn to Nwabueze again who explains:

> All the Constitution provides is that 'no movable property or any interest in an immovable property shall be taken possession of compulsorily and no right over or interest in any such property shall be acquired compulsorily in any part of Nigeria except in the manner and for the purpose prescribed by a law.[27]

He adds, however, that:

> The provision is thus clearly not a guarantee of the right to acquire, use or dispose of property. Its sole concern is to restrict the power of the state to take compulsory possession of, or to acquire compulsorily, property which a person has lawfully acquired. No doubt, it implies a right to own or hold what one has acquired. Property once lawfully acquired cannot be expropriated or confiscated by the government. But that falls short of a right to make future acquisitions or to use or dispose of existing acquisitions free from the government's regulatory control. Under the Constitution, therefore, the right of property exists only to the extent that compulsory acquisition and compulsory possession of private property by the state is restricted.[28]

Judging by the preceding, it appears that a less restrictive reading of this provision of the Constitution would not mean that the Constitution DOES NOT guarantee freedom of private enterprise, but that it guarantees a qualified freedom of private enterprise. For, to emphatically state that the Constitution does not guarantee freedom of private enterprise would give rise to a rather misleading impression that in Nigeria individuals are not at liberty to acquire and keep property or to engage in private enterprise.

Chapter Five, which establishes an Afrocentric/Africa-centered theory of leadership and political integration and analyzes a select number of Nigerian governments, specifically examines the extent to which the leadership of Shehu Shagari (1979–1983) (which operated that constitution for the first time), lived up to or deviated from the objectives and directive principles of state as well as the norms of political culture enshrined in the 1979 Constitution.

Nigeria reverted to military rule on December 31, 1983. There was a plan to return the country to civilian rule by 1993, but it did not materialize for the administration of General Ibrahim Babangida nullified the results of the June 12, 1993 presidential election. Nigeria thus continued to be under the rule of a military interregnum until it returned to its current civilian rule in 1999.

In what some observers effusively heralded as a modern-day political miracle, General Olusegun Obasanjo assumed office in 1999 as an elected civilian president, having won that year's presidential election, shortly after being released from political incarceration. In July 2003, he was re-elected for a second term as a civilian president of Nigeria.

Chapter Two

Post-Colonial Political Leadership in Nigeria

OVERVIEW

Political leadership in Nigeria—a multi-ethnic West African country whose 2005 population was projected at 131,530 million by the United Nations—has been beset by governmental instability for much of its post-colonial era. As Chinua Achebe puts it, "Nigeria has been less than fortunate in its leadership."[1] The country became independent of British colonial political control in October 1960 after about sixty years of formal colonial rule. It was on January 1, 1900 that the British government formally took over the administration of Nigeria from a British firm, the Royal Niger Company. The company had administered Nigeria as a set of loose commercial territories for half a century.[2]

In 1966, six years after independence, the elected civilian government of the late Prime Minister Abubakar Tafawa Balewa was overthrown in a bloody military coup d'etat (the country's first), which was led by the late Major Chukwuma Kaduna Nzeogwu. The coup marked the end of Nigeria's experimentation with the British parliamentary system of government, which it inherited from colonial rule. That coup of 1966 was followed by several subsequent military takeovers of government in Nigeria. The coup of 1966 exacerbated the unstable political situation in the country by unleashing a chain of events that culminated in a three-year "civil" war that ended in 1970.

Between 1966 and 1999, Nigeria had the following military leaderships: Major-General J.T.U. Aguiyi-Ironsi, January 1966 to July, 1966; General Yakubu Gowon, 1966 to 1975; Brigadier Murtala Muhammed, July 1975 to February 1976; General Olusegun Obasanjo, 1976 to 1979; General Mohammed Buhari, 1984 to 1985; and General Ibrahim Babangida, 1985 to August 1993; General Sani Abacha, November 1993 to June 1998; and General Abdulsalam Abubakar, 1998 to 1999.

Military rule in Nigeria was itself quite unstable, for it was punctuated by abortive coups, most notably the 1976 unsuccessful coup d'etat led by late Colonel Buka Dimka—which resulted in the death of a charismatic and nationally admired Head of State, Brigadier Murtala Muhammed (the one rare case where a Nigerian national leader was nationally admired). Although Muhammed had a short tenure, he exerted a positive impact on the life of the nation during his time. He dealt a heavy blow on the general indiscipline, corruption, and governmental inefficiency and ineffectiveness, which had pervaded and almost crippled the affairs of the nation before he took over power. Nigerians who witnessed his administration still recall his name with nostalgia.

Like previous governments, the administration of General Ibrahim Babangida (1985–1993) experienced various forms of insurrection, including an abortive coup of 1990 led by the late Major Gideon Ngwozor Oka.[3] A distinctive record of Babangida's administration was its inability to complete its program of transition to a civilian government before leaving office in August 1993. The last phase of the program, the presidential election, ran into a political hitch, but other phases of the transition program had been implemented, including the 1989 revision of the 1979 presidential-style national constitution, elections to state and national legislatures, and governorship elections. The transition program was originally scheduled for completion in 1990. It was later rescheduled for 1992, from where it was moved to January 1993 and later rescheduled for August 1993. But the August date never materialized. A presidential election was held in June 1993, but Babangida nullified the results. As a result of the political storm triggered by his political crime of nullifying the will of the people, Babangida had to take his exit, handing over power in August 1993 to a quasi-civilian caretaker government, headed by Ernest Shonekan. But the Shonekan's administration lasted for only three months, for it was overthrown by General Sani Abacha who ruled Nigeria with an iron-fist from November 1993 until his death in June 1998.

The last phase of Babangida's uncompleted program of transition to civilian rule was marked by a watershed crisis. The abuses that characterized the process re-opened old wounds in Nigerian political life to such an extent that a leading Nigerian newspaper, *The Guardian*, never known for editorial extremism, called for a reconfiguration of the Nigerian polity from a federal to a Confederal structure. As the newspaper put it:

> Each component part (of Nigeria) must enjoy a large measure of self government, use its own resources to develop itself, contribute a certain

proportion to the center to run the government and share power at the center in a manner designed to promote national harmony.[4]

The Guardian implies, by this statement, that Nigeria, which has been a federal state since the time of colonialism with a fairly strong center, should become a confederacy with a relatively weak center. The ill-fated 1993 presidential election in Nigeria, which prompted Guardian's call for a structural change, is discussed in detail in Chapter Seven of this book.

Since it achieved political independence from Britain in 1960, Nigeria has been ruled for a much longer period by the military than by civilian administrations. Out of its 45 years of post-independence governance (1960 to 2005), Nigeria was under military rule for 29 years. The first civilian government headed by Prime Minister Tafawa Balewa lasted from 1960 to 1966; and the second, led by President Shehu Shagari, began in 1979 but was terminated by a military return to power on the eve of 1984. This military interregnum continued until 1999 when Nigeria, once again, returned to civilian rule.

Of the twelve governments that Nigeria has had since 1960, there have been only two instances of a formal, constitutional and orderly governmental change of hands. The first was in 1979 when the military government of General Olusegun Obasanjo handed over the reigns of power to the elected government of President Shehu Shagari of the now proscribed National Party of Nigeria (NPN).[5] This was the first time a military leader willingly handed power over to an elected Nigerian government. The second was in 1999 when General Abdulsalam Abubakar handed over power to the elected, civilian government of Olusegun Obasanjo. (Even though Nigeria conducted a presidential election in 2003, the incumbent was returned to office). In the remaining cases, governments changed hands in Nigeria violently, unconstitutionally, arbitrarily, and abruptly. In those instances, the gun, rather than the ballot, was the operational tool. What does this mean? Of course, it implies that Nigeria's political environment was dominated by instability for much of its post-independence phase. At least until the new civilian dispensation that came onto the scene in 1999, the country represented a striking example of a politically unstable state as defined at the onset of this book. J. Gus Liebenow believes that soldiers are the chief source of instability in African political leadership.[6] That is true to the extent that military take-overs of power often take a sudden, violent and arbitrary form as well as disrupt a constitutional, albeit often abused, system of governance. The violence and the resultant assassinations sometimes, like the 1966 coup in Nigeria (which will be discussed in detail later), exacerbate ethnic tension and even provoke a war like the Nigerian civil war of 1967 to 1970. But it should not be forgotten that the irresponsibility of civilian governments and their flagrant abuses of their constitutional mandate (as exemplified by the Nigerian cases that will be delineated in the subsequent pages of this chapter), often gave the army reasons or excuses for intervening in the body politic.

But much more fundamentally, Toyin Falola's and Julius Ihonvbere's analysis of political instability in Nigeria holds that the basic causes stem from the colonial state's and international capitalists' under-development of Nigeria, the existence of a world-view in that country that serves the interests of international capital, and the inability of the indigenous bourgeoisie to impose its own hegemony on social formation.[7] (I define world-view as the prism through which a people perceive and interpret reality. It is a function of the people's socio-geographical environment. In other words, world-view derives from history and culture.) Falola's and Ihonvbere's analysis contends that the post-colonial state of Nigeria is inherently weak because while it's being subjected to the international division of labor, it has not inherited the central and governing role of the colonial state within that division of labor. In recent times, this international division of labor that constitutes a source of the weakness of the average developing country of today, has reformulated itself in the guise of what is known generally as globalization. Their analysis argue further that in transitioning to independent rule, Nigeria did not inherit the finances nor the ideological support of the metropolitan bourgeoisie.[8] Furthermore, the analysis correctly points out that the colonial state had given Nigerians a false consciousness through the distortion of their history and the glorification of the metropolitan's past. It rightly observes that, as of now, the world-view of the colonial state holds sway and the Nigerian governing class has not been able to replace it with its own ideological hegemony.[9] This school of thought believes that the contradictions and struggles produced by this state of affairs make military coups inevitable in Nigeria.[10]

As I have indicated, the preceding analysis is correct in many respects, but its weakness lies in its inference that socialism *per se* would solve Nigeria's problem of political instability. Given that socialism is the public control of the means of production and distribution, does the dismal performance of most Nigerian public enterprises, serve as a vindication of the socialist economic theory of national development? It is no secret that those publicly-owned enterprises are known for chronic inefficiency and ineffectiveness and are characterized by undue governmental interference. In fact, they are generally a drain on the public treasury, and it is no surprise that the current civilian government of Olusegun Obasanjo has pursued an active program of privatization of government owned enterprises. In view of these facts, how could socialism, by itself, become the way out of Nigeria's economic problems and consequent political malaise? The recent collapse of socialist governments around the world has raised questions about the efficacy and durability of socialism/Marxism as a political-economic strategy. Besides, the Marxist view of political economics over-stresses class conflict but ignores or distorts the racial factor in global politics. It is of historical significance to note, for instance, that the United States and other Western nations took steps to bolster a sagging Russian currency and the economies of the former Eastern block nations, but have offered debt relief or debt cancellation packages to African economies that are tied to counter-productive conditionalties. In fact, the United States is on record for advocating restraint in the transfers of international capital to developing countries of the world.[11]

NIGERIA'S HISTORICAL BACKGROUND

An examination of the beginnings of the political entity known as Nigeria reveals the root causes of the political ailment afflicting it. About 290 ethnic groups[12] exist in the country, including the three dominant ones: the Hausa-Fulani, Igbo, and Yoruba. Before the advent of Europeans in West Africa, both the word "Nigeria" and the political state itself did not exist.

In pre-colonial times, the territory that constitutes present-day Nigeria was composed of centuries-old empires and kingdoms such as the Yoruba Empire of Oyo, Benin Empire, the Onitsha Kingdom and the Kanem-Bornu Empire (which flourished on the southern banks of Lake Chad from the ninth or tenth century to 1846 AD.). There was also a confederation of seven Hausa states which rose to prominence by the thirteenth century (but later came under Muslim/Fulani domination as from the 18th century). These are Biram, Daura, Gabir, Kano, Katsina, Rano and Zaria. These empires and states traded among themselves and internationally with other parts of West Africa and North Africa, including Egypt.[13] Kano and Katsina were the chief commercial centers and served as links with the North-Western Trans-Saharan Trade. Kano was, in addition, a manufacturing center.

Even though British colonial rule brought about the amalgamation of the northern and southern segments of Nigeria, history indicates that some of the constituent kingdoms and empires had maintained contact with one another before the arrival of the Europeans.[14] For instance, the Yoruba kingdoms, located in the south of Nigeria, interacted with the Hausa states in the north. The Yoruba empire of Oyo transmitted to and received goods from North Africa through the Hausa States.[15] The Oyo empire, which was at its peak by the middle of the seventeenth century, covered not only

Yorubaland, but also much of Nupeland in the North, parts of Borgu and areas of the modern-day Benin Republic.[16]

A first millennium B.C. culture—the Nok Culture—flourished around the confluence of the Niger and Benue rivers—in the heartland of what is now known as Nigeria. The Nok culture is believed to have occupied an area that was three hundred by one hundred miles wide. Of notable importance is the fact that whereas the culture was located in an area that is situated in the Nigerian Middle Belt, its influence extended beyond it to the south. Thus, the stylistic features of the sculptures of Ife, located in the Southern section of Nigeria, have been likened to those of Nok.[17]

Nigeria, as a name, came into being about the end of the 19th century.[18] The Portuguese were the first Europeans to set foot in Nigeria. This occurred in 1472.[19] Their initial purpose was commerce—trade in what have been described as legitimate goods: spices, ivory, salt, etc. The Europeans were later to turn this "legitimate" commerce into a trade in African captives, which dominated European international trade from the 16th to the 19th centuries.

The Spanish and the Portuguese inaugurated the era of trans-Atlantic trade in African captives. Before long, almost all the nations of Europe joined in this barbaric commerce.[20] The consequences of this assault upon the tranquility of African society are discussed in detail later in this book.

British rule in Nigeria was ushered in by traders and missionaries. The first British trade mission to Nigeria (1832) was led by Macgregor Laird, a Liverpool merchant and shipbuilder.[21] The first Christian expedition to Nigeria came from Britain in 1841, and this was led, ironically, by a Nigerian, Bishop Ajayi Crowther, who had been freed from slavery, and Rev. J. F. Schon.[22] Historian M. A. Fajana writes that "the natives, especially the chiefs, did not always approve of these visitors from Europe."[23] But European trade later expanded to include the French and the German and resulted in what Fajana describes as a proliferation of companies.[24]

This proliferation became a matter of concern for Sir George Taubman Goldie, a British merchant and ex-army officer. Through his influence, the British companies came together under the umbrella of the United Africa Company (UAC) in 1879. The formation of this company, which later changed its name to the National African Company in 1882, was crucial to the eventual formal British rulership of Nigeria. The company entered into trading agreements of all sorts with African Kingdoms within Nigeria. (These agreements were secured by all kinds of means, including force.[25] It is also of note that "these treaties later formed the basis of British claims at the Berlin Conference"[26] where the European powers carved up Africa into spheres of economic and political influence.) The National African Company later received a charter from the British government (under the name of the Royal Niger Company), to administer justice and maintain order in the "areas covered by its treaties."[27] The company, however, lost this charter in 1899 for contravening a British stipulation against monopoly trading. While the Royal Niger Company was allowed to remain as a trading company, the British formally took over the administration of its Nigerian charter territories in 1900.[28] That year marked the beginning of formal British rule in Nigeria. Notice that it was through the Royal Niger Company that a set of "charter territories" (which were often coerced into such treaties with European traders) located in the geographical space now called Nigeria were brought under the administrative umbrella of the British empire.

Arthur Gavshon has written that "Europe's arbitrary, often illogical partition of Africa split whole peoples and concentrated diverse and often hostile [ethnic] groups into territories which ultimately became sovereign states, so making internal . . . strife inevitable."[29] Isawa J. Elaigwu believes that cultural diversity in Africa, particularly Nigeria, created the problem of "the fragility of authority of the center over the periphery."[30] However, as will be demonstrated later in this book, the cultural diversity which Elaigwu addresses here often does not significantly go beyond language differences—differences that obscure the fundamental commonalities, which characterize the African cultural landscape—a fact that has been amply demonstrated by Diopian African historiography.

Britain ruled Nigeria as two separate protectorates—northern and southern—until 1914 when they were amalgamated, thus bringing into formal existence the single political entity known as Nigeria.[31] Historian J.F.A. Ajayi observes that in bringing the Northern and Southern protectorates together,

> the British were not seeking to unify Nigeria. They were not religious or political reformers seeking an empire where new religious or political principles could be enforced. They were essentially traders from abroad anxious to establish a situation favorable for the growth and development of their trade.[32]

E. A. Ijagbemi reinforces the preceding position in his observation that the amalgamation was motivated by economic expediency.[33] Even then, that amalgamation did not result in the country being administered uniformly. As Ijagbemi puts it, "administratively, the north and south (the former more than twice as large in area as the latter), remained distinct—thus planting the seeds of rancor, fear and suspicion in the future politics of the country."[34] Chapter Four provides a detailed discussion of these seeds of rancor that Ijagbemi points out in the foregoing passage.

Despite policy divergences in the northern and southern colonial administrative approaches, the whole colonial country was ruled as a system of provinces—twenty-four on the whole. The north and the south had twelve provinces each. While colonial rule in Nigeria grew stronger between the period of the First and Second World Wars, the period from 1948 to October 1, 1960 saw major internal changes (including a heightened nationalist struggle against the backdrop of a Britain that was weakened militarily by the devastations of the Second World War), which culminated in independence on October 1, 1960.[35]

CONSTITUTIONAL METAMORPHOSIS

Between 1922 and 1958, Nigeria went through a series of colonial reforms or constitutional metamorphoses marked by six constitutional changes. Those constitutional changes are as follows:

1. 1922 Constitution: Bowing to pressure from Nigerian nationalists, the British introduced this constitutional reform which provided for elected representation in the Nigerian Colonial Legislative Council, but it brought in only four Africans in a house of forty-six members. This constitutional reform also brought Northern and Southern Cameroon under the administration of Nigeria.[36]

2. 1946 Constitution: Owing to press and nationalists' criticisms of the grossly inadequate African representation in the Legislative Council and of other shortcomings of the 1922 constitution, a new constitutional reform (this could be described as yet another reform of colonialism) came into being in 1946. This reform brought to life the concept of "regionalism" in Nigerian affairs through the establishment of a House of Assembly for each of the Northern, Western and Eastern Provinces of Nigeria. Some scholarly observers believe that this factor of regionalism laid an official foundation for colonial tribalism—that is, disunity fostered by colonial divide and conquer tactics. Under this regional configuration, the Yoruba constituted the dominant group in the Western provinces, the Igbo held sway in the Eastern Provinces, and the Hausa-Fulani dominated the Northern Provinces. Ironically, one of the expressed principal aims of this constitutional reform was to promote the unity of Nigeria even though in reality it exacerbated its lines of divergence. This reform also empowered the Central Legislative Council to make laws for the whole

country in all matters; previously, the Council made national legislation only on financial matters and/or matters pertaining only to the Southern Provinces.

The 1946 Constitution also established a House of Chiefs for the North. This constitutional reform also brought about unofficial majorities in the Central and regional houses of assembly. Note, however, that the regional houses of assembly were merely advisory bodies and had no legislative authority at this time.[37]

3. 1951 Constitution: Nigerian nationalists as well as the Nigerian Union of Students condemned the preceding reforms of 1946 as an imposition by the British Colonial Governor, Sir Arthur Richards. They castigated the 1946 constitution for exacerbating forces of disunity in the country through its institutionalization of the concept of regionalism. Thus, the ensuing 1951 constitution (which this time was formulated through the recommendations of a select committee), among other things, authorized the regional houses of assembly to make legislation but subject to the approval of the Governor-in-Council. It also brought into being a council of ministers at the center. Note that resultant elections to the Central and Regional Houses of Assembly established a pattern that would haunt Nigerian politics for all time. The Northern Peoples Congress (N.P.C) (dominated by the Hausa-Fulani) won majority seats in the Northern House of Assembly; the National Council of Nigeria and the Cameroons (N.C.N.C) (with an Igbo majority) obtained the majority seats in the Eastern House of Assembly, while the Action Group (consisting of mainly the Yoruba) won majority positions in the Western House of Assembly.[38]

4. 1954 Constitution: This constitution established Nigeria as a federation made up of the Northern Region, the Western Region, the Eastern Region, the Southern Cameroons and the Federal territory of Lagos. Each of the regions became autonomous, further strengthening the divisive, regional factor introduced by the 1946 constitutional reform. However, the federal legislature shared legislative responsibility with the regional assemblies on items in the concurrent list, while it reserved matters on the exclusive list for itself. Residual items (that is, subjects not specified anywhere in the constitution) went to the regional houses of assembly. This constitution also regionalized the judiciary, the public services and the marketing boards.[39]

5. 1957 Constitution: This modified slightly the 1954 constitution by providing for a bicameral federal legislature and a Prime Minister

as the nation's chief executive. The reform also granted self-government to the Eastern and Western Regions. It made Southern Cameroons an autonomous region with its own premier. But, to the disappointment of the nationalist movement, this constitutional reform failed to set a date for national independence.

6. 1958 Constitution: This reform set October 1, 1960 as the date of independence from colonial rule for Nigeria. It also granted a self-governing status to the Northern Region.[40] Note that each of the six constitutional reforms had the effect of advancing Nigeria's march towards independence from British colonial rule. Note also that in each case, the reforms were introduced as a result of unrelenting pressure from politically conscious Africans. In other words, the reforms were not necessarily made at the initiative of the colonial power. They were not voluntary gifts from a liberal and reforming colonial regime. Other Africans—on the continent and in the Diaspora—have also had to take either direct nonviolent actions or engage in armed struggles in order to break the yoke of oppression. As I observed elsewhere, "historically conscious Africans would not hesitate to aggressively, but lawfully (excluding unjust laws) and morally, advance and protect the African interest."[41]

As previously noted, Nigerian nationalists and historians like Fajana and Biggs identified the 1946 constitutional reform as part of the early foundation for ethnic politics of dis-unity in Nigeria. Although the constitutional document professed a commitment to the promotion of Nigerian unity, it simultaneously had a goal of expressing Nigeria's "diversity" rather than the shared Africanness of the constituent groups.[42] Commenting on this Constitution, one of the leading Nigerian nationalists of that time, who later became its first president (although a ceremonial one), Nnamdi Azikiwe said, rather prophetically:

> The Richards constitution divides the country into three zones which are bound to departmentalize the political thinking of this country. Whether Richards intends it or not, it is obvious that regions will now tend towards Parkistanization [that is, balkanization] than ever before, and our future generations will inherit this legacy that is born out of official sophistry.[43]

Another significant development in Nigeria prior to independence that should be relevant in any analysis of the early roots of its political instability was the basis upon which party politics emerged in the country. The three political parties that came to dominate the politics of the first republic were, by and large, regionally and ethnically centered although the NCNC (the National Council of Nigeria and the Cameroons) had begun with an apparent nationalistic vision and membership, but later came to be primarily supported by the Igbo of the East. The then leader of the NCNC, Nnamdi Azikiwe had said that the party was "founded in order to unify the various elements of our communities . . . to create a spirit of oneness among our heterogeneous peoples."[44] But the other two major parties had begun strictly as ethnic unions. The Action Group originated as an offshoot of a Yoruba group known as Egbe Omo Oduduwa with no pretext at a national orientation. The Northern Peoples Congress (NPC) also originated as an Hausa-Fulani cultural organization. Elaigwu recalls that "the Northern, Eastern and Western regions [of Nigeria] had taken on their own dynamics as competing centers of power."[45]

Even then, the regionalization policy of the 1946 Constitutional Reform and the formation of political parties along ethnic lines were not the only early seeds of disunity to be sown in Nigeria prior to independence. The competition generated by the pattern of urban economics and politics that grew out of the colonial state also had the effect of exacerbating ethnic consciousness.[46] As an illustration of this factor, it's apropos to recall that from 1916 to 1966, ethnic unions were set up in Nigeria[47] primarily to help their members to cope with that competition. Examples of such unions include the Igbo State Union, the Egbe Omo Oduduwa for the Yoruba, the Ibibio Welfare Union for the Ibibio ethnic group, etc. Incidentally, these ethnic unions had the backing and membership of educated Nigerians and business people. "Most unions were the brain child of professional men such as lawyers, doctors, teachers, businessmen and civil servants."[48] Nigeria's first president, Nnamdi Azikiwe was once the president of the Igbo state Union: from 1948 to 1952.[49] Another prominent Nigerian politician, Obafemi Awolowo, was one of the leaders of the Yoruba ethnic union, Egbe Omo Oduduwa. As earlier stated, these ethnic unions turned out to be the fore-runners of the political parties that vied for federal and state elections before and after independence. Confirming that the Action Group was a direct offshoot of the Egbe Omo Oduduwa, its leader, the late Chief Obafemi Awolowo said:

> When the idea of starting a political party occurred to me in 1949 and I began to make contacts, I had frequent contacts with members of the Egbe . . . [If] the new party [Action Group] was to make any appreciable showing at all at the regional elections, it must make use of the

branches and organization of the Egbe Omo Oduduwa throughout the West Region.[50]

That statement was reinforced by an Action Group premier of the Western Region, the late Chief Samuel Akintola, who stated that the Egbe Omo Oduduwa and the Action Group were 'as inseparable as wine and water'[51] in their goals and objectives. All these factors helped to nourish feelings of separatism around the country; they contributed to inter-ethnic tensions and sub-nationalism in Nigerian politics.[52]

Early ethnic politics in Nigeria was not confined to party political organizations, however. It infiltrated the academic community as well.[53] For instance, at Nigeria's University of Lagos in 1965, the choice of a vice-chancellor degenerated into an ethnic contest between the Yoruba and the Igbo. The sitting Vice-Chancellor, Eni Njoku, who was Igbo, was denied reappointment in a manner which the Igbo construed to be ethnic. He was replaced by Dr. S. Biobaku, a Yoruba. The Action Group only fueled the ethnic embers aroused by this incident by sending Dr. Biobaku a lengthy letter of congratulation.[54] Thus, as political scientist, Ali A. Mazrui comments, "Nigerian academics had failed by the middle of the 1960's to produce or practice an ideology of national unity which transcended ethnicism or communalism."[55]

The army was also infected by this disease of ethnicity chauvinism. Toyin Falola and Julius Ihonvbere note that at the height of the political delinquency of Nigeria's first Republic's politicians, "rumors about the intentions of particular ethnically based political parties to use the army against other ethnic groups were rampant in the country and especially within the army."[56] Such fears of one ethnic group using the army to secure political dominance of the country had long been expressed by a prominent Nigerian politician, Obafemi Awolowo. He advocated that in order to allay this concern, Nigeria should replace the standing army it had inherited from Britain with compulsory military training for Nigerians. As he saw it, "when all able-bodied Nigerians have been given military training, no group or groups would be prone to accuse or suspect the other group or groups of actually using or wanting to use their predominance in the army to dominate the country."[57]

Besides ethnicity, there was/is the factor of bureaucratic corruption. During the first republic, for instance, ministers of government openly boasted about their ill-gotten foreign bank accounts "in the midst of mass poverty, illiteracy, unemployment and hunger."[58] Achebe's aptly entitled book, *The Trouble With Nigeria*, comments: "Nigerians are corrupt because the system under which they live today makes corruption easy and profitable; they will cease to be corrupt when corruption is made difficult and inconvenient."[59] While Achebe may be guilty of over-generalization (I contend that there are legions of Nigerians who are neither corrupt nor corruptible), his assertions are largely reinforced by this book's forth-right discussion of the multitude of social and political ills that plague Nigeria. Specifically, the work is correct in arguing that, in general, and no doubt there must be exceptions, Nigerian political leadership lacks integrity. In theory, its political culture, as articulated in constitutional declarations and stipulations, derides corruption, but in practice, the Nigerian political elite, at large (and with exceptions here and there) tends to pay a lip service to its normative opposition to corruption.

The political parties of the first Republic abused the electoral process during the 1964 federal elections in Nigeria—the first to be supervised by Nigerians themselves. There were rigging and wanton destruction of lives and property by political activists. The politicians could no longer keep the public services functioning; there were indiscriminate use of state power by politicians and unchecked police brutality against civilians.[60]

In announcing the 1966 coup that overthrew this rather disorderly and shameless bunch of politicians, Major Chukwuma Kaduna Nzeogwu told a traumatized nation that: "Our enemies are the political profiteers, swindlers, the men in high and low places who seek to keep the country divided permanently so that they can remain in office as ministers and V.I.P's of waste, the tribalists, the nepotists."[61] Not surprisingly, Falola and Ihonvbere point out, perhaps with nostalgia, that "no one doubts Nzeogwu's sincerity, though he did not stay in power long enough to put his ideas into practice."[62] But, they erred in using the phrase 'did not stay in power,' for Nzeogwu's coup was still-born, and he never stayed in power—that is, he never ruled Nigeria.

When, years later, General Yakubu Gowon was toppled in 1975, almost the same reasons as above: ethnicity, corruption, lack of direction, wastefulness and arrogance, were cited by the new military leaders.[63] Similar reasons were advanced for the overthrow of President Shehu Shagari in 1983 and for subsequent coups in Nigeria. Regarding public corruption, a U.S.-based magazine, *Emerge* reports that "in the late 1970's when Nigeria was riding the crest of an oil boom, corrupt politicians transferred $25 million a day abroad."[64] General Sanni Abacha,[65] who announced the coup that toppled Shehu Shagari in 1983 (and ushered in the leadership of General Buhari) told the rather jubilant nation:

> I am referring to the harsh intolerable conditions under which we are now living. Our economy has been hopelessly mismanaged. We have

become a debtor and beggar nation. There is inadequacy of food at reasonable prices for our people who are now fed up with endless announcements of importation of foodstuff. Health services are in shambles as our hospitals are reduced to mere consulting clinics, without drugs, water and equipment. Our educational system is deteriorating at an alarming rate. Unemployment figures, including the graduates, have reached embarrassing and unacceptable proportions . . . Yet our leaders revel in "squandermania"[66], corruption[67] and indiscipline.[68]

Surprisingly, in this announcement, General Abacha did not mention the controversial 1983 presidential election in Nigeria—the second to be conducted, or should one say mis-conducted, by civilians themselves—which was characterized by the same evil forces that had marred that of 1964. There were allegations and counter-allegations of rigging, police vandalism, etc. Shehu Shagari was re-elected—in the midst of widespread economic discontent and widespread perceptions of official corruption—with a questionable landslide. In fact, the initial election of Shagari as president in 1979 had also evoked charges of cheating and abridgement of the electoral law. Thus, for Nigerians in general, 1983 was more than dejavu. Ken C. Kotecha provides an apt summary of the outcome of the 1979 presidential poll:

Under the election rules, the federal president had to win a plurality of all votes cast in two-thirds of the country's states. The winner was Shehu Shagari, the leader of the National Party of Nigeria, who drew heavy support from the Muslim Hausa-Fulani and Nigerian businessmen. Shagari technically failed to satisfy the second requirement of 25% in two-thirds or 13 states, having only [less than] twenty per cent in the thirteenth, but was still declared victorious by the Federal Elections Commission over Mr. Obafemi Awolowo.[69]

Commenting on the subsequent election of 1983, Falola and Ihonvbere report that, "generally, political and other trade organizations and unions were dis-satisfied with the conduct and results of the election."[70] A former Nigerian Army chief, who had served in Obasanjo's military government, General Theophilus Y. Danjuma, said of the 1983 election: "Democracy had been in jeopardy for the past four years (1979 to 1983). It died with the 1983 elections . . . The politicians killed democracy."[71] Given all this, why then did the soldiers who overthrew Shagari later on the eve of 1984 keep mute on his controversial re-election? A possible answer lies in the fact that at the time of the military coup that overthrew Shagari, Nigerians would privately say that "the N.P.N [the National Party of Nigeria] wing of the army" had taken over the government from their civilian counterparts. Gus J. Liebenow is guilty of a faulty analysis when he theorizes that the Buhari coup of December 1983 was a "personalized affair,"[72] for the preceding record demonstrates that it was a coup that was prompted by severe political abnormalities. Liebenow's interpretation, no doubt, trivializes or shows a misunderstanding of the burning issues that precipitated the 1983 military coup.

At this juncture, it's necessary to recall that the impact of the existence of ethnically based political parties in Nigeria had been felt prior to the departure of the British. In 1951, friction had arisen between the central government and the regional assemblies due to the fact that no nationally based party controlled a majority in the central legislature. Those parties later tested the limits of the parliamentary government of Prime Minister Tafawa Balewa after independence, and matters came to the fore during the 1964 national and 1965 Western Regional elections, which were more or less "tribal" contests for the soul of Nigeria disguised as party politics. The elections were characterized by wide-spread rigging, arson, thuggery, bribery and blatant soap-box "tribalism." Initially, the NCNC and AG—the two major Southern parties—rejected the results of the 1964 national elections. The nation tethered as the president refused to invite the prime minister to form a new government. Eventually, a government was put together, but the nation continued to slide, torn by the bitterness generated by the "rigged" elections. The country had nearly been enveloped by anarchy by the time the army stepped-in in 1966. Unfortunately for Nigeria, what had been conceived as a redemptive military intervention in national politics floundered during its execution and fell into the hands of a conservative army leadership, which failed to adequately manage the political crisis that was precipitated by the 1966 coup. The end result was a three year, bloody "civil" war that culminated in the termination of an attempt of the Eastern section of Nigeria to secede from the country.

In Nigeria's quest for political stability, it has experimented with both the British style parliamentary system of government and the United States model of presidentialism. The latter was the basis of the second republic, which lasted from 1979 to 1983. The third Republic that began with the 1999 election of Olusegun Obasanjo continues as a presidential system of government. To explain why Nigeria replaced its British-style parliamentary system with presidential-style constitutional democracy, I turn to Elaigwu who observes:

> the 1979 and the 1989 constitutions have been carefully drafted to
> include provisions aimed at giving various groups a sense of belonging

to the nation. The constitution also had provisions for the emergence of political parties, legislatures and leaders with national outlook.[73]

However, these political instruments have conspicuously lacked a crucial element: a vehicle for reconnecting and integrating the contemporary national political structure with the traditional political system from which it had been disconnected by the colonial order. In other words, there is a yawning void in Nigeria's political structural arrangement. Basil Davidson perhaps states the problem poignantly when he writes that "if Africa needs to restructure its institutions . . . then Africa needs to reinvent itself. The essential solution . . . is to abolish that acute disjuncture, between the history of the past and the history of the present, which was imposed by the dispossessions and their consequences."[74] Thus far, Nigeria's political experimentations at the national and state levels have tended to perpetuate a break with traditional political systems and their underlying values, which began with colonialism—a break that Davidson characterizes in the foregoing as an "acute disjuncture." From this standpoint, it's relatively easy to see that politics at the national and state levels lacks historical continuity. The traditional political institutions and authorities have been marginalized, stripped of meaningful authority and relegated to ritualistic and ceremonial duties at the local level. Is there a way by which African states could transform their traditional political institutions and leaderships into agents of unity, continuity and stability for the nation-state? Given the multi-ethnic nature of most African states and consequently the existence of numerous traditional rulers in each component ethnic group, how could this gigantic challenge be tackled? This subject is addressed in Chapter Five, which discusses an Afrocentric/Africa-centered theory of governance and in Chapter Six which provides a comparative summary and recommendations of the study.

Although Nigeria has fought a three-year civil war and has had sporadic incidents of Islamic-ethnic extremism resulting in violence confined mostly to the northern states, and has also had sporadic occurrences of student uprisings and labor unrest, perennial civil unrest is not a mark of its brand of political instability. Certainly, Nigeria is not anywhere comparable to the Sudans, the Congos, and the Liberias of this age, or the Yugoslavias, the Lebanons and the Angolas of the 1980s and 1990s' chapter of world history. Secondly, Nigeria's military or civilian changes of government have not led to fundamental shifts in economic ideology or international postures. Notice also that although Nigeria's governmental changes have not always been constitutional and systematic, these changes can hardly be characterized as excessively frequent. During the 45 years that Nigeria has been self-governing (that is, October 1, 1960 to October 1, 2005), it has had twelve heads of state. In other words, it has had a change of leadership every 3.75 years on the average. The problem is that, for the most part, those changes of leadership have not occurred systematically or have occurred systematically in the context of elections that Nigerians did not acknowledge as free and fair. Besides, this 3.75 average sequence of leadership changes is rather misleading, as shown by the distribution of the data of the different years of leadership. Prime Minister Tafawa Balewa ruled for six years; General J.T.U. Aguiyi-Ironsi for six months; General Yakubu Gowon for nine years; General Murtala Muhammed for seven months; General Olusegun Obasanjo for three years as a military leader; President Shehu Shagari for four years; General Mohammed Buhari for two years; and General Babangida for eight years; President Ernest Shonekan for three months; General Sani Abacha for five years; General Addulsalam Abubakar for one year; and President Olusegun Obasanjo for six years so far.

Political instability in Nigeria has been caused by public mismanagement, economic setbacks, public corruption, ethnic pluralism, and abuse of the electoral process against the backdrop of a host of destabilizing colonial legacies. These factors have come to light through an examination of both the political climate that preceded military overthrows of Nigerian governments and the reasons advanced by the soldiers, newspapers, academics, labor unions and other opinion leaders. Kotecha offers additional insights:

> Anyone seeking to stage a coup in Africa does not have to look far for reasons. After assuming power, the officers typically cite the corruption, inefficiency, tribalism, arbitrary use of power, and general moral bankruptcy of the preceding regime as evils obliging them to intervene. Their accusations are often not unfounded.[75]

Be that as it may, Dorothy Dodge observes that certain prerequisites are necessary for the existence of an effective governmental system. These include common acceptance by its citizens of political institutions and procedures, popular confidence in and respect for the ruling elite, and a sense of nationalism and common destiny.[76] This study reveals that those conditions are lacking or in short supply in the Nigerian political culture.

The problem of corruption remains a major threat to political stability. In April 1990, the Christian Association of Nigeria reported that more than 3,000 Nigerians had secret Swiss bank accounts, which were on the top lists of those banks' patrons from the developing world.[77] Major Gideon Okor, the spokesperson of the group that attempted that year to topple

General Babangida's government, had accused the government of "corruption."[78] But Babangida dismissed the coup plotters as "dissidents . . . motivated by greed, self-interest and base avarice."[79] However, a prominent government critic, Gani Fawehinimi, had an interesting reaction: "I believe in using legal and constitutional means to oppose the policies and programs of this regime."[80] Like a deteriorating patient, bureaucratic corruption in Nigeria has only gotten worse and more daring in the new millennium, and the current civilian government of Olusegun Obasanjo[81] has had to embark upon an understandably difficult "war on corruption"although the war has attracted a mixture of praises and skepticism from a cross-section of Nigerians. While some Nigerians have cheered Obasanjo's war on corruption, some have pointed to what they perceive as his government's double standards and selective justice in terms of who is investigated and who is not. My take on it is that an effective war on bureaucratic corruption in Nigeria has to involve much more than the efforts of the presidency; the state governors and leaders of the local governments must also participate as prosecutors of the war.

In the late 1980s, Nigeria's climate of political tension was compounded by the introduction of the highly unpopular and painful structural adjustment program under the auspices of the International Monetary Fund (IMF). Ebere Onwudiwe reports on the factors that led to IMF's intervention:

> The IMF is there at the insistence of foreign banks who lent billions of dollars to my country in the 1970's. (*This was at the time of Nigeria's oil "boom"*)[emphasis mine]). The Nigerian government spent all the money, some of it unwisely, and now the foreign banks want to be repaid.[82]

As the government proceeds with an inevitable debt repayment program and structural adjustment, unemployment has reached record highs; so has inflation, and Nigeria has even joined the ranks of nations where some are starving.[83]

What is particularly striking about the foiled coup of 1990 is one of the reasons advanced by the plotters for their action. They alleged that the Babangida administration of Nigeria had been biased against Christian Nigerians in particular and Southern and Middle Belt Nigerians in general.[84] The moslem northerners, their spokesman said, had reduced other Nigerians to the status of slaves. These sentiments did not come as a surprise to watchers of the Nigerian political scene. In September 1990, the country's then defense minister, Lt. General Domkat Bali retired from the army after accusing the Babangida government of dictatorship and insensitivity to matters concerning religion. His resignation came after a cabinet shake-up in which he lost his position as head of the army. The cabinet changes evoked criticisms from "Christian" Nigerians who accused the government of attempting to "Islamize" the country. There were also street protests.[85] The government reacted by saying that in making those cabinet changes, it merely considered the abilities of those appointed to do the job; it did not care about their religious affiliations.[86] Thus, the cleavages in the Nigerian body politic were only becoming deeper and had assumed a dangerous, religious dimension. Worse still, the second program for a transition to civilian rule was characterized by irregularities reminiscent of the evils that wrecked the First Republic.

This chapter has pin-pointed the causes of political instability in Nigeria as ethnic competition for control of the center, public corruption, economic setbacks compounded by neo-colonial reforms, abuse of power, governmental ineptitude, indiscipline, abuse of the electoral process, religious intolerance and the prevalence of an alien world-view. The 1979 presidential style constitution was revised in 1989 in preparation for a second return to civilian rule. It was revised again in 1999. As in the previous case (that is, the 1979 Constitution), the revised constitution contains provisions designed to cure some of the ills that have plagued the federal republic. These include anti-corruption stipulations,[87] provisions for accountability on the part of the custodians of power, provisions for religious tolerance, provisions for a clean electoral process and so on.

However, the conduct of the politicians during the 1993 presidential campaigns and primaries once again highlights the sharp dichotomy between "theory" (as laid down in the constitution) and "practice" (as demonstrated by real life politics) in Nigeria's political affairs. Is the fault in the system or in the human beings who fail to play the game of politics by its clearly laid down rules? Why does the system of checks and balances prove ineffective? As the foregoing discussion shows, the disregard for the rules apparently stems from several weaknesses occasioned by non-adherence to Afrocentric/Africa-centered values. (These values are defined in Chapter Five). These weaknesses include indiscipline, a lack of true commitment to the public interest, an abandonment of the politics of honor, and the fear of ethnic or religious domination.

The question remains whether the Nigerians who operate the revised constitution would strive to respect its letter and spirit, or obey it in the breech as their predecessors had done. How that question is resolved would determine, to a large extent, whether Nigeria would continue on its current path of democratic experimentation or would become, once again, a victim of violent military usurpation of power. It has been shown clearly in the preceding analysis that military coups succeeded in Nigeria when the political climate induced it or proved conducive for such an intervention. In other words, these coups occurred in the wake of a public outcry and disgust against economic difficulties, governmental improprieties and ineptitude and ethnic or religious insensitivity on the part of the government of the day. Thus, it appears that the true antidote to military usurpation of power is an effective and integrative political leadership under girded by Afrocentric/Africa-centered values. How could this be achieved? This is the challenge that this book tackles.

It is one thing to propose a theoretical remedial measure, but what concrete steps are necessary for such a measure to become a reality? Some political observers have wondered if in the face of all these centrifugal forces and political disfunctionalities, Nigeria should go the way of a confederation, instead of remaining a federal state with a strong center. Remember that in the aftermath of the 1993 presidential campaigns, a leading and respected Nigerian newspaper called for the replacement of Nigeria's federalism with confederalism. Some have gone as far as projecting that given the disintegration of the former Yugoslavia and the Soviet Union along ethnic lines, the days of multi-ethnic nationhood are numbered. This viewpoint apparently ignores two factors: one, ethnic chauvinism is not a new phenomenon in Europe or world history; and two, the incidence of ethnic polarization has been confined mainly to the countries of what used to be the Eastern bloc, while the rest of Europe has forged ahead as an economically unified European Union.

AN IMPERIAL WORLD-VIEW

Earlier, it was pointed out that the colonialist world view, an **Imperial World-View**, still holds sway in Nigeria. It was also mentioned that this alien world-view was systematically imposed on Nigerians and other African states for the benefit of the colonizers; thus its dominance in the post-colonial era effectively works to the advantage of powers which have physically left the stage, but remain in control of the psyche of the ex-colonial nations by virtue of the world-view they left behind. Hence, the existence in contemporary times of what is known as colonial mentality. As a result of this world-view, Nigerians and other Africans, to a significant degree, apparently remain psychologically dislocated—a factor which seems not to bode well for the political, social and economic development of African peoples. This alien world-view, which time has proven inappropriate, is perpetuated by those whom Carter G. Woodson described in his book—*The Miseducation of the Negro*—as mis-educated negroes. In his reference to this class of Africans, Historian D. Chanainwa states as follows: 'Like the missionaries, they (the mis-educated Africans) often categorized the African masses as 'benighted people' and 'noble savages' and then assumed the responsibility of overhauling traditional Africa."[88]

Chanainwa goes further to say that the miseducated Africans had, "helped to undermine psychologically the African capacity to resist missionary-settler propaganda and in a way hindered the development of a truly African historical, racial and liberationist consciousness."[89] Afrocentric/Africa-centered historian, Tsehloane C. Keto describes how African centers of learning have also served this end:

> African universities which should become the academic nurseries for the re-emergence of . . . Africa centered intellectual flame even as they continue to open their doors to perspectives, methodologies, and viewpoints from other parts of the world, unfortunately, continue to be bastions of a hegemonic Europe centered perspective and have, on the whole, effectively shut out any serious participation of Africa centered perspectives of research and scholarship.[90]

What all this suggests is that in order to bring about an era of political leadership guided principally by an Afrocentric/Africa-centered philosophy, Africa needs a reformed form of education aimed at dislodging the colonialism-instituted world-view with an Afrocentric or Africa-centered perspective dedicated, among other objectives, to the promotion of African consciousness as opposed to a neo-colonial consciousness. Some people may wonder why it is so important that the alien, hegemonic world-view should be drastically modified. The answer may be found in the following question: when you look at the world through someone else's cultural eyes rather than yours, whose reality do you perceive? Besides that, as Cheikh Anta Diop says in his book, *The African Origin of Civilization: Myth or Reality*, "African culture will not be taken seriously until their utilization in education becomes a reality."[91]

Adherence to "the African orientation to the cosmos,"[92] as Asante puts it, could enable Africa to look inward rather than outward in its search for solutions to its problems. This, of course, does not suggest that Africa should not borrow ideas and techniques as and when necessary, provided that what it takes-in not only synchronizes with African ontology, but also serves African interests. In Nigeria's continuing experimentation with various forms of governmental systems, it appears the following question has seldom been asked: are there no composite elements in Nigeria's traditional governmental systems that could be incorporated into contemporary institutions in order to evolve a culturally condusive and workable political system? African consciousness would enable us to see ourselves as a people with a common destiny, or bring about what Asante describes as "collective consciousness,"[93] and Diop calls the "collective national African personality."[94] Collective consciousness would not necessarily mean that the African would forget that his/her particular cultural group is Igbo, Yoruba, Hausa, or Zulu, as the case may be, but it would mean for him/her a consciousness of the commonalities shared by those particularities.

THE SIGNIFICANCE OF POLITICAL STABILITY

This book contends that a healthy political leadership is central to the well-being of the people of a given geo-political entity. Other factors being equal, political leadership affects not only the peace of the nation, but its economic prosperity as well. As the literature on leadership will demonstrate, other things being equal, correct political leadership fosters peace, happiness, lasting and self-sustaining economic prosperity, technological growth and innovation. Even where a polity contains an abundance of economic resources as shown by Nigeria's example, without correct political leadership the nation will not be able to harness its resources. Africa in general is indeed a good example of this although we recognize the external, historical and internal constraints that tend to weaken political leadership on that continent. Despite those constraints, the factor of political leadership can be isolated and examined to determine its performance and effect on the well-being of the geo-political entity.

A politically unstable polity is like a human mind that is unstable. A person with such a mind can hardly realize his/her potential because he/she lacks the capacity for the calm judgment and calculations required for success in life. Leadership and political stability go hand in hand; they mutually reinforce each other. A supposedly good leader cannot thrive in a politically unstable climate and vice versa. Think of it in terms of a good driver in the wheels of a malfunctioning car. Even if you were a good driver, you would need a car that is in a good working condition for you to steer the wheels successfully. Conversely, if the car were in a good working condition, but the driver were incompetent, you might have a crash!

A state lacking in political stability may not support good political leadership. It can hardly attain and sustain economic prosperity and national tranquility. The citizens will be hard put realizing their full potentials because the political dispensation inhibits creativity. Political instability is not conducive to strategic, economic planning.

Businesses make decisions on the basis of a number of factors, including most importantly, the economic policies and legal environment set forth by the political order. But when the political entity's life is indeterminate, businesses will be hard pressed making long term plans, not knowing what political wind of change might sweep the country the next day. It is, therefore, not surprising that investors, especially the external ones, tend to be wary of undertaking ventures in countries that appear to wobble politically.

Empirical studies of this question have yielded varied, but generally affirmative findings. Robert T. Green came up with some what contradictory conclusions when he tested the hypothesis that a direct relationship exists between political stability and U.S. foreign direct marketing investment. Utilizing marketing investment data from United States government's publications and sample sizes consisting of countries with 90 percent of the total U.S. direct marketing investment in 1965, Green concluded from a statistical analysis that "political instability does not appear to be a major decision criterion of international managers."[95] Green quickly added, however, that "in prior studies executives claimed that it was a primary decision factor.[96]

Again, Green reports: "political instability may be an important factor in explaining the variance in the allocation of marketing investment within the different regions of the less developed world outside Latin America."[97]

Yair Aharoni's study of thirty-eight firms in 1966 found that political and economic stability was among the prerequisites a nation must meet in order to attract foreign investors.[98] R.S. Basi's 1963 study, using a mail questionnaire survey of 214 business executives, found that the executives ranked political stability of a foreign country as of crucial importance to investment decisions.[99] Yet another study (in 1969) by the National Industrial Conference Board confirmed the preceding findings. The study, involving 76 countries, found that political instability was the obstacle to investment most frequently mentioned by the sampled business executives.[100] A 1983 article on international investment political risk assessment holds that companies that rely heavily on overseas manufacturing, mining sites, or market outlets in a few countries are vulnerable to disastrous loss if their facilities are located "in historically unstable countries or regions."[101] Similarly, a 1989 study cites "the policy environment" in respect of domestic and foreign investment as a factor that determines the flow of international direct investment into developing countries.[102]

The major implication of these findings, which are certainly not exhaustive of the literature on this subject, is that the factor of political instability can dissuade a potential investor from a given country. The fortunes of indigenous businesses in such a country can also be undermined by political tremors and consequent uncertainty surrounding policy making, especially in a continent like Africa where, generally speaking, there is a high level of public sector involvement in the economy. For instance, a business can base its short term and long term plans on existing import/export regulations, economic nationalization policies and credit policies only to have such plans derailed by an arbitrary (military laws are usually arbitrarily enacted) policy reversal brought about by a sudden change of government.

Another reason the political condition of a state is of interest to us is that it can affect the planned development program. Developing countries engage in long-term economic development planning. The execution of such plans and even their very lives could be hampered by an abrupt political change. Even the regional economic co-operation commitment of a country could be undermined by a whimsical military leadership. An example is the death of the first East African Economic Community as a result of a chain of events precipitated by the coming to power of Uganda's Idi Amin.[103] However, the East African Economic Community was resurrected in 1999.

The overwhelming influence of political leadership is sometimes felt by its failure rather than its success. Under the leadership of the late Mobutu Sese Seko, the Central African state of Zaire (now renamed as the Democratic Republic of the Congo), the West African state of Liberia under the late Sergeant Doe, and the failed state of Somalia are, to varying degrees, stark, real-life examples of the failure of political leadership. Although Olusegun Obasanjo's current civilian government does not form an integral part of the historical period covered by this book, it's important to point out that his government has faced a Herculean task trying to normalize a Nigerian political economy that was bruised and battered under the infamous regime of Sanni Abacha. With the exception of a minority of privileged and well-connected Nigerians, the preponderance of Nigerians still await the day that daily news of the bountiful revenue that accrues from their nation's oil wealth could turn around the concrete realities of their hard daily lives.

Despite these examples of the failures or shortcomings of political leadership, in fairness, we have to recognize the historical, external and internal obstacles that have imposed constraints on political leadership on the continent in general. Writing about these constraints, Molefi K. Asante observes: "the boundaries by which Africa lives are artificial in the best sense of the word, serving little purpose in terms of the interjection of the African ethos into the world. The boundaries . . . are major obstacles to solving the food crisis in Africa."[104] Asante then went on to prescribe a reorganization of Africa into six states, none of which would be landlocked.

Like Asante, other analysts have contended that Africa's economic malaise can not be viewed in isolation from its history of colonialism and the Great Enslavement—the trade in African captives which dominated European international trade from the 16th to the middle of the 19th century. Historian John G. Jackson estimates that more than one hundred million African lives, including skilled labor, were lost.[105] The Africans who were thus uprooted from the continent became the tools that helped to bring about the Western industrial Revolution. Africa was robbed of able-bodied men and women who wound up contributing to the development of Europe and the Americas, not that of Africa. As historians F.K. Buah and J.F. Ade Ajayi have reported:

> Year after year, for more than three centuries tens of thousands of Afri-can farmers and craftsmen were shipped away to work in American plantations, mines and cities. With their labor they created vast wealth and profits, but seldom for themselves and never for Africa.[106]

Neither the assaulted and robbed continent nor the direct human victims of the Great Enslavement have received compensation. Instead, African scholars and leaders in the Diaspora and on the continent who have called for reparations have been dismissed by some Western commentators, along with their African hatchet-writers, who seem to lack correct historical consciousness, as rabble rousers and extremists.

Festus Ohaegbulam observes that African countries inherited cash crop economies from the colonialism, and that African economies were incorporated into an international economic system where the rules are decided by forces over which the largely infant African economies have little or no control.[107] Dependency theorists hold that one of the consequences is that the efforts of these countries at development have inevitably produced under-development rather than true development.[108] A one-time Tanzanian Minister of Economic Planning, Abdur Rahman Babu states that the biggest force against the economies of developing countries is the world market itself.[109] In this market, he notes, the prices of cash crops are determined not by the inter-action of demand and supply as the law of economics would prescribe, but by Western markets—a condition which the Western nations themselves will not tolerate in their internal economies.

Political economists Coralie Bryant and Louise White suggest that the industrialized nations "are part of the reason . . . the third world finds development so difficult."[110] These authors could not be more correct. Efforts by the developing countries to bring about changes for equity in the prevailing conditions of international business (like the movement for a new international economic order) have fallen on deaf Western ears, and instead corporate globalization, which perpetuates the economic inequities engendered by colonialism and imperialism, has become the order of the day. Worse still, as Ohaegbulam writes, "the widespread poverty in Africa and the slums associated with the African urban centers are not entirely a function of independent Africa but were essentially established features of colonial rule."[111] He contends that the roots of the misgovernment that pervade the continent are traceable to colonial times, including the nationals' lack of preparation for governance before the termination of colonial rule. The former colonies of Belgium and Portugal in Africa are good examples. In addition, African countries have weak national foundations owing to the fact that the existing political boundaries and institutional structures were erected by Western European powers for the benefit, not of the Africans, but of the European people—a one-sided fulfillment of Lord Frederick Lugard's Dual Mandate doctrine of the colonial era.

The fact that Africa contains artificial states has created enormous difficulties for African leaders who devote substantial energy to the process of nation-building, otherwise known as national integration—a process of forging a national spirit among disparate ethnic nations, a sense of disparity that is perpetuated by a Eurocentric epistemological paradigm, which emphasizes the differences among African cultures rather than their commonalities as is the case with Diopian African historiography—a historiography of synthesis rather than analysis. This synthesis focuses on the Cultural Unity of Africa in the midst of diversity.[112] Writing about the persistence of Eurocentric bias in the epistemology of African institutions of higher learning, Tsehloane C. Keto observes that the minds of Africans are still entrapped by "colonial mentality."[113]

The 1885 Western European balkanization of Africa (see Figure 2.1 for a map showing the current 54 states of Africa), as well as preceding factors, have helped to produce devastating consequences. The Nigerian Civil war of 1967 to 1970 is a case in point; the anarchy that engulfed Somalia in the 1990's, the Sudanese war, the Ethiopian/Eritrean war, the Chadian war, the Angolan war, Hutu slaughter of the Tutsis, etc. are other examples. These are wars that were/are fought at the expense of the scarce resources that could have been channeled to the improvement of the lives of the people. In Mozambique and Angola, forces sponsored by the then apartheid Minority government in South Africa, for years, wrecked immense havoc on the developmental efforts of their governments.

However, besides these colonially and externally derived forces that have impeded Africa's development, there is the problem of political instability fueled largely by internal factors like incessant military coups, governmental corruption, abuse of power, poor accountability and mismanagement, ethnic politics, religious intolerance, and ethnic intolerance manifested most dramatically by the Hutu mass slaughter of Tutsis of Rwanda in 1994. An estimated 800,000 Tutsis and some Hutus lost their lives.[114]

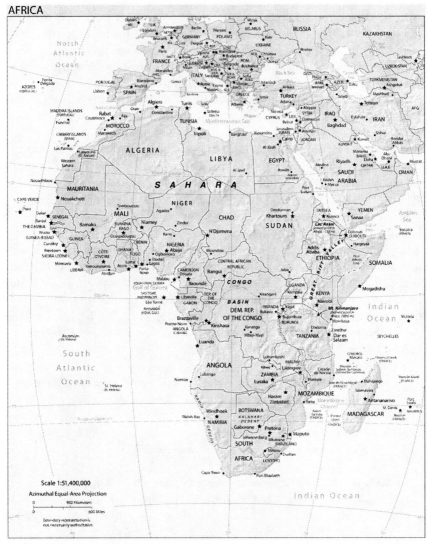

Figure 2.1. Map of Africa. Courtesy of the University of Texas Libraries, The University of Texas at Austin.

Although African countries in general and Nigeria were historically prone to political instability, since the 1990s, Africa has seen a wave of democratic changes of government previously unknown in its checkered history. Whereas before 1990, only seven of the 54 countries of Africa practiced multi-party democracy, between 1990 and 1997 alone, over forty-seven

African countries converted to multiparty democracies.[115] However, it remains unclear as to whether these multi-party democratic elections have been driven more by long-suppressed internal yearnings for democratic rule than by external political conditionalties demanded by Western bilateral and multilateral institutions, as well as global institutions, such the World Bank and IMF. It would appear that both factors have been contributory to the wind of multiparty democratic elections that has swept Africa in the recent decade. An unresolved question is whether multiparty elections have necessarily institutionalized an effective political culture on the continent.

Here, I will bring in Adebayo Adedeji, for as a former executive secretary of the Economic Commission for Africa (ECA), he must have attained an intimate understanding of the forces that affect Africa's development. Adedeji contends that lack of a democratic culture in Africa has impeded popular mobilization and effective accountability.

As he puts it: "the existing patterns of social differentiation and political organization have tended to encourage a rather narrow base for decision-making."[116] Adedeji believes that "the democratic process is the only means of involving the people in their entirety in change and transformation and in bringing about sustainable development."[117] This is an incisive observation, but Adedeji misses a significant factor, which Ohaegbulam captures as follows:

> Attempts by African leaders to diversify their political, economic and military relations are looked at with disfavor by the great powers, particularly of the West. Leaders who persist in such efforts face, and have faced, the risk of assassination or the overthrow of their administration by forces externally instigated, armed and financed.[118]

Such neo-colonial interventions in African affairs can succeed only as long as disloyal and self-fish Africans collude with their perpetrators. Neo-colonialism, like colonialism, takes advantage of ethnic divisions. What kind of philosophical orientation could enable Africans to withstand and resist these neo-colonial and other forces that disrupt the political life of the continent?

I suggest that if an Afrocentric/Africa-centered philosophy of leadership (which promotes, among other factors, the African interest and African consciousness, as opposed to ethnic or clannish consciousness), becomes dominant on the continent, it could facilitate the evolution of an Africa-centered political culture, which is necessary for effective leadership and political integration in African states. As formulated by Asante, its foremost contemporary proponent, the Afrocentric/Africa-centered philosophy, which is rooted in African history and culture, holds that it is legitimate to view phenomena from the African standpoint, in the context of constantly evolving African ideals and values.[119]

"African" is used in a holistic sense, a Pan-Africanist sense, which holds that continental and diasporic Africans share a common ancestral, cultural, historical and metaphysical heritage. It conceptualizes an African Cultural System[120] which regards African groups situated in different geographical locations of the world as centers of an African Cultural System that grew out of a common ancestral world-view, history and culture. This perspective seeks to lay the foundation for a universal African consciousness. In the context of the continent, Africa-centered leadership would stress Pan-African consciousness—that is, consciousness of the commonalties shared by African continental cultural centers.

The preceding discussion shows that colonial legacies, ethnic politics, religious cleavages, governmental corruption, political mismanagement, indiscipline, etc. contributed to Nigeria's present political condition of no-peace, no war type of instability—some might label it as a political condition of uneasy peace. However, the anarchy that engulfed and crippled Somalia in the early 1990's adds a fresh insight to African political studies. Although the Somali crisis is the outcome of complex international and national factors, it demonstrates that clannish cleavages can be as perilous to the nation-state as ethnic or religious polarities.

Chapter Three
Leadership and Political Integration in Africa: A Literature Review

As the preceding chapter shows, the forces that militate against political integration in Nigeria and consequently generate political instability have been a thorn in the flesh of the polity since its colonial inception as a nation-state. It was demonstrated in that chapter that the Nigerian case is merely a reflection of a malaise which is relatively continent-wide in scope.

A TELEGRAPH OF THE STUDIES

Several studies have been carried out on this problem. Among those reviewed in the ensuing chapter are: Claude Ake's *Theory of Political Integration*, Alaba Ogunsanwo's *Transformation of Nigeria*; Claude Welch, Jr.'s *Civilian Control of the Military*; and Larry Diamond's *Class, Ethnicity and Democracy in Nigeria*. Others are Richard A. Joseph's "Principles and Practices of Nigerian Military Government;" F. Niyi Akinnaso's "One Nation, Four Hundred Languages: Unity & Diversity in Nigeria's Language Policy;" Basil Davidson's *Modern Africa*; Ngugi Wa Thiong'O's *Moving the Center*; Robert H. Jackson's and Carl G. Rosberg's *Personal Rule in Black Africa*; and Ben Nwabueze's *Nigeria's Presidential Constitution*. The rest are Nzongola Ntalaja's "The Crisis in Zaire;" Bode Onimode's "Crisis of Global Capitalism;" Kempton Makamure's "Contradictions in the Socialist Transformation of Zimbabwe;" Abdoulaye Bathily's "Senegal's Fraudulent Democratic Opening;" Samuel Decalo's *Coups and Army Rule in Africa*; John Harbeson's "Military Rulers in Africa;" Olusegun Obasanjo's "Our Desperate Ways" and *My Command*, and Mansour Khalid's *Africa in the Eyes of a Patriot: a Tribute to General Olusegun Obasanjo*. These works and others reviewed and cited in this chapter shed light not only on the nature of post-colonial political leadership and political integration in Nigeria in particular and Africa in general, but also on the nature of the socio-economic and political environment in which they function.

A Theory of Political Integration by Claude Ake is a penetrating and highly-informed theoretical and historical analysis of the subject. Ake views political integration as the problem of "developing a political culture and of inducing commitment to it."[1]

Ake identifies two major challenges for leadership in trying to promote political integration within a nation: "(a) how to elicit from subjects deference and devotion to the claims of the state, and (b) how to increase normative consensus governing political behavior among members of the political system."[2] This definition of political integration suggests that both old and new nations deal with the challenges of political integration, but with different degrees and areas of emphasis. For a new nation with a diverse population, the challenge for national leadership involves much more than the twin challenge of eliciting the deference and devotion of citizens and increasing the normative consensus for political behavior. Leadership in such a situation—that is, in the case of a new, heterogeneous nation—has to grapple with the task of forging a coherent political society from a plurality of traditional societies; it also has to worry about how to enhance cultural homogeneity in the midst of diversity.[3]

One of the critical elements of Ake's definition of political integration is the concept of political culture, which is described as 'the system of empirical beliefs, expressive symbols and values which defines the situation in which political action takes place.[4] For the individual, the political culture determines the boundaries of political behavior. The political culture provides the political system with 'a systematic structure of values and rational considerations which ensures coherence in the performance of institutions and organizations.'[5] Ake believes that an integrated political system is one in which there is a consensus among individual political actors over the norms of political behavior as well as a commitment on their part to the patterns of political actions legitimized by those norms. In their work, Hanes Walton and Robert Smith shed further light on the concept of political culture as follows: " . . . Political culture refers to political orientations—attitudes towards the political system and attitudes toward the role of the individual in the system. Simply put, the concept refers to the individual's attitudes, beliefs, and values about politics and the political system."[6] Both are perceptive postulations, but they leave out an important variable. What impact does the state of the economy exert on the level of political integration within a state? To what extent is the "commitment" of the individual political actors to the accepted norms of political behavior affected or influenced by the condition of the economy? If, for instance, there is a normative consensus against the acceptance of bribes by political actors from interest groups or individuals, would economically distressed political actors resist the temptation to violate such a norm? If such violations occur on a mass scale, what would be their effect on the ability of the state to elicit the deference and devotion of the subjects—a crucial ingredient of political integration?

Ake makes a distinction between a mal-integrated political system and an integrated political system, pointing out that the former stresses effective, rather than legitimate, means of accomplishing goals.[7] The book sets up an explanatory model of level of political integration. The model, which is not exhaustive, consists of the following explanatory variables: 1. a legitimacy score, 2. a extra-constitutional behavior score, 3. a political violence score, 4. a secessionist demand score, 5. an alignment pattern score, 6. a bureaucratic ethos score, and 7. a authority score.[8]

Another thoughtful definition of political integration is that provided by Ernst Haas: 'a process whereby political actors in distinct national settings are persuaded to shift their loyalties, expectations, and political activities toward a new center, whose institutions possess or demand jurisdiction over the pre-existing nation-state.'[9] This definition may appear commonsensical, but it aptly describes a major task of leadership in post-independence Africa, particularly Nigeria. This is sometimes referred to as nation-building. As I stated earlier, an undeniable fact of Nigerian political life is the multiplicity of its ethnic make-up. However, super-imposed on this is the legacy of what Basil Davidson describes as "colonial tribalism"[10]—the divide and rule policy of playing one ethnic group against another. Nationalists fought against this virus during the independence struggle, but they did not succeed in crushing it. The nationalists mustered enough forces of unity to defeat colonialism, but their effort "was not strong enough to end the legacy of internal division."[11] Chapter One demonstrated how this legacy of internal division tore away at the heart of Nigeria and led to a three-year Civil War that ended in 1970. Even now that the colonial rulers have physically quit the stage, their institutions of mass communication tend to seize every available opportunity to fan embers of ethnic animosity in Africa. *Africa Confidential*, the British-based weekly journal of African Affairs, ran the following cynical remark in its report on Kenya's general election of December 1992 in which President Daniel Toroitich Arap Moi emerged as the victor.

> No Kikuyu or Luo has been elected on a KANU (the president's party) ticket. The president is reportedly going to attempt to appease these groups with presidential appointments. Whatever nominees he finds,

nothing will change the fact that three provinces (the home base of the first and third most numerous ethnic groups in the country) voted over-whelmingly against Moi and his party.[12]

Notice the apparent subtle attempt in the preceding paragraph to incite the ethnic groups, which apparently did not vote for Moi, against the president.

Ake's diagnosis of the problem of political instability in the post-independence states identifies several causal factors: (1). the end of colonialism removed a factor which had helped to unify the nationalist movements; (2). as independence approached, centrifugal forces became more pronounced as political leaders sought to strengthen their positions at the center through appeals to particularist tendencies; (3). after independence, these centrifugal forces became even stronger and the ruling party's influence and popularity decreased as the nation engaged in the onerous task of social mobilization for economic development. The expansion of voting rights following independence, in most of the new states, produced new centers of power which in some cases tried to pursue different political interests through new political parties. There was also the fact that the end of colonialism removed "the atmosphere of crisis"[13] which had engendered and fostered popular support for the nationalist movement during the independence struggle. Added to all these was the public disillusionment caused by the inability of the governing party to meet the many promises of independence.[14]

Ake also identifies an external destabilizing factor, which he describes as imperial diplomacy. This factor, he states, encouraged opposition to the party in power in the hope of weakening the forces of nationalism. Examples of such imperially-inspired opposition include the Northern Peoples Congress (NPC) in the first Republic of (1960–1966) and the Northern Peoples Party during Nkrumah's Ghana. Ake is merely one of several scholars who have written about external influences on the political health of post-independence Africa.

Writing about the phenomenon, Davidson observes that external forces, through visible and invincible means, have circumscribed the ability of independent nations to govern themselves as they see fit. He explains: "These limits were an attempt by the former colonial powers to keep an indirect control; to govern indirectly through 'convenient partners;' to undermine a true independence of thought and action."[15] Davidson's observation is a familiar one, but it contains a striking message: imperialism has been actively seeking to undermine "a true independence of thought and action"[16] in post-independence Africa. In other words, neo-colonialism is much more than an attempt to maintain political control through the economic backdoor; it has a vibrant intellectual dimension. This helps explain Toyin Falola and Julius Ihonvbere's earlier observation that the colonialist/imperialist world-view still holds sway in Nigeria and is one of the factors accountable for political instability.

Lack of elite solidarity has worked against political integration in Nigeria. A notable cause of this has been associated with the fact that Nigerian and other African intellectuals had played the leading role in the independence struggle. This role habituated them to opposition to constituted authority; thus, after independence, the intellectuals continued their onslaught against the powers-that be, often putting them at odds with politicians who regard "opposition as unreasonable."[17] Apart from this factor, ethnic competition, differences among the elite over policy questions, and generational distinctions between older and younger intellectuals have had the effect of polarizing the ranks of the elite.[18]

Making matters worse, says Ake, is the fact that the elite are preoccupied with all things Western. This preoccupation with Westernization and the elite's Western education has alienated them from the masses. By the time Ake did his work in the sixties, the internet had not yet been born. Given the pervasive presence of the internet in the new millennium, one only wonders about the extent to which the World Wide Web, along with its globalizing influences, has even deepened this preoccupation with Westernization that Ake identifies on the part of the elite of the post-colonial nations. While being preoccupied with Westernization, the elite are simultaneously disillusioned with the new domestic order, for not treating and rewarding them fairly.[19] A notable source of the elite-masses gap is a communication gap, which stems from the inability of the masses to comprehend the elite's language of secularism and rationality. On the other hand, "the leaders are constantly frustrated by the masses' persistence in those attitudes of mind which are clearly detrimental to the execution of the policies that will realize the cherished 'brave new world.'"[20]

The preceding situation is compounded by a backdrop of colonial indoctrination. Such is the magnitude of this indoctrination that the decolonization of African minds would require what Sekou Toure once described as 'the total reconversion of the human being who has been taught a way of thinking foreign to the real condition of his milieu.'[21] At the same time, however, there is a need, as Ake agrees, to imbue the general population with a bureaucratic attitude of mind (that is, respect for rationally adopted rules) and skills necessary for the construction of an industrial society. Ake conceives of the journey towards a bureaucratic state in Max Weberian terms: social evolution is a movement away from "traditionalistic social systems, whose legitimacy is based on custom."[22] But it is apropos to

wonder whether the so-called masses are solely to blame for the fact that
bureaucratic ethos do not prevail in the new states. Do the educated ones,
whom we describe as the elite, always play by the rules of rationalism in
the way they discharge their official duties? As Ake is quick to point out,
parochial loyalties and tendencies of the elite have also seemed to obstruct
the attainment of "a tradition of bureaucratic impartiality."[23] He rightly
observes that such deviations from bureaucratic norms tend to dilute the
citizenry's respect and loyalty to its political leadership. Favoritism breeds
mistrust of the government. In consequence, interest groups, which feel left
out or cheated, seek to strengthen their position through extra political
action. This reaction, in turn, leads to "a proliferation of political organizations"[24] and ultimately produces a government beset by "segmented and
rivalrous interests."[25]

While the end-goal of a bureaucratic society is laudable, I do not
believe that rationalism should necessarily produce only a society where
rugged individualism prevails. Nigeria and other African nations ought
to promote rationalism in the context of a society of community-minded
individuals. These societies should seek to foster rationalism with a human
face—a regime of rationalism that would place no less an emphasis on the
intrinsic worth of the human being than Western humanism even though
the latter places a premium upon individualism. The rugged marketplace-
oriented individualism that characterizes the Western experience (and
which was transplanted to Africa through colonial education) has tended
to dilute human empathy for one another, particularly the natural human
instinct to be protective of fellow human beings. As Walter Rodney puts it,
capitalist individualism had infused Europe with a sense of entrepreneur-
ship and adventurism, but in Africa, it had the overall effect of destroying
social solidarity and promoting the worst kind of alienated individualism
without social responsibility.[26]

Another impediment to political integration cited by Ake is the fact
that some of the new states, like Nigeria, have found it difficult to adopt
an indigenous language as a national language. For the most part, these
nations still communicate, officially, through the languages of the imperial powers. Ake believes that the adoption of an indigenous language as
the common language of the nation would "reduce cultural fragmentation
while enhancing the country's identity."[27]

The language issue is understandably a contentious subject. In a
discussion of this subject, F. Niyi Akinnaso comments that the multiplicity
of languages in Nigeria "accentuate the difficulty in achieving national
unity in the face of ethno-linguistic diversity."[28] But a question that must be
asked is this: if a neutral language like the language of the colonizer could

not minimize cultural fragmentation, how could an indigenous language achieve that objective in an tribalism-infested climate like Nigeria—a milieu marked by endemic mutual mistrust among the competing ethnic groups? In any case, do we really have a problem of cultural fragmentation in Nigeria? Or, could it be that what Ake describes as cultural fragmentation is, in reality, what Akinnaso correctly recognizes as linguistic pluralism? Ake needs to establish that fundamental cultural differences exist among Nigerian ethnic groups in order to substantiate his position that genuine cultural fragmentation applies to the Nigerian political landscape. I believe that linguistic diversity, rather than real cultural fragmentation, more accurately describes the Nigerian cultural landscape. The British took advantage of this linguistic schism to introduce and nurture what Basil Davidson described earlier as colonial tribalism into the Nigerian psyche. In other words, I believe that the problem of ethnic hostility (popularly known as tribalism) in Nigeria did not arise from fundamental cultural differences among Nigerian ethnic groups. In fact, Nnamdi Azikiwe, one of the foremost leaders of Nigeria's independence struggle and first indigenous governor-general of Nigeria, points out in *Renascent Africa*, a 1937 publication, that European colonial rule had amplified what, in reality, are simply insignificant "cultural differences" among African ethnic groups.[29]

Walter Rodney offers a thoughtfully historical perspective on "tribalism." Condemning as erroneous a rather popular conception that Africans are naturally more grafted to tribe than to nation in a world of perpetual inter-tribal hostility, Rodney observes that that idea is ahistorical, for Africa's pre-colonial history boosts of multi-ethnic states—thus, showing that Africans had had an active sense of trans-ethnic nationalism. However, in destroying those states, as colonialism did, colonialism removed a major vehicle through which the continent had begun to dismantle fragmented loyalties. Worse than that, colonialism actually set the hand of the clock backwards through its divide-and-rule policy of fueling and exploiting ethnic antagonisms. Thus, in the particular case of Nigeria, "tribalism" was a "product of administrative devices, of entrenched regional separations, of differential access by particular ethnic groups into the colonial economy and culture."[30]

Diop has another insightful exposition on this subject. He writes that pre-colonial Africa manifested a monarchical Africa and a tribal Africa. Monarchical Africa, as exemplified by Ghana, Mali and Songhai Empires, contained African populations that had become de-tribalized. This progressive trend was thrown off balance by the intrusion of European adventurers onto Africa as from the fifteenth century.[31] However, in those places where the trend toward de-tribalization had taken roots, social bonds would continue to determine inter-personal relations. On the other hand, Diop explains:

> Where clanic organization still predominated, where social limits were still determined by the territory of the clan or tribe, there would be a sort of turning inward, an evolution in reverse, a retribalization reinforced by the new climate of insecurity. Collective life again took precedence over individual life.[32]

A key element that is missing from this historical explanation of the trajectory of ethnic consciousness in African social evolution is the deliberate role that colonialism played in facilitating "retribalization" (as Diop describes it) on the continent.

Like the cultural arena, it has been found that Nigerian endogenous languages do not manifest fundamental differences. Although there are about four hundred indigenous languages in Nigeria,[33] they share a high level of "structural similarity."[34] Nigeria has three exogenous languages—English (which is the predominant language of governmental affairs and educational instruction), French, and Arabic. There is also "pidgin English"—a hybrid of mainly English and local languages. Three of the 400 indigenous languages of Nigeria—Hausa, Igbo and Yoruba—are spoken by about 53 percent of the population.[35] The Hausa-Fulani, Igbo and Yoruba constitute the major ethnic groups of the country. Remarkably, Nigerian political leadership has tried to turn Nigeria's language diversity into an instrument for national integration. Section fifty-one of the nation's 1979 Constitution provides that in addition to English, the three major indigenous languages—Hausa, Igbo and Yoruba—should be used as official languages. (Section 53 of the Revised Constitution of Nigeria (1989) retains that proviso).[36] The subsequent, 1999 version of that Constitution stipulates that "the business of the National Assembly shall be conducted in English, and in Hausa, Ibo and Yoruba when adequate arrangements have been made thereof."[37] Furthermore, Nigeria's national policy on education stipulates that every school child should learn at least one of those three languages, besides her mother tongue.[38] While this policy reflects pride in the African culture, it demonstrates Nigerian leadership's determination to pursue the overall goal of national integration within a multilingual/multi-cultural framework.

As Akinnaso puts it, the preceding national language policy of Nigerian leadership is driven by:

> (1) the desire to achieve 'national unity' through the use of indigenous 'national' languages; (2) preservation of the people's diverse cultures

through preservation and maintenance of their languages; (3) development and projection of Nigerian languages; and (4) enrichment of the
children's ability to communicate effectively in a multilingual society.[39]

He recognizes that the adoption of three major Nigerian languages as
national official languages—in addition to English—is not the ideal step
but a politically expedient measure. Given the fact that none of those three
major indigenous languages is spoken by the majority of the estimated
one hundred and thirty-one million plus Nigerians and no ethnic group
forms a majority in the population, "the relatively large size of these . . .
groups and political rivalry among them have made language domination by any one group impossible."[40] Even then, there is a lesson to be
learned from India's experience. In that case, even though Hindi is spoken by a majority of Indians, the country's decision to adopt Hindi as the
national language unleashed "a storm of protest and political crisis"[41] from
non-Hindi speaking groups. While it is healthy to Africanize key aspects
of Nigeria's national affairs like the language of official transaction, the
important question of political feasibility must be taken into consideration
at each given step. Therefore, Akinnaso's hope that "one of the national
languages [of Nigeria] would eventually emerge supreme and be adopted
as the nation's official language"[42] is laudable but needs to be viewed with
cautious optimism. The litmus test ought to be: can such a step further
or weaken Nigeria's political march toward political cohesion? Does the
Nigerian experience with nation-formation indicate that such a step would
augur well for national harmony?

I believe that the nation's current policy of creatively using Nigeria's
linguistic and cultural pluralism to promote national integration is a sensible
and pragmatic one. In a Nigeria where the vocabulary of political discussions includes speculations about a latent or real Hausa-Fulani hegemony
over the nation, would the idea of adopting a single Nigerian language as the
national language exacerbate or lesson such fears? Does such an idea hold
a glistening prospect for fostering political integration? I for one, I do not
believe that having all Nigerians adopt and speak one common indigenous
Nigerian language could or should, by itself, result in the ethnic domination of Nigeria by the original speakers of the nationally adopted language
if Nigeria learns to respect and uphold her constitutional provisions for
equal citizenship rights for all. In fact, since everyone will end up speaking
and using the nationally adopted Nigerian language, in the long run, there
may no longer exist a distinguishable dichotomy between the majority and
minority speakers of the nationally adopted Nigerian language. A common
Nigerian language could also be politically feasible if official policy makes

it clear that using a common Nigerian language would not require that you should give up the language of your own ethnic heritage.

However, in addition to adopting an indigenous Nigerian language as a common national language, the Nigerian national leadership should additionally adopt a widely-spoken African language, such as KiSwahili of East Africa, as a tactical means of forging African unity. It can do this by adopting KiSwahili[43] as a Pan-African national language of Nigeria. One of the attractions of KiSwahili is that it is spoken across ethnic lines, and for this reason, it is not perceived as the language of a given ethnic group. In any case, whatever political leadership ends up doing on the question of a lingua franca for Nigeria must be designed to allay, not exacerbate the fear of ethnic political domination that pervades Nigerian political life. KiSwahili is large and flexible and has been written for centuries either in the Arabic alphabet or the Latin.[44] Another attractive character of KiSwahili, as described by Ngugi Wa Thiong'O, is that it has not served as a language of oppression and domination. He explains that "KiSwahili has created space for itself in Africa and the world without displaying any national chauvinism."[45] Tanzania has set an excellent example in this regard by choosing KiSwahili as her official language even though the language has few or no "native-speaker population."[46] If followed by Nigeria and other African countries, such a measure would help water the seed of African unity and African consciousness. Increasingly becoming a continental language, KiSwahili already serves as a major language in Eastern, Central, and Southern Africa.[47] If adopted by Diasporic Africans, KiSwahili could then become the common language of the African world. In contrast with other widely-used, but externally-derived languages in Africa like Arabic, English or French, KiSwahili ranks high in terms of cultural or political acceptability because of its African origins. As Wa Thiong'O himself puts it, KiSwahili is a product of African history and has historically served as a vehicle for unity, cultural contact, intra-African and international trade.[48]

An additional impediment to political integration arises from the new state's difficulty in finding "cultural symbols around which the country may be united," Ake reports.[49] This point is cogent, and it is in recognition of the need for such cultural symbols that this writer has suggested the setting up of a federal house of traditional rulers to help give the Nigerian nation a symbolic sense of historical continuity in political leadership. This is explained in detail in Chapter Six.

Another issue tackled in Ake's work is the relationship between what is known as charismatic leadership and political integration. What effect, if any, does charismatic leadership exert on political integration? Charismatic legitimation is a theory which holds that a leader with a broad and national appeal (as opposed to a narrow ethnic appeal) could motivate citizens to transfer their ethnic loyalties to the state. Explaining that charismatic leadership is an important pre-requisite for the legitimation of the state, Ake notes: "the legitimation of the state is a matter of getting the citizen to regard it as a genuine representative of his interests and, therefore, deserving his loyalty; it is to some extent a matter of making him think of the state as 'we' rather than 'they.'"[50] He adds that for political integration to be realized, citizens need to believe that the state is a legitimate instrument of force and authority—the legitimate medium of legislative and social decisions. The theory states further that state legitimation requires not just a charismatic leader but one who commands the respect and trust of citizens. In a critique of the manner in which ex-President Babangida (1985–1993) implemented his never-completed program of transition from military to civilian rule in Nigeria, General Olusegun Obasanjo alluded to this factor. Decrying the absence of "persons whose authority was recognized and accepted by the rank and file"[51] from the leaderships of the two political parties that the Babangida administration had approved for the transition to a Third Republic, Obasanjo laments that two parties (rather than the five under the Second Republic), had not succeeded in bringing about a much hoped for national cohesion. In fact, the nation, he observes, was more polarized as of 1992 than ever before. However, Obasanjo's comments miss a number of important facts of Nigeria's recent political history. One is that the winner of the 1979 presidential election, Shehu Shagari, was the least charismatic of the five contestants. Among those who lost to Shagari were the two most charismatic and elderly political leaders of Nigeria at that time—the late Chief Obafemi Awolowo and the Owelle of Onitsha, Nnamdi Azikiwe, the country's first indigenous Head of State. One of the factors which enabled Shagari—a Fulani—to emerge triumphant was his command of most of the votes from the Hausa/Fulani ethnic block in the North. (The northern section of Nigeria has a population advantage over the south.) Thus, in this case, the ethnic factor proved more decisive than the charismatic element. For if charisma had been the decisive factor in the 1979 presidential race in Nigeria, Azikiwe, Awolowo or even Aminu Kanu would have won the election.

Not surprisingly, Ake criticizes the theory of charismatic legitimation. He argues that the logic of the theory amounts to a circular interpretation of political integration, for it "presupposes the existence of a symbol of national identity—the charismatic leader."[52] In addition, he notes, the theory collapses if a state is not entrusted in the hands of a charismatic leader or if the charismatic leader lacks an extensive appeal. Furthermore, ethnic politics and other polarizing elements of a typical heterogeneous society limit the functional value of the theory as a tool of political integration. Other obstacles to the application of the theory are 1. the demise of the unifying presence of colonialism, 2. the public disillusionment brought about by unfulfilled promises of independence, and 3. unpopular governmental actions in the quest for socio-economic development.[53] The African experience illuminates the pitfalls of trying to build a political system on the basis of the charisma of a leader or what is otherwise known as personalized leadership. As Ake puts it, "the political history of Africa shows that the downfall of the 'national hero' has tended to lead to the complete collapse of his mass party."[54] The point is well made. However, the problem with the African experience which Ake cites is that one is not sure whether Ake is confusing hated dictators for true charismatic leaders. The theory at hand assumes that a charismatic leader is one with a broad cross-ethnic appeal and one who commands the respect and trust of his/her people. How many current leaders of African nations fit this description? On its own, charismatic leadership is inadequate for purposes of political integration. However, despite its inadequacies, I think that the theory of charismatic legitimation can serve as a useful glue for meshing together all the other devices applied by leadership toward the goal of political integration although Nigeria's "tribalism" seems to have proven invincible to the force of charisma. Ake is mindful of the supportive role that charismatic leadership can play in the process of forging political integration. Thus, he writes: 'The personal authority which is to be used for buttressing the state should not be sought from one charismatic leader but from a multiplicity of sources—traditional authorities, leaders of important secondary associations, etc."[55] This appears like an attempt on the part of Ake to "democratize" charismatic leadership roles, but how could this suggestion be implemented especially at the national level? My proposed house of traditional rulers could serve as a vehicle for the operationalization of this idea.

It is in the interest of a political system to narrow the gap between the elite and ordinary people through such measures as universal education and political education for the rural population. The gap between the elite and the masses works against the attainment of true social change. Ake believes that this is why military takeovers of power in the new states are merely palace coups rather than mass uprisings.

Ake holds that since political power lies in the hands of the elite, the ultimate panacea for the instability of the new states resides principally in the modification of their conduct. He cautions that "as long as they are so avowedly elitist and so bitterly contentious, their political power will always be precarious."[56] He urges the elite to temper their competition for power, promote mass participation in the process of governance and to respect constitutionalism.

While Ake urges the elite to narrow the gap that exists between them and the masses, he, at the same time, makes a suggestion that seems somewhat contradictory. He calls on the elite to strive for greater cohesion in their ranks, arguing convincingly that greater group cohesiveness would minimize tensions among the political elite. But the ironic twist to this is that the attainment of elite cohesion would require that a group of members of society should consciously differentiate themselves from the masses—thus, psychologically, if nothing else, inducing a gap between "them and us."

Another issue that Ake tackles relates to the contentious question of whether the single party system contains the key to political integration, especially in a multi-ethnic society. The major argument in favor of the single party system or unipartyism as Ake describes it, claims that it promotes social solidarity, maximizes mass participation and social communication and emphasizes political education.[57] It is also claimed that unipartyism enhances political integration and political stability. The mass participation which unipartyism generates induces a sense of involvement and motives party leaders to think in national rather than in particularist terms.[58] This line of reasoning contends that the real choice for Africa is between the one party system on the one hand and anarchy and perennial military interventions on the other.[59] Tanzania's ex-President, the late Julius Nyerere, whose nation thrived on the one party system, believes that the new states face an emergency which requires that all sectors of the population must close ranks. By an emergency, Nyerere refers to the problem of poverty and the task of socio-economic development.[60] In fact, he does not mince words about his distaste for multi-partyism as shown by the following:

> If you define democracy in a stupid manner, [and] if you equate democracy with the multiplicity of parties, you're going to quarrel with serious people in Africa. You're not going to quarrel with non-serious people because they'll give you the multiplicity of parties and that will not be democracy.[61]

In addition to the preceding, the sometimes reckless conduct of the self-appointed police of world democracy, namely the United States (a recklessness manifested in America's brazen invasion and occupation of the Sovereign nation of Iraq in 2003 in violation of the United Nation's founding principle of the sovereignty of nations), makes one cynical about her much-vaunted belief in justice, equity, and the right of nations to self-determination—cardinal principles of democracy.[62] Here again, in characteristic and perhaps prophetic fashion, Nyerere does not mince words. He observes: "Countries like the US which are forever talking about the rule of law and the need for improved international relations, think nothing of flouting those very principles themselves when it is in their interest to do so."[63] He cites the U.S. disregard of a World Court ruling against it for mining Nicaraguan ports.[64] In fact, America's rather hypocritical postures in world affairs do not set a good example for the rule of law in international affairs. In general, the United States tends to recognize and implement U.N. resolutions only when it suits the designs of policy makers in Washington. A stark example is its over-zealous pursuit of the UN resolutions against Iraq in the early 1990s and well into the new millennium, culminating in the afore-mentioned invasion and occupation—an occupation that, in its wake, triggered an insurgency that has transformed Iraqi into a dangerous and terrorist stronghold that it wasn't prior to George Bush's lawless invasion. Another example is her tendency to look the other way when Israel bullies the long-suffering Palestinians, regardless of applicable United Nations resolutions. The U.S. ought to have approached the Palestinian-Israeli dispute in an even-handed manner. An even-handed approach would require that the U.S. should employ its financial and diplomatic muscles in a balanced fashion to bring about the much-talked about two-state solution—that is a free independent Palentine living and trading side by side with a secure Israel. So far, it seems that the U.S. is willing to apply its financial muscle only on the weaker side of the dispute. Isn't that politically convenient?

Ake concedes that the single-party system has its strengths, including the inhibition of social differences, but points out that it suffers from several weaknesses. First, unipartyism is still vulnerable to parochial intra-party competition. As he puts it, "it sometimes happens that the competitors find the temptation to gain a temporary advantage by a subtle appeal to social differentiation irresistible."[65] Second, the system tends to be authoritarian and intolerant of dissent. Since the party equates itself with the state, it tends to regard organized opposition as unlawful. This, in turn, compels opposition forces to resort to desperate tactics, which provoke a counter-response from the ruling party. Third, single partyism makes for a winner-take-all result. This winner-take-all outcome makes intra-party competition a bitter contest which sometimes involves unscrupulous means and a flagrant disregard for the rules of the game.[66] In the final analysis, the system, Ake contends, "endangers stability and impedes integration by discouraging the growth of that mutual self-restraint which makes the coexistence of different interests within the same political society possible."[67] A major step that leadership must take in working toward political integration is that of social mobilization.[68] But this has its own risks, for social mobilization tends to disrupt the political order in the short run, notes Ake. Given the fact that social mobilization represents a primary challenge for the developing nations, Ake postulates that the problem of political integration presents two major questions to the new states. 1. "What characteristics must the political system possess to enable it to undertake social mobilization effectively? 2. What type of political system is most capable of neutralizing the disruptive short-run effects of social mobilization?"[69] In another sense, how could the leadership of the new states maintain a necessary degree of political stability as they undertake the disruptive task of social mobilization? What factors would enable the political system to contain the dysfunctional and disequilibrating effects of social mobilization? Ake suggests that a political system must possess four structural characteristics to enable leadership to carry out social mobilization successfully. He lists those characteristics as the authoritarian, paternal, identific and consensual characteristics.[70] These four elements, he states, provide a political system with the resiliency that it needs to be able to implement social mobilization, adding that the absence of any or a combination of these would raise the destabilizing impact of the process.

The following is a description of Ake's conceptual scheme containing four conditions which leadership must meet for a successful prosecution of the social mobilization necessary for the attainment of political integration. "The authoritarian element: a political system is authoritarian if the government's power is large, concentrated, and easily mobilized, and if the government manifests a determination and ability to use this power to carry out its policies. "[71]

Ake goes on to identify three sources of governmental power and their implications for new states. They are: "The esteem of the citizens for the government, the economic resources and information that the government commands, the government's constitutional rights, etc."[72]

He explains that the government exercises these powers through the army, the police force, the civil service, the mass media, etc. But the ability of the governments of the new states to exercise authority over their citizens is circumscribed by a number of factors,[73] he observes. Factor one, those governments have not, by and large, won the respect of the individual for the state. Two, the weak economic clout of the governments limits their ability to win influence with economic resources. Three, the forces of coercion available to those governments are inadequate and incompetent. Four, the forces of ethnic parochialism hamper the observance of the rules and regulations of bureaucracy. Five, inadequate communication facilities limit the ability of the governments to control their citizens. Reflecting on these shortcomings, Ake observes that "the problem is not that the governments of the new states are too powerful but that they are too powerless."[74] This powerlessness explains, in part, why those governments achieve limited success in their drive for change.

One wonders how political scientist Nzongola Ntalaja would have taken Ake's preceding conclusion, for in his discussion of the state of post-independence Zaire (now known as the Democratic Republic of the Congo), he identifies an authoritarian, bureaucratic structure of control as a significant cause of the failure of Zairian (Congolese) leadership to provide for the basic needs of the country.[75]

The second element of Ake's conceptual scheme is what he calls the paternal. A paternal political system is one, which is " . . . dominated by a political class that is willing and able to lead."[76] "Political class" refers to leaders of the important social, religious, professional and ethnic groups—in fact, everyone who heads a significant base of power.[77] The role of this class, he explains, is to destroy or change "certain habits of mind" and undermine "certain traditional symbols of collective identity."[78] This class also strives to "induce the people to accept new norms, new goals, new motivations."[79] It is also the task of this class to make the people feel that their voice counts lest they would be alienated.[80]

The third component of the conceptual scheme is described as the identific. An identific political system is "characterized by mutual identity between the political class and the governed."[81] Such a system is identific to the extent that:

a   There is a free flow of communications between the political class and the governed.
b.   The political formula of the political class is acceptable to the governed. (Political formula is the principle—moral, legal, philosophical, etc.—on which the government's claims to political power rests.)
c.   The civic body considers that it has some interests in the continued existence of the government.[82]

To what extent do the new states practice this code of political behavior? Ake reports that those states lack a "well-articulated and widely accepted political formula"[83] and consequently have a limited ability to influence their citizens. Interestingly, Ake finds a positive role for ethnic particularism in the promotion of identific relations between the political class and the governed. He writes:

> Ethnic particularism helps to make the political system more identific
> by helping to produce a pattern of segmentary political alignments

cutting across the elite-mass gap, and thus keeping the political system from being dangerously polarized.[84]

My reaction to this position is that such a pattern of segmentary alignments calls for careful management otherwise it could prove counter-productive. Of greater pertinence, however, is the following question: "Are there cultural symbols and historical experiences that can be exploited for reinforcing social solidarity?"[85] I believe that the latter idea, that is, using cultural symbols to reinforce social solidarity, is what ought to be stressed.

The fourth dimension of the conceptual scheme is a consensual factor, which is present in a political system if "the political class is solidary and if the hegemony of the political class is not threatened by a counter-elite."[86] What are the conditions that make the political class solidary? Ake lists them as follows: a. the ability of the political class to promulgate policies that carry the widest possible support within its class; b. the existence of an effective mechanism for conflict resolution and enforcement of discipline within the political class; and c. an emphasis on the collective responsibility of the political class.[87]

In sum, Ake postulates that effective leadership and political integration rests, by and large, on the nature of society's political culture. But Robert H. Jackson's and Carl G. Rosberg's study of leadership in Africa is one based on the premise that effective governance and political goods like political integration are the products of institutionalized politics.

In their *Personal Rule in Black Africa: Prince, Autocrat, Prophet, Tyrant*, Jackson and Rosberg assert, quite persuasively, that:

> The most settled kind of national politics takes place within a framework of institutions. Institutional offices and rules by definition restrain and moderate the acts of powerful men and are the tools of civil government. This is not to say that governments cannot be civil without them, but if they are, it is due entirely to the civic virtues—the civility—of the men who rule. Politics and government without the benefit of institutions . . . are at best uncertain and problematic and at worst dangerous; for this reason one of the historic tasks of political men has been to build and develop political institutions so that political life need not depend upon civic virtue alone.[88]

Their study concludes that political leadership and political activities in Africa do not follow an institutionalized pattern. Rather, leadership and political activities in Africa are carried out in a manner that amounts to a system of personal rule—an institutionless type of governance. The authors compare politics in Africa to international diplomacy where the rules of the jungle predominate.[89] They state with some measure of accuracy that "African politics are most often a personal or fractional struggle that is restrained by private and tacit agreement, prudential concerns, and personal ties and dependencies rather than by public rules and institutions."[90] What about the new, but struggling democracies on the continent? Could some qualify as exceptions to Jackson and Rosberg's observation? Predictably, both authors report that a major consequence of this kind of personal politics in Africa has been relative political instability. Thus, this implies that personal rule is injurious to political integration.

Jackson and Rosberg acknowledge that African leaders may not have answers to some of the problems of economic underdevelopment; however, the way they govern has [generally-speaking], exerted negative effects on the quality and general conditions of public life on the continent.[91] They observe that historical evidence shows that African leaders are not simply victims of their environments. The actions of African leaders, they contend, have been decisive in the provision or destruction of "political goods" like peace, stability, order, security, welfare, justice and liberty. These leaders have, by their performances, either reversed the fortunes of economically and socially depressed countries or rendered disorderly and insecure countries with great potentials.[92]

In making these evaluations of African leadership, Jackson and Rosberg are, however, careful to point out that personal rule is not peculiar to Africa; in fact, they report that it is one of the prevalent forms of leadership in the world. They also recognize that European colonialism undermined or subordinated African political systems.[93] But worse than that, as was pointed out earlier by Davidson, colonialism left behind a legacy of colonial tribalism and other divisions. Colonialism also infused the body politic with habits of dictatorship which inevitably clashed with "democratic parliaments"[94] left behind by colonial officials as they departed the scene. A problematic observation from Jackson and Rosberg's is that "the structures of the successor African states, based on various democratic designs, have so far failed to take root."[95] The problem here is that the statement carries a thinly-veiled suggestion that democracy is a foreign concept to Africa. The spread of multi-party democracies within Africa in the 1990s and beyond further negates Jackson's and Rosberg's pessimism about democratic possibilities on that continent. The ultimate objective of democracy is to involve the people in the governance of their own affairs. African traditional political systems tended to hinge on consensus politics and contained mechanisms by which grassroots opinions were sought on issues affecting the general community. For example, the ruler of the Fantis of Ghana governed by popular will even though he was not chosen by popular vote. In effect, the Fantis' structure of governance is consultative.[96]

Jackson and Rosberg hold that political leadership is most likely to meet the expectations of the people when governance is effectively institutionalized. By institutions, the authors mean an impersonal system of rules and offices as well as roles and relations. Institutions do not refer simply to rules and behavior or patterns of behavior; they cover conduct based on rules that spell out the rights and duties of actors in the system. An institutionalized system governs conduct on the basis of rules. As Jackson and Rosberg put it:

> Rules are the tools of a civil society. In an institution the rule and its authority always stand above the person and his power or ability. In an effectively institutionalized state, the rules are respected by all persons no matter how important they may be; indeed the rules in a well-established state with a strong institutional tradition appear entirely natural. In a state without effective institutions, rules are defied or ignored; they appear artificial and without value and meaning.[97]

In an institutionless state:

> Persons take precedence over rules, where the officeholder is not effectively bound by his office and is able to change its authority and powers to suit his own personal or political needs. In such a system of personal rule, the rulers and other leaders take precedence over the formal rules of the political game: the rules do not effectively regulate political behavior, and we therefore cannot predict or anticipate conduct from a knowledge of rules . . . The state is the government of men and not of laws.[98]

When one surveys the African political scene, one finds an irony which Jackson and Rosberg have encountered: political institutions or edifices like glamorous houses of parliament abound. The problem is that, in most cases, the political leaders do not observe the rules always or observe them only when it is politically expedient to do so or when they have changed them to suit their liking.[99] A good illustration of this is a 1979 Supreme Court decision in Nigeria over an Opposition party's challenge to the Federal Electoral Commission (FEDECO's) decision to declare Shehu Shagari of the National Party of Nigeria (NPN) as the winner of the presidential election of that year. In this case, the plaintiff charged that Shehu Shagari had failed to meet the constitutional criterion for victory, namely winning at least 25 percent of the votes cast in two-thirds of the states of

Nigeria. By then, Nigeria had nineteen states; prior to the election, the electoral commission had interpreted two-thirds of nineteen to mean thirteen states since a state could not, in practical terms, be reduced to a fractional number.

In the election, Shagari secured 25 percent of the votes in twelve states; he fell short of the required 25 percent in the thirteenth state. In this case, where the first ballot had failed to produce a clear-cut winner, the 1979 constitution required a run-off election. But the electoral commission did not call a run-off election; instead, it reversed itself by stating that two-thirds of nineteen was now twelve two-thirds instead of thirteen as it had held in the past. This new interpretation of two-thirds of 19 states meant that Shagari fulfilled the requirement for victory. The Supreme Court agreed with this interpretation but cautioned, curiously I would add, that its judgment should not be used as a precedent in future cases. One of the consequences of this weird ruling of the highest court in the land was that the second Republic of Nigeria took off on a note of bitterness and mutual distrust between the winning party (which was now charged with "stealing the election") and the Opposition. Matters only got worse as time passed; the presidential elections of 1983, which were so terribly rigged that a commentator characterized them as "selections," rather than elections,[100] only exacerbated the political climate. The civilian leaders were subsequently thrown out of office by a military coup on December 31, 1983, which, not surprisingly, was greeted with great public acclaim.

If the rules laid down by the electoral commission had been strictly followed, Nigeria—other things being equal—would probably have been ushered onto an era of genuine political peace, and perhaps there would not have been another military overthrow of an elected, civilian government. Nwabueze's in-depth and incisive book, *Nigeria's Presidential Constitution: The Second Experiment in Constitutional Democracy*, includes a thoughtful discussion of the negative impact that the controversial presidential election of 1979 exerted on the true operation of federalism in Nigeria. Needless to say, the consequent estrangement in the relations between the federal government and the states, which were not under the control of the president's party, NPN, did not help the cause of political integration. Although Nwabueze attributes this "confrontation" between the federal government and the non-NPN states to the ethnic base of the political parties, he also notes that the specific cause was the ill-feeling generated by the disputed outcome of the presidential election. He writes:

> The antagonism arising from the tribal support base of the parties was
> aggravated by the feeling on the part of the UPN, NPP, PRP and GNPP

that the declaration by the Federal Electoral Commission (FEDECO) of Alhaji Shehu Shagari as the winner of the presidential election was illegal and improper.[101]

The confrontational attitude of the non-NPN governors is indicative of their lack of respect for a president who came to office via a questionable verdict. The UPN-controlled states were unequivocal in their disdain for Shagari's presidency. For instance, those states refused to hoist the president's picture in public buildings.[102] As Jackson and Rosberg correctly reasoned in the preceding passages, if the leader defies the rules, the only power that can put him out of office is a superior force.[103] In the case of the contested election verdict of 1979, what the culprits defied was principle. Commenting on the place of written constitutions in African political leadership, the authors observe: "insofar as constitutions remained important features of rule, they were important less as constraints on the abuse of power and more as legal instruments that a personal ruler could amend or rewrite to suit his personal needs."[104] Thus, personal rule, as opposed to institutionalized leadership, abounds in Africa not because the instruments of institutionalized governance such as written constitutions (along with all their rules and regulations) and elected executives and legislative houses do not exist, but because as Jackson and Rosberg correctly report, African political leadership is, by and large, regulated by a informal network of politicians, their patrons, associates, clients, supporters and others.[105] This accounts for the fact that personal rule breeds political insecurity, for personal rule is not conducted within the framework of "established rules and effective referees."[106] As Nwabueze sees it, African leaders' "propensity to personalize rule and to perpetuate it indefinitely is a disastrous factor in the politics of African countries."[107]

Nonetheless, politics is not meant to be a prisoner of rules. Thus, institutionalized leadership needs to be adaptive. In recognition of this fact, Jackson and Rosberg observe that rules and offices can become obsolete and constitute a stumbling block to necessary change. Institutions can also decay and lose their ability to perform their expected roles.[108]

One means of guarding against the emergence of personalized rule is through a constitutional limitation on the term of office of an elected leader. The 1979 Presidential Constitution of Nigeria (along with the currently operative amended version of 1999) limits the period in which the president can rule to eight years of two four-year terms. Explaining the merit of this limitation, Ben O. Nwabueze writes:

A president who has held office for twenty years is a different kind of functionary from one who is limited to a maximum of two terms of four years each. His authority is bound to be greater, for after twenty years in office he is apt to become an institution himself, attracting loyalties of a personal nature. His authority tends to be all-pervading. A cult of personality is built up around him. A belief in his infallibility and indispensability is generated.[109]

Continuing, Nwabueze correctly observes that personalized leadership has not only proven inimical to the evolution of democratic rulership and stability in Africa, but it has also robed the affected countries of the benefit of change in leadership. Describing the advantages of change, he asserts that "change may prevent or check sterility and complacency by enabling a fresh vitality and a fresh approach to be brought to bear upon the problems of government."[110] Needless to say, Nwabueze's position stands to reason, but it should be noted that he appears presumptuous that change necessarily yields positive results for a given polity. Change is welcome as long as it moves the country forward, not backward. There is nothing in recorded human history that demonstrates that a term limit of only eight years is the only suitable term limit, particularly for a developing country. One suspects that in prescribing the current term limit of eight years for elective offices in Nigeria, the constitution makers were probably mostly guided by the lure of the American presidential constitution, which limits the president to two terms of four years each, but they probably did not realize that the United States arrived at the practice of an eight-year term limit for its presidency through a home-grown, constitutional evolutionary path that began in 1951 when the twenty-second amendment to the U.S. Constitution came into effect. It was a term limit that the United States arrived at through its own national experience and its own trials and errors with governance, not in imitation of the practice of some other country. One cannot help asking the following question: did the framers of the 1999 constitution of the Federal Republic of Nigeria consider whether and how term limits impact upon the different development challenges of developed vis-à-vis developing countries? Ideally speaking, where an electoral system functions effectively, it's the people, through their ballots on election day, that should determine whether an incumbent government that seeks re-election, should stay or be replaced. The people, through an effective and transparent system of elections, should determine how long or how short an elected official should serve in office. Where there is an effective political culture, an effective electoral system and a rational electorate, no amount of the advantages of incumbency would enable a failing and ineffective government to survive the electoral judgment of the people.

Although neocolonialism, also described as imperialism, has been a feature of post-independence Africa from the onset, the monster has only grown worse in recent years and now constitutes a major impediment to effective leadership and political integration on the continent. Wa Thiong'O captures this most succinctly: "imperialism . . . is the one force that affects everything in Africa—politics, economics, culture, absolutely every aspect of human life."[111] Since neo-colonialism results in political control by one society over another through the economic backdoor, it follows that African countries are, in reality, not in-charge of their destinies even though they have regained political independence from the colonial powers. Again, the words of Ngugi Wa Thiong'O are instructive. He writes:

> A society needs political survival—that is the retention of power in its hands—to regulate the life of that society in a manner beneficial to that society . . . The power to decide between options, alternatives, tactics and strategies for survival should be wielded by the society.[112]

The following discussions of the manifestations of neo-colonialism in Zaire (now known as the Democratic Republic of the Congo), Senegal, Nigeria and Zimbabwe aptly illustrate how neo-colonialism/imperialism has operated through "convenient partners" (as Davidson calls them), to undermine genuine economic development and, in consequence, obstruct stability and political integration.

When the Central African country of the Democratic Republic of the Congo (then known as Zaire) was under the leadership of the late Mobutu Sese Seko, it represented a typical neocolonial state and its consequences for political integration. Nzongola Ntalaja provides a bold and eye-opening discussion of Mobutu's leadership in this regard. In it, Ntalaja reports that Mobutu's leadership in Zaire was participating in U.S.-sponsored subversive activities against Central and Southern African governments. Describing these activities as "counter-revolutionary,"[113] Ntalaja writes that Mobutu's actions undermined the liberation struggle on the African continent that was still going at the time.

Ntalaja notes that Mobutu's complicity in U.S. and Western-sponsored Anti-African activities in Africa date back to the first year of Zaire's independence. He reports:

> It is a role that began soon after independence with the Katanga and South Kasair secessions of July and August 1960, respectively, and culminated in the CIA-led plot against Prime Minister Patrice Lumumba, who was eliminated from the political scene and then assassinated, between 5 September 1960 and 17 January 1961. Since then, every revolutionary trust in Zaire has been met by a formidable

counter-revolutionary challenge under the supervision of the United States and its Western allies.[114]

He explains the United States' motive for sponsoring the assassination of Patrice Lumumba: "Perceived as a 'dangerous man' from the standpoint of Western interests in Africa, Lumumba became a target of a CIA assassination plot ordered by President Dwight E. Eisenhower."[115] On the other hand, Mobutu Sese Seko, who was subsequently foisted on the people of Zaire by the CIA, was seen as the kind of "strong man" who would be amenable to Western interests in this part of the world. Ntalaja writes that the CIA's station chief in Leopoldville, Lawrence Devlin, had identified Mobutu as matching the profile of a leader who could facilitate Western interests. Ntalaja continues:

> As described by Rouleau, the 'strong man' is supposed to be intelligent, cunning, and independent of any group or popular consensus likely to prevent him from serving his external patrons. Deemed to possess these prized qualities, Mobutu was carefully groomed through his U.S., U.N., Belgian and Israeli connections as the perfect candidate for the role of Zaire's strongman.[116]

Shedding further light on imperialism's strategy in Africa, Ntalaja reports:

> The ruin of Zaire is better for Western interests than a strong and independent state likely to support struggle against white Southern Africa. At the same time, a weak state like Mobutu's Zaire may still be equipped to play a gendarme role against poorly armed and poorly organized revolutionary forces, and to provide moral and logistical support to counter-revolutionary forces in the region.[117]

Ntalaja reveals that Mobutu's service to the Western Interest (as opposed to the African interest), earned him the friendly embrace of Washington and Brussels where he was reassured constantly that he was "loved"[118] and would not be abandoned. On the other hand, for the people of Zaire, the regime of Mobutu meant the continuous worsening of their standard of living, the decay of social services and widespread corruption of Zairian society.[119]

The role of the U.S. as the leader of the neocolonial/imperialist movement has been amplified by Ngugi Wa Thiong'O. He notes that the means by which the U.S. carries out this neo-colonial/imperialist leadership include the establishment of proxy governments attuned to Western interests (like

Mobutu Sese Seko's) in the developing countries. Where it does not engage in direct military invasions, the U.S. acts through phony freedom movements like Nicaragua's Contra and Angola's [now defunct] UNITA to further its neocolonial designs. Elaborating on how such actions of the U.S. negate political integration in the affected countries, Wa Thiong'O writes:

> Over the years, the U.S. became the main agency for the destabilization of any country in Asia and Africa and South America that leaned a bit too heavily on the side of social change; or that wanted to break the neo-colonial chains around its economy, politics and culture.[120]

On his part, Ntalaja believes that Mobutu's Zaire exemplifies the collapse of an alliance formed between African nationalist leaders and their people during the independence struggle. In Zaire and other [similarly situated] African countries, he points out, the ordinary folk have not experienced the promises of independence. Instead, since independence, they have received either more promises or outright repression from the ruling class.[121]

Ntalaja avers that one of the causes of the present state of affairs is that the ruling class which fought for independence in Africa did not possess a "revolutionary consciousness;"[122] its primary concern was to take power from the colonial authorities. He explains that with the exception of the states where independence was achieved through a war of liberation, popular participation in the anti-colonial struggle was restricted to public meetings, demonstrations and electoral politics.

Citing Amilcar Cabral, Ntalaja asserts that the most critical problem that faces post-independence Africa (for which Zaire is a major example) is that of neo-colonialism—the consequences of an alliance between the ruling classes and international capital. He writes:

> Faced with a choice between the difficult road to development for all the people and the easy glittering embourgeoisement offered by international capital in its search for local allies, or a choice between revolution and counter-revolution, the African petty bourgeoisie opted for the most part to be co-opted into the service of imperialism.[123]

Echoing this perspective, Ngugi Wa Thiong'O writes that in reality independence has meant "the ruler holding a begging bowl and the ruled holding a shrinking belly."[124]

Ntalaja remarks that the post-colonial state in Mobutu's Zaire was as despotic as its colonial predecessor and was primarily concerned with the maintenance of law and order instead of the task of development.[125] He derides the absence of checks and balances in the neo-colonial state—a void which he attributes to the lack of popular political control and lack of accountability. Another feature of the neo-colonial state as described by Ntalaja is that the leaders of the neo-colonial state abhor democracy and in fact view "democratic politics as being destabilizing."[126] In the neo-colonial state, state officials are preoccupied with pleasing those who appointed them to office and give little attention to the duties of their offices. He points out that while the neo-colonial state is as despotic as the colonial state, the latter had a more efficient and effective administration.[127]

The post-colonial economy is simply a neo-colonial economy dominated by the state which is used by its functionaries for personal enrichment. Ntalaja holds that agencies of this neo-colonial economy are merely engaged in "resource extraction and social control"[128] rather than economic development. Writing on the failure of state-owned enterprises in the neo-colonial state, Ntalaja contends that their failure is not due to the mere fact of their being state-controlled but the consequence of their being run as means for wealth accumulation by those in power. He submits:

> It is this privatization of the state that constitutes the major obstacle to economic development. But the deeper roots of this obstacle are to be found in the state's external connections. These are crucial not only in determining the particular pattern of accumulation known as 'pillage imperialism' and which benefits both African ruling classes and metropolitan capital, but also in propping up those regimes likely to serve the interests of imperialism.[129]

He points out that through such privatization of the state (notice that Ntalaja uses privatization in a different sense from the legitimate sell of state corporations to private entrepreneurs), the national ruling class in Zaire stripped the nation of "those essential means and capabilities with which to generate economic growth, improve the living conditions of the masses, and facilitate effective participation in the Pan-African liberation struggle."[130]

Ntalaja then goes on to identify the grand objectives that imperialism seeks to achieve through the neo-colonial state as follows: 1.) the preservation of a country's role in the international division of labor as a source of cheap raw materials and labor, 2.) the broadening of the home market for luxury goods manufactured in the metropolis, 3.) and the use of the neo-colonial state as a dumping ground for technologies inconsistent with the absorptive capacities and development needs of the country. Ntalaja's list includes a fourth objective (of imperialism), which deserves a special mention. This is "the suppression of revolutionary ideas and movements likely to challenge [the preceding] arrangement—"[131]that is, the neo-colonial statuesque.

Nigeria, Senegal and Zimbabwe present additional examples of the disequilibrating effects of neocolonialism. Bode Onimode's incisive analysis of the manifestation of neo-colonialism in Nigeria is cast in the mold of the "crisis of global capitalism."[132] Viewing the problem as the African component of a world-wide economic crisis, Onimode then proceeds to discuss the Nigerian experience. First, he dissects and lists four facets of the African crisis itself. One, the continent's yearly agricultural output falls below the population growth rate of 2.5 percent. Two, the continent has a negative debt-service ratio as a result of heavy indebtedness to international financial institutions. In effect, there is a net outflow of capital from Africa. Three, the continent is rife with political instability, political repression and authoritarian leadership. In Onimode's view, the coups and counter-coups that interrupted the political life of the continent [until the beginning of the wind of democratic changes that have swept Africa since the 1990s] are not provoked by a crisis of legitimacy (as some political pundits would argue), but are the bye-products of "gross political repression."[133] He believes that military interventions occur primarily where African leaderships do not accord a free reign to democratic precepts. Four, the continent is plagued by an intellectual crisis, which Onimode describes as follows:

> This is very clear if you look at the dominant social science operating in Africa today, particularly in economics, political science, sociology, and psychology, which have become bankrupt manipulative tools not only for misleading our governments into policies that wreck our economies, but instruments for mental colonization of Africans.[134]

A scholar of no less renown than Ngugi Wa Thiong'O has attested to this phenomenon. He writes: "The USA and the West control . . . the placement of most Third World intellectuals. A good number become trained and cultured into drawing pictures of the world in harmony with the needs of US imperialism."[135] Suffice it to say that in this respect, Onimode and Wa Thiong'O are one with Afrocentric/Africa-centered scholars, such as C. Tsehloane Keto who in particular has criticized African institutions of higher learning for operating as bastions of a hegemonic Europe-centered perspective of epistemology. However, Onimode fails to suggest a remedy for this intellectual malaise except for a vague call for a "progressive scholarship."[136]

To what extent do the preceding factors apply to the Nigerian situation? Onimode contends that Nigeria had, for long, been mired in "the crisis of the capitalist under-development"[137] and cites the failed leadership of Shehu Shagari from 1979 to 1983 as a chief culprit in this respect. He claims that this government, which had inherited a balance of 5.1 billion dollars in Nigeria's external reserves, left the country in the red to the tune of fifty billion dollars of debt to Western creditors by the time it was sacked by the military in 1983.[138]

He notes, quite correctly, that inappropriate economic policies (including neglect of the agricultural sector) and economic mismanagement left Nigeria with stagnant rural and urban economies. The resultant balance of trade and balance of payment crises forced the government to seek and obtain additional loans—this time the lenders included the International Monetary Fund and the World Bank.[139] Onimode rejects the official view, at the time, that Nigeria's economic setback resulted mainly from the glut which developed in the world market for oil in the early eighties. He points out that the economies of other oil-dependent countries like Libya have not suffered the same fate as Nigeria's. However, that view appears to me like an unfair comparison, because Libya's population of 5.6 million pales in relation to Nigeria's—more than one hundred and thirty million—along with its attendant needs.

Second, Onimode cites dependent economic development as another feature of the African crisis in Nigeria. He attributes this phenomenon to "the wreckage of individual African economies by colonialism, the perpetration of a new colonial domination after so called independence and the systematic control of economic activity by the advanced countries."[140]

A third feature of the crisis, as articulated by Onimode, is the existence of a dependent capitalist system in Nigeria. Like the preceding factor, Onimode traces the origins of this type of capitalism to colonialism. He notes that the system was given a boost after the expiration of the so-called oil boom in Nigeria by the enthronement of "the forces of import-substitution industries and capitalist agriculture and to some degree a massive construction boom."[141] He explains that those measures have deepened Nigeria's integration into the imperialist centers and generated weak intersectoral linkages between and within the sectors of the economy.

The Structural Adjustment Program of the International Monetary Fund (IMF) continues to be cited as a factor that militates against political integration and complicates the difficulties of leadership in African countries. *Africa Confidential* puts it poignantly:

Any genuine democracy would be highly critical of the effects of the Standard IMF 'structural adjustment' programs, which include cuts in subsidies on basic foods, the closing of state enterprises, large-scale unemployment and reductions in social spending.[142]

Onimode's discussion also highlights similar effects of the IMF pill on the health of the Nigerian economy. Describing IMF measures as fundamentally contradictory, he reports that they exerted the greatest toll on the "weaker sections of the population."[143] The IMF intervention also produces a contradictory situation in which companies report huge profits while workers are retrenched, cost of living soars, and the incomes of the bulk of the population decline or are frozen.[144] The overall life of the nation has received a shattering blow. In his own reflections on the consequences of the IMF pill, Obasanjo, writing as a private citizen after his military rulership of Nigeria and before he ascended the throne again, this time, as its civilian leader, could not help crying out that "all the values we hold dear are under assault. Hope has become a scarce commodity, and fear a constant companion."[145] Obasanjo's well-made point draws attention to a question that I posed earlier in this work while discussing Ake's theory of political integration as to how the vagaries of a nation's economy could affect the political elite's commitment to its normative consensus for political conduct.

It is little wonder then that Onimode pronounces the structural adjustment program a farce that served the interest of the multinational corporations by enabling them to achieve a greater control over Africa's economies "through programs of privatization which involve the sale of public enterprises to these 'hawkers' of technology transfer."[146] For this reason, he charges that IMF and the World Bank, which are supposed to be politically and technically neutral, have served as tools of the multinationals in their neo-colonial adventures.[147]

Zimbabwe presents another spotlight for an examination of the disequilibrating impact of neo-colonialism. In articulating this, Kempton Makamure echoes Onimode's line of reasoning which portrays the African crisis as a continental manifestation of the global crisis of capitalism. Zimbabwe, he reports, is engulfed by a national struggle between the forces of economic equality and justice and those of imperialism. The generality of Zimbabweans, he notes, have come to view imperialism as the country's number one enemy.[148] Makamure then describes an alliance that he believed was forged between the forces of imperialism and the bourgeois class of Zimbabwe:

> The British made sure that the constitution would operate for ten years, knowing that they would have bribed sufficient influential politicians, so that by 1990 when it comes to changing the constitution, the African bourgeois class will not be interested in social transformation. Some will be big landowners. This is already happening, some ministers are

saying that if the leadership requires them to dispose of what they have
accumulated they will resign from government.[149]

But Makamure's analysis fails to predict the current gallant, but controversial efforts of Prime Minister Robert Mugabe to reclaim Zimbabwe's
farmlands that were stolen forcibly from Africans by European invaders.
His courageous land reclamation efforts have, however, led to his demoni-
zation in the Western media, ostracism by Western governments and victimization by the same "neutral" international financial institutions that
have already been indicted in this work. One wonders whether such a fate
awaits the leadership of post-apartheid South Africa (which has a worse
history of economic and land dispossession) if it follows the example of
Robert Mugabe. This is, of course, left to history to determine.

The vast distance separating Zimbabwe in the southern end of
Africa from Senegal in the far west apparently did not make a significant
difference to how neocolonialism has exerted its weight on the masses
of Senegal. Abdoulaye Bathily's "Senegal's Fraudulent 'Democratic Opening'" sheds light on it. So disruptive was its impact in Senegal that Bathily
issued an alarm that Africa faces a risk of being recolonized not by the
former imperial powers but by multinational corporations under the leadership of the United States.[150] Like the preceding scholars, Bathily argues
that the IMF and the World Bank are tools of the alleged multinationals' design to take over control of the economies of African states.[151] He
reports that the IMF scheme has had a more devastating effect on the Senegalese economy because of a special circumstance of colonialism in Senegal: unlike the Nigerian and Zimbabwean cases just reviewed, the local
bourgeoisie that formed in Senegal during colonialism consisted of French,
rather than Senegalese nationals. It was only after independence that a
Senegalese entrepreneurial class emerged through a government-backed
program of credits and loans. But this credit scheme was butchered by
the IMF Structural Adjustment Program, causing the newly created core
of African of entrepreneurs to evaporate.[152] Bathily also reports that the
structural adjustment scheme has destroyed the mainstay of the Senegalese economy—groundnut production—as a result of the discontinuance
of state subsidies and credits like fertilizers and seeds.[153] The discontinuance was effected at the urging of IMF which contended that the groundnut business should operate at the market price. But the farmers could not
afford to operate at the market price, Bathily remarks. Commenting on
the effects of such cuts in government subsidies, Julius Nyerere, former
Prime Minister of Tanzania, now deceased, decries Western double-stan-
dards in this respect:

Poor developing countries are forced by IMF conditions to abandon all subsidies to their consumers, producers and exporters, to cut public expenditure, and to move rapidly toward uncontrolled free trade. The rich countries of the North, on the other hand, continue or even increase the subsidies to their agricultural producers and exporters, 'rescue' major manufacturing and commercial companies threatened with bankruptcy, persist in great imbalances in their national and foreign accounts, and have increased their open or disguised protectionism.[154]

Nyerere could not be more correct. In fact, the United States, which is supportive of IMF's Structural Adjustment Programs for developing countries, provides an elaborate array of subsidies to its small and large-scale farmers. It's pertinent to draw attention to the fact that disagreement between the Western industrial powers and developing nations over such agricultural subsidies have stalled completion of the current Uruguay Round of negotiations for a new world trade agreement under the auspices of the World Trade Organization (WTO). In Senegal, according to Bathily, whole industries collapsed because IMF insisted that "Senegal must have an industrial system which can compete on the world market."[155] Bathily contends that "since most of the firms which exist had in fact developed only because of the monopoly they had on the market, once protection is removed, they cannot sustain any competition with the world market."[156] Medical doctors, engineers, economists, agriculturalists, etc. were among the victims of the resultant unemployment. Ironically, while the state could not hire these workers, it, nonetheless, beefed up its police force in order to contain the civil upheaval which was unleashed by the harsh results of IMF's measures.[157] Another notable dimension of this neocolonial ravage in Senegal is best captured in Bathily's words:

In the urban area, there is a process of Lumpenization of the urban population. In the countryside it is a process of proletarianization of the peasantry. The consequences of these two phenomena on the social landscape, are vagrancy, prostitution, delinquency, etc.[158]

Bathily points out that it is not only the privately controlled groundnut industry that was strangulated; the public sector of Senegal's economy was also emasculated by IMF's Structural Adjustment program.[159]

The social and political tremors unleashed by the hardship and privation generated by the neocolonial programs of IMF in Senegal include Islamic fundamentalism in a place where religious peace had reigned. Bathily reports that external powers cashed in on the situation: "Every oil sheikdom has an Islamic movement in Senegal, Saudi Arabia, Bahrain, every Gulf state. They fund them with petro dollars."[160] Bathily just touched upon a factor which, as *Africa Confidential* earlier pointed out, has become a real threat to political peace in Africa. It is an incendiary which has caused a havoc in several African countries, including Nigeria, Sudan, and the Horn of Africa. Despite the reinforcement of the police force, the Senegalese government was barely able to cope with all the social and political upheavals triggered by IMF's neocolonialism—for the capacity of the state to manage crisis had been dampened. The weakness of the political state meant a membership boom for the sprouting religious movements.

The upshot of all these, as Bathily reports, was the emergence of cracks in the wall of national integration in Senegal where ethnic peace used to prevail mainly due to the predominance of one ethnic group. Thus, ethnic polarization became a feature of the nation's political life with the emergence of ethnic and cultural movements alongside religious movements. As if this is not enough, a secessionist movement came to life in Southern Senegal orchestrated by an ethnic group which feels left out of the national scheme of things. In order to keep itself in power in the face of these centrifugal forces, the state resorted to desperate tactics, including political repression.[161] The preceding picture demonstrates clearly the symbiotic relationship between political instability and the economy.

Ngugi Wa Thiong'O provides a heart-shattering description of neocolonialism in Kenya. He accuses the then Arap Moi regime of acting in the interest of the West rather than those of Kenyan people. Wa Thiong'O observes that Kenyatta's and later Moi's leaderships were repressive of dissent and methodically and consistently silenced voices raised on university campuses or in the theaters in defense of the people or against neo-colonialism.[162] Government policies not only resulted in widening the gap between the rich and the poor, they left the country more divided as the Moi regime set "nationalities and regions against one another"[163] as a way to maintain itself in power. Not surprisingly, in December 2002, Moi's party, KANU was dislodged from 40 years of uninterrupted rule when Mwai Kibaki emerged as the new president of Kenya under the banner of his National Rainbow Coalition, which won a landslide victory and achieved a parliamentary majority. His predecessor, Daniel Toroitich Arap Moi could not stand for re-election, for he had exhausted his constitutionally-permitted term of office.

Whether Kibaki can change the fortunes of Kenya's political economy remains to be seen, but Ngugi Wa Thiong'O's and other discussions of neocolonialism in the foregoing passages, demonstrate that as a force that exacerbates poverty, increases the elite-mass gap and weakens the ability of the government to meet its obligations to the governed, neocolonialism militates against African leadership's efforts at achieving political integration and other state objectives. But some of those leaders are not blameless, given their reported role as proxies of the West who were foisted on African nations for the advancement of Western economic interests rather than the promotion of the welfare and interests of their people. Wa Thiong'O's words best surmise this situation:

> The African people are still struggling for a world in which they can control that which their collective sweat produces, a world in which they will control the economy, politics and culture to make their lives accord with where they want to go and who they want to be.[164]

A fact of modern imperialism, which students of African political economy must not loose sight of is the role of Japan as a center of imperialism. Understandably, Western Europe and the U.S. have exerted the most negative impact on the course of African development—via slavery, colonialism and neo-colonialism—and thus deserve the substantial attention they receive in our discourse. Nonetheless, the discourse will prove incomplete without the inclusion of the Japanese part in the imperial equation even though its main sphere of influence tends to be South-East Asia. Similarly, account must be taken of the support, which Arab Oil sheiks provide to the Islamic Fundamentalist movements that contribute to the disturbance of the political peace of Africa.

The military has been a major player in African leadership. How has the intervention of the military in the leadership of African states furthered or undermined political integration? Ntalaja's discussion of Mobutu's inglorious leadership in Zaire is highly critical of the impact that military rule exacted upon African political development. He holds that, generally-speaking, military rule helped to strengthen the hands of neo-colonialism. The military in Africa, he writes, is preoccupied with personal enrichment, lacks a professional ethic and operates in an environment based on intrigue.[165] Suffice it to say that this is hardly conducive to political stability in the affected states.

A prominent feature of post-independence Africa is the relative inability of civilians to control the military. Hence, the flood of military coups that swept the continent following the end of political colonialism during the last half of the twentieth century. In fact, scholars of African politics, like Ali Mazrui have identified military interventions in African national leadership as a major cause of political instability on the continent. Ironically, as we saw in the experience of Nigeria, one of the major reasons that soldiers usually advanced for intervening in African politics is a need to restore order where civilian governance resulted in political disorder. Claude Welch, Jr.'s *Civilian Control of the Military: Theory and Cases From Developing Countries*, throws light on this all-important subject, specifically methods and tactics by which civilians could maintain control over the military. Since abrupt and unconstitutional changes of government militate against orderly governance, it must be assumed that, other things being equal, if civilians in Africa, particularly Nigeria, succeed in achieving institutional control over the military such an achievement would represent a major step forward in the continent's drive for political integration.

Drawing from a cross-section of empirical data, Welch, Jr. outlines a number of factors which determines the capacity of the civilian establishment to control the military. One, the civilian government must specify the parameters within which the military exercises its responsibilities. Two, the objectives of the military must be specific and limited. Three, the civilian authorities must deal with the military through a clearly specified chain of command that respects the integrity of the force. Four, this chain of command must be subordinated to civilian control.[166]

The military has never been entirely detached from politics, even in the West, which has a history of a relatively stable relationship between the civilian and the military establishment. Welch, Jr. does acknowledge that the military establishment commands some influence in the Western body politic, but he points out that a clear boundary exists between military and political roles. And he explains that it is in the arena of specialized knowledge that military opinion influences policy making. And whatever degree of political influence that the military so commands in Western countries usually comes from the top echelon of the military establishment. He also explains that, in the Western experience, interactions between civilian authorities and the military are limited to the highest rungs of the military leadership.[167]

Drawing from the empirical experiences of countries, which have had a successful tradition of civilian control of the military, Welch, Jr. identifies five methods by which civilians control the military. They are:

> 1) Constitutional constraints on the political impact of the military; 2) ascriptive factors (e.g. class, ethnicity) affecting relationships between civilian and military leaders; 3) utilization of party controls, possibly through the creation of parallel hierarchies of command; 4) geographic and historical factors permitting the maintenance of relatively small armed forces with narrow responsibilities; 5) delineation of clear spheres of military responsibility, leading to widespread acceptance within the armed forces of an ethic of subordination.[168]

Details of these methods include constitutional provisions like the investiture of the president as the commander-in-chief of the armed forces, the investiture of the legislature with power of war declaration and budgetary controls. But he points out that heavy reductions of the military budget could backfire on the civilians. Ironically, Welch, Jr. draws attention to an finding, which holds that developing countries with high levels of military spending achieved less civilian control of the military than those with low military budgets.[169] Welch also points out that the prevalence of an ethnic group or class in the military forces does not always guarantee civilian control of the military as military coups are known to have occurred in ethnically homogenous societies.[170]

The imposition of limits on the responsibilities of the military helps to strengthen their subordination to civilian control. Welch notes that "the more focused the international duties of the armed forces and the clearer the differentiation between their duties and those of police or paramilitary units, the greater the likelihood of civilian control."[171] The greater the organizational complexity of the military the more difficult it is to stage a coup de' tat.

Welch stresses that technical specialization in the military helps to promote officer job satisfaction. He suggests that civilian control is enhanced through control of major military decisions like war declaration, major weapons acquisition and formation of military alliances.[172] He cautions that even though these measures and designs for civilian control of the military are drawn from empirical experiences of certain countries, each society needs to apply its unique circumstances to its expectations on military behavior.[173]

The past prevalence of military governments in Africa and the little ease with which soldiers were able to take over African governments demonstrate that Africa is not the place to go to for success stories on civilian control of the military. If anything, until the wind of multiparty democratic elections began to sweep across Africa in the 1990s, the military, generally-speaking, were in control of the civilians on the continent.

Despite this sweeping wind of democracy, the military continues to influence politics on the continent. Two recent examples will suffice. In 2005, when General Gnashingbe Eyadema died after ruling the West African country of Togo for 38 years, the military quickly and openly installed his son, Faure Gnassingbe, as his successor. This brazen defiance of and insensitivity to the democratic movement on the continent sparked off internal[174] and external protests and condemnations, including a decision of the African Union (AU) not to recognize the new military appointed leader of Togo. Apparently to quitten this international indignation, the

Togolese authorities reversed course later, Eyadema's son relinquished his position, albeit temporarily, and an election was held to fill the office democratically. The election produced the same Faure Gnassingbe as the winner. Despite opposition cries of a rigged election,[175] Eyedema's son remains the country's elected president—one that succeeded his father in office. Election or no election, it's clear that the original design and wishes of the Togolese military eventually prevailed. A second example also occurred in 2005 in another West African country, Mauritania where there was a successful military coup against the elected civilian president of the country.[176] This time, however, the military junta survived an initial outburst of international indignation and condemnation, including feeble protests from the African Union. While Nigeria has been under a civilian, elected government since 1999, it's still under the shadows of the military. Why? The incumbent president, who has been ruling since 1999, is a retired army general. Thus, even though the current Nigerian government did not come about through a military coup, the fact that the elected president comes out of the military ruling elite demonstrates that Nigeria continues to exist under the shadow of its military establishment. Thus, Africa continues, although less so than in the past, to present a good case study of the military control of civilians. Welch's book thus serves as a good prescription for how civilian governments in Africa could someday achieve overall long-lasting control over their military.

Samuel Decalo's elaborate and well-supported study, *Coups and Army Rule in Africa: Motivations & Constraints* demonstrates that military leadership in Africa militated against rather than promoted effective leadership and political integration. The work also reveals that, on the average, no significant difference exists between the records of African military leadership and civilian leadership in the provision of political goods such as peace, stability, order, security, welfare, justice and liberty although one questions the fairness of this comparison, given the fact that the military in Africa have had a longer reign in political leadership than elected civilian governments.

Decalo's study demonstrates that contrary to popular imagination, military interventions in the governance of African countries was, for the most part, motivated by personal, corporate and idiosyncratic considerations often camouflaged by vitriolic slogans against the commissions and omissions of the ousted civilian administrations. West Africa's first military coup of January 13, 1963, which unseated the elected government of Sylvanus Olympio provides a good illustration of this personal motivation. It was a putsch carried out by disgruntled and unemployed soldiers. Having gotten rid of Sylvanus Olympio, the soldiers installed a puppet government, which subsequently tripled the size and budget of the army and elevated noncommissioned solders to officer ranks. But these "gains" did not satisfy the junta, for four years later, January 13, 1967, the soldiers overthrew their civilian proxies in government and took the leadership of the country into their own hands. Decalo notes that military leadership was, for a time, the norm rather than the exception in African politics. The island nation of Mauritius in 1982 and the East African nation of Zambia were, for a while, the only exceptions to a rule that no ruling political party in Africa was removed from office through an election.[177] But, as we have seen, the 1990s wind of democratic changes has reversed this trend in African politics.

Although at the onset of independence weak nations—characterized by insecure economies, intense ethnic cleavages, lack of mass parties and lack of charismatic leadership—became easy victims of power-seeking military juntas, Decalo reports that it did not take long before relatively powerful countries like Nigeria and Ghana got infected by the cancer of military interventionism in politics. As Decalo puts it, "the spread of the coup syndrome into Anglophone Africa dashed myopic assumptions that the long period of British tutelage had insulated former colonies from the instability of Gallic Africa."[178] But Decalo's reference to "the long period of British tutelage" (in the preceding statement) distorts the true nature of the legacy of British colonialism, which infested the foundation of African politics with destabilizing forces like colonial racism and colonial tribalism. Secondly, his concept of "Gallic Africa" is a peripherializing term that upholds the Eurocentric image of African nations as imperial spheres of influence.

Decalo asserts that too many earlier studies of military leaderships in Africa had erroneously attributed coup d'etats mainly to the socio-economic and political weaknesses of the affected countries. Such studies, he notes, ignored "fundamental behavioral dynamics and motivations"[179] of the coup plotters because of their "uncritical positive images of African armies."[180] These include images of the armies of Africa as cohesive, non-ethnic, disciplined, bureaucratic and the best managed institutions of their societies. Decalo holds that the African armies, do not, as he puts it, conform to this "Eurocentric model."[181] By characterizing those necessary organizational norms as Eurocentric, Decalo leaves an impression that organizational effectiveness derives exclusively from the Western cultural tradition. This kind of posturing is tantamount to hegemonic Eurocentric thinking.

Be that as it may, Decalo's otherwise penetrating description of the internal dynamics of the armies of Africa leaves one with a sense that some of the causes of political disequilibrium on the continent lie within the belly of the military itself. Picture his observation that beneath the facade of "neat hierarchical command-flow charts"[182] of African armies lies "deep cleavages—extensions of wider societal chasms."[183] Most notable of these cleavages is ethnicity, popularly referred to as tribalism. Most African armies, he points out, lack an "ethnic balance"[184] in their officer and ordinary cadres. He comments that this ethnic imbalance exacerbates cleavages based on rank, age, education and religion in societies where ethnicity/regionalism reigns supreme.

But the problem is worse than this picture. For Decalo suggests that African armies are not national armies in the true sense of the term. Rather, they are "a coterie of distinct armed camps owing primary clientelist allegiances to a handful of mutually competitive officers of different ranks."[185] Decalo suggests that these armed camps, as he calls them, are not beholden to military discipline and hierarchical command. The cleavages that ravage them are of such depth that they prevent the military from providing effective national leadership when they seize power, for they spend a preponderant amount of time trying to consolidate their power and to fend off challenges from within.[186]

As a result of the factional nature of African armies, the rise to power of one "faction" evokes the jealousy of other factions for whom the event represents not the super-ordination of the armed forces as an institution over the nation but the "triumph" of one faction of the army over other factions.[187] In consequence, the less fortunate factions will start scheming for their own "chance" at national leadership. The upshot, concludes Decalo, is that "every military incursion"[188] sows the "seeds of future intramilitary strife."[189]

Decalo recognizes that external factors also account for military interventions in African governance. While we now know that the administrations of Mobutu Sese Seko and Idi Amin are proven examples of coup d'etats, which resulted from "an overt or covert nudge from the metropolitan power,"[190] the exact number of such externally-sponsored coup d'etats in Africa remains unknown. However, Decalo offers us an insight into the other side of the "external variable" coin. He states that external forces of "protection" have shielded some African countries from military intervention in their governments. He cites Cote-d'Ivoire (formerly known as the Ivory Coast), Senegal and Gabon as examples. In those countries, he writes, the fear of reprisals by French soldiers kept potential coup plotters in check.[191] This leaves one to wonder about the motive of the French government in this regard: to serve the African interest or the French interest? Whose interests are these "protected" governments serving? However, in recent years, Cote-d'Ivoire has seized to be the show-piece of political harmony and economic development that it was during the more than thirty years of post-independence rule by late Felix Houphouet-Boigny. A civil strife that began in 2002 has kept the country polarized.[192]

Thought-provoking is Decalo's question as to why students of politics tend to "accept" the 'normality' of "diverse motivations" on the part of civilian seekers of political power but tend to "assume that their military cousins are saints and immune to identical behavioral temptations and drives?"[193] Indeed, official explanations for military take-overs have often masked the underlying personal, corporate or idiosyncratic motivations. Decalo observes that the unsuspecting public tends not to question such official "justifications" especially in situations where the ousted civilian government was guilty of "systematic flaws."[194]

Corruption, for instance, is a most frequently cited raison d'etre for military overthrows of governments in Africa. However, it turns out that the military governments sooner or later become as corrupt as the "sinful" civilians. Besides, as Decalo correctly points out, "the charge of corruption is often used ex post facto to publicly legitimate coups mounted for other reasons by officers neither particularly aggravated by it nor untainted themselves."[195] Other such reasons include hidden ambition, fear, greed, and vanity.[196] Decalo reports rather interestingly that sometimes, the charge brought against a civilian government by an emergent military junta is not corruption per se but that the civilians' illegally derived wealth had made them more attractive to mistresses.[197] Some coups were planned and led by officers involved in the very scandals leveled against the ousted civilian governments. For instance, "the coup of 1972 in Cotonou cited the Kovacs Kickback scandal, though allegations of Mathieu Kerekou's own involvement in it have periodically surfaced."[198] Other examples include a 1967 coup in Benin Republic by promotion-seeking junior officers, Jean-Bedel Bokassa's personally-motivated coup of 1965 in the Central African Republic, and General Idi Amin's 1971 "classic power grab"[199] in Uganda. Thus, as Decalo observes, African soldiers have taken advantage of the "powerlessness of most polities to defend themselves from assaults."[200] He points out that the "fragmented, unstructured, and unstable political systems"[201] of Africa have enabled these army officers to advance their personal and corporate interests at the expense of the state. Davidson has harsher words for the power-hungry soldiers. He uses terms like "war-loads, criminal and bandits" to characterize the regimes "from whom nothing but disaster came or ever could have come."[202] One's hope that systemic stability can shield the state from military interventions is almost immediately dashed when Decalo reports that coups could occur even in cohesive, stable and integrated societies but with a lesser chance of success.[203] This is a classic catch-22 situation: systemic stability supposedly forestalls military encroachment on the body politic, but at the same time, the military claims that coups are necessary for stability.

Decalo also holds that military regimes in Africa have not proven themselves to be different from civilian administrations in any significant manner on economic, social and political questions.[204] As he sees it, when personalist, corporate or idiosyncratic motives bring a military junta to power, it tends to focus its attention on those non-state objectives rather than the problems of the country. It is little wonder, then, that he notes as follows:

> Most military juntas—irrespective of their other policies in office—find it imperative, often as one of their first edicts, to increase military salaries and fringe benefits, augment the defense budget, and expand the armed forces, even if profligate expenditures by civilian politicians were the alleged justification for their seizure of power.[205]

In the face of such budgetary preferences to military personnel, little is left for the promotion of socio-economic change, which is the principal task of the government. At the end of the day, the masses are left worse off, but the military, the police and civil servants are better off. A good illustration of this is Ankrah's and Acheampong's Ghana where the appropriations for social services declined by 78 percent at a time the military and civil service's budgets increased by 22 percent annually. Even in instances where a military regime asks everyone else to "tighten his belt," the military government exempts itself from austerity measures. A case in point is the Republic of Benin where in 1965, Soglo's government imposed a squeeze on civil service salaries due to severe economic conditions, but allowed army officers customs exemptions for the importation of private cars and other luxury goods.[206] What does all this indicate? Decalo has a rather cogent observation, namely that it is naive to view army officers as having austere and puritan tastes; they are similar to civilians in "bourgeois tastes."[207]

A critical contention of Decalo's is that the socio-economic culture of African states indirectly stimulates public corruption. He puts it this way. "There are few saints in conditions of acute economic scarcity, especially in cultural systems where the rise to eminence of one individual triggers an obligation to provide for the welfare of an entire kinship group."[208] He also observes that "traditional African values do not usually place a high premium on ascetic life styles."[209] Could this be a veiled critic of the social philosophy that undergirds the African extended family system, which holds that the members of the family are jointly and severally responsible for the welfare of that unit? The responsibilities created by this social philosophy did not prove a heavy burden for the individual in traditional society with its rather simple life and an agrarian economy that made food plentiful.

However, in this age of wage labor and fixed income, it has been difficult for Africans to meet their obligations under the extended family system. Limited disposable incomes have encouraged individualistic living. People tend to focus on their nuclear families. While traditional African society might have valued ascetic life styles, the day-to-day challenges faced by the average African wage of today were forged in the context of a wage-labor economy, different from the subsistence farming that characterized traditional society. Given the low per capita incomes of most African states, the difficult question that faces the average African wage earner of today often is not "how could I live an opulent life, but how could I meet my basic bills and needs on my monthly income?" The challenge of meeting the daily economic obligations of life could induce actions that border on corruption. It's arguable whether such petty corruption is the focus of the analyses that identify corruption as a destabilizing force in African socio-political and economic development.

Military regimes in Africa are known to have been guilty of naked tribalism. Decalo cites several examples of military regimes which purged the officer ranks in order to displace one ethnic group or another from army leadership or to promote the military junta's ethnic group to positions of leadership in government and the army. He observes that "every time a northern group rose to power after an upheaval in Dahomey/Benin it purged the army's senior Fon and Yoruba officers and promoted northerners in the administration."[210] Another example is Jaffer Nimeiry's Sudan where northerners were favored over southerners in military and governmental appointments.

Given the military's lackluster record on political leadership, as the foregoing shows, it' s not a surprise that Decalo concludes that military rule has not helped the cause of political stability in Africa. It is particularly instructive to note that the greatest threat to a military government is the military institution itself. As Decalo puts it,

> Military hierarchies carry within them the seeds of their own destruction or instability. Every single one of them has been rocked by internal power struggles, factionalism, decay of cohesion and discipline, personal power gambits, and successful or attempted counter-coups, though the intensity and frequency of such disturbances may be low or moderate.[211]

In fact, Decalo goes on to say that military leadership in Africa obstructed the emergence of institutional leadership, for, as he argues, military regimes do not emphasize "the development and legitimation over time of stable, complex political structures and procedures."[212] Even where military regimes have instituted "political organs," the same military regimes have ensured that such organs are no more than paper or hollow structures. Indeed, such paper structures have served to prolong military rule. Decalo notes that "in no instance in such 'constitutional zed' or quasi-civilianized systems, however, is there the slightest doubt as to where the locus of power lies."[213]

Another noteworthy point of Decalo's is that military leadership in Africa has not shown itself to be better than civilians in nationalistic leadership or the ability to attract foreign investment. If anything, the arrival of the military on the political scene often "dries up the trickle of foreign investment or assistance, especially if the regime is seen as unstable, or has initiated a program of ideological radicalization."[214] But how should one react to the fact that Burkina Faso's Thomas Sankara's "poignantly sincere commitment to honest, open government and a more aggressive socioeconomic development"[215] program did not invite any greater global interest in that country? He apparently belonged to the category of "radical" leaders—a category that is usually not in the good books of the West.

Decalo recognizes the existence of the phenomenon of neocolonialism in Africa, but he gives it an upside down, "blame the victim" interpretation. He holds that scarcity of "easily exploitable natural resources"[216] and development capital have caused many an African government to become more dependent on the Metropolitan countries, "creating virtual neocolonial relationships."[217] This is really an upside down view of neocolonialism. The works of scholars like Ngugi Wa Thiong'O, Nzongola-Ntalaja, Onimode, et all (which I reviewed earlier), point out convincingly that neocolonialism is the function of the alliance between external political and economic interests and their internal proxies—often a handful of elites.

Another insightful and provocative study of military leadership in Africa, which, in some respects, presents a contrast to the preceding study, is John W. Harbeson's article "Military Rulers in African Politics." In it, Harbeson suggests that it is incorrect to study the phenomenon of military rule in Africa as an aberration. He saw military rule as the norm in Africa. Therefore, he suggests, "we must . . . examine military rule as both a reflection of, and an influence upon the emergence of given countries' fundamental political contours."[218] In this regard, he argues, it is incorrect to regard military rule in Africa as a kind of 'time-out' from a given country's political history. Like Decalo, he observes that there is little difference between military and civilian governments in Africa. The African experience, in fact, presents a breakdown in practice in "the analytical and institutional line between civilian and military rule."[219]

Harbeson goes on to pose a rather "explosive" question about the future of African politics—a question which would make uncomfortable scholars who adhere to the doctrine that military leadership is an interregnum. He asks:

> Have such patterns of governance come to represent the emergence of concepts of the state in which military rule is an alternative to civilian rule as a means of seeking shared broad objectives that is somewhat analogous to the alternation of political parties in established industrial democracies?[220]

As disconcerting as it maybe, the preceding represents a pertinent question. As we shall later see when we examine military leadership in Nigeria, it appears that in as much as some scholars and politicians would like to wish it away, military rule promises to remain a revolving menace to African politics until an enduring political system takes a firm root. However, the democratic wind of change that has ushered in elected, civilian governments in Africa as from the 1990s calls into question the validity of Harbeson's prediction about the permanency of military rule in Africa. It's perhaps too early to speculate as whether this current spread of representative democracies on the continent is a mere fad that will fade away eventually or whether democracy has truly come to stay on this troubled continent.

But Harbeson differs from Decalo on the factors that generate military interventions. In contrast to Decalo's theory of persona list motives, Harbeson cites "renewal of national purpose"[221] as a key motivator of military interventions in African governments. By the renewal of national purpose, he states, the coup leaders attempt to "reestablish clear national objectives,"[222] often objectives such as those which had been conceptualized by nationalist leaders during the independence struggle. Harbeson cites Jerry Rawlings of Ghana as a good example of this. Nigerian military regimes also received a favorable mention in this regard. Harbeson describes the military governments of Nigeria as Constitution-builders and nation unifiers, citing as an example Yakubu Gowon's successful three-year war against Biafra's attempt at succession. In their assessment of the military record of political leadership in Nigeria, Harbeson's and Decalo's views are in agreement, for Decalo even regards Nigeria as an example of a polity where "altruistic/patriotic considerations motivate[d] many coup leaders."[223] However, that stance, in my view, represents a sweeping generalization, for some Nigerian successful or unsuccessful coups were attributed to personalist or even "ethnic" motivations. The July 1966 counter-coup and the 1985 coup led by Babangida are good examples of counter-revolutionary interventions. However, it is significant that the successful coup d'etats in Nigeria tended to be received with wide public acclaim. Harbeson holds that the military in Nigeria contributed to the establishment of political rules by enacting decrees about "how the political game is to be played."[224] He also gives credit to African military regimes where Decalo would not have done so. For instance, he gives credit to the military for playing roles that helped to neutralize and subdue "residual ethnic tensions and conflict."[225] However, the October 21, 1993 bloody coup d'etat in the central African country of Burundi did every thing but neutralize and subdue the long-standing ethnic tension and conflict between the Hutu majority and the Tutsis minority. Although the coup eventually crumbled—thus, restoring the surviving members of the elected civilian government to office, it succeeded in taking the life of the elected President, Melchior Ndadaye, a Hutu, and subsequently provoked a wave of inter and intra ethnic clashes[226] and mass killings. Be that as it may, Harbeson holds that military regimes in Africa brought about social, economic and political changes, though they exerted a greater impact on politics than on the economic structures of their countries.

While Harbeson's analysis is a general picture of military rule in Africa, Richard A. Joseph provides a highly informed discussion of military governance in Nigeria. Joseph's "principles and practices of Nigerian Military Government" describes and analyzes the nature, philosophies, policies and programs of all the military governments that ruled Nigeria up to 1993, starting from Major General Aguiyi Ironsi's first, but brief military government of January 1966 to July 1966 to that of General Ibrahim Babangida, which came into being in August 1985. Babangida left the stage in August 1993.

Joseph presents a positive picture of the stewardship of the military in the governance of Nigeria. He observes that "the relative cohesiveness and continuity of the armed forces, as a corporate body, have accorded it a certain advantage in a country known for its deep cultural divisions."[227] To a large extent, but with the exception of the 1960s, the Nigerian armed forces deserve to be portrayed, as Joseph did, as a cohesive corporate body. However, the intra-military killings of 1966 showed that the Nigerian armed forces could be contaminated by the virus of ethnic animosity just as much as any other Nigerian institution. In addition, I doubt that the ethnic animosity that reached fever pitch in the 60's (and culminated in a three-year old civil war) was a function of "deep cultural divisions." Instead, I believe that it was the consequence of ethnic jockeying for power and the resultant distrust, misunderstanding and fear. I suggest that the so-called deep cultural divisions in Nigeria are not of a fundamental nature, and that the cardinal principles and features of Nigerian cultural centers (when stripped of their Islamic and Christian impositions) are by and large in unity. This point is elaborated in the next chapter.

But Joseph was right on target in his observation that the second civilian administration under Shehu Shagari had steered the country backwards to divisive politics, massive corruption and fraudulent electoral practices. In fact, as well documented by the Nigerian mass media (I served as a political journalist during the period), Shagari's regime's excesses, including alleged acts of impropriety and flagrant electoral mal-practices left the otherwise democratic-minded Nigerian public disillusioned about civilian democracy. Thus, Joseph describes the coup which overthrew Shagari's group as "both a rupture and a recuperation."[228] He explains:

> The military praetors now felt less bound to acknowledge, even verbally, the norm of democratic contestation for power. It was a recuperation as the military is now able to draw, in a conscious way, on the various elements of its own system of governance and even look to maintain aspects of that system when it moves, or is pushed, to permit civilian politics.[229]

But to what extent did the military's dominance of Nigerian rulership help the cause of political integration and political stability? Before I discuss that question, let me state that Nigeria came to a point in its political history where military rule was viewed not as an interregnum, but as Joseph puts it, as an "alternate governing system"—almost in much the same way as a temporarily "out-of-government" civilian political party would be regarded. One must ask rhetorically whether Nigeria's return to civilian rule in 1999 has changed this expectation of the political culture.

Upon coming to power in 1985, Ibrahim Babangida's administration—which left office in August 1993—had generated high hopes about the future of Nigeria and about political leadership in the country. Joseph reports that it had even been hoped that Babangida would lead Nigeria in much the same way as the beloved and respected, but short administration of Murtala Mohammed—July 1975 to February 1976. Those hopes were not realized, for, along with other failings, Babangida left office with an unenviable record of having failed to complete his administration's program of transition to civilian rule. The administration survived two reported attempts from within the military to topple it. A line from Joseph's article surmises the mood of the Nigerian political life—although in a way that would upset the peace of mind of many a Nigerian. He asserts that "unpredictable developments could disrupt the course of any Nigerian government, military or civilian."[230] In March 2005, a conference of experts on Africa convened by the United States National Intelligence Council also predicted the likelihood of an unstable future for Nigeria. The report puts it this way:

> Other potential developments might accelerate decline in Africa and reduce even our limited optimism. The most important would be the outright collapse of Nigeria. While currently Nigeria's leaders are locked in a bad marriage that all dislike but dare not leave, there are possibilities that could disrupt the precarious equilibrium in Abuja. The most important would be a junior officer coup that could destabilize the country to the extent that open warfare breaks out in many places in a sustained manner. If Nigeria were to become a failed state, it could drag down a large part of the West African region. Even state failure in small countries such as Liberia has the effect of destabilizing entire neighborhoods. If millions were to flee a collapsed Nigeria, the surrounding countries, up to and including Ghana, would be destabilized. Further, a failed Nigeria probably could not be reconstituted for many years—if ever—and not without massive international assistance.[231]

What becomes of the preceding prediction will lie in the hands of Nigeria's ruling elite. Larry Diamond's *Class, Ethnicity and Democracy in Nigeria* provides an elaborate discussion of the conduct of Nigeria's sociopolitical elite and its impact upon the nation's political health. In this detailed and heavily supported work, Diamond highlights the forces, which crippled the First Republic (1960–1966) and have continued to haunt the federal republic like a ghost.

Diamond contends that the political leadership of the First Republic failed because of the nature of the interaction among four principal factors: ethnicity, class formation, a rapidly expanding state, and an electoral democracy.[232] A major underlying cause of Nigeria's recurrent political crises, he argues rather cogently, is not ethnicity per se, as conventional wisdom would suggest, but class action as a function of those four variables. Diamond defines class action as the struggle by the elite for power, prestige, security and challenge. In the course of this struggle, "politics became a zero-sum game without rules or boundaries. Constitutional guarantees were trampled and ethnic and regional insecurities heightened in a vicious cycle of tribalism, violence and repression."[233]

Persuasive as the preceding appears, it does not completely account for the destructive behavioral pattern of the Nigerian political elite. Diamond perhaps would agree with me on this, for he cites additional causal variables, including inept and visionless political leadership and factors that derived their origins from colonial rule, such as structural flaws in the federal system, along with political and economic imbalances arising from the commissions and omissions of colonial policy. For instance, "colonial rule . . . failed to develop institutions that could have integrated Nigeria around common cultural, social and political symbols and structures."[234]

Another thought-provoking view of the Nigerian political elite comes from a soldier's perspective—a soldier who had played a leadership role in Nigeria. General Theophilus Y. Danjuma, who was Chief of Army Staff during the Muhammed/Obasanjo's military administrations of 1975 to 1979,[235] thinks of the Nigerian political elite as one which has not achieved a sense of solidarity. They have no focus and no sense of direction, he says. Describing them as their own biggest enemies, Danjuma points out that the Nigerian political elite would rather invite a military take-over of power than lose power to their own political rivals.[236]

Looking back at the early history of the Nigerian political elite, Danjuma observes:

> The political class fought the British using the press and other means and obtained independence for us. And one would think by the length of time that they had existed they should be more mature. The growth in experience has been stunted most probably because of the several interventions of the military.[237]

While Danjuma deserves credit for his candid opinion of the Nigerian political elite, it's worthy of note that this soldier is also candid enough to admit that military interventions in Nigerian politics (for which he himself has been a major player) had the effect of obstructing the maturation process of the political class. There is a catch-22 situation here: on the one hand, the political elite have not had enough time to mature; on the other, when they assume power, their misdeeds, arising partly from immaturity, prompt the military to intervene—an intervention that interrupts their learning process. It is, indeed, a vicious circle!

Another soldier who played a key role in Nigerian military rule, General Olusegun Obasanjo, having served as a military head of state from 1976 to 1979, does not even think that a Nigerian political class has evolved into a group held together by class consciousness. He writes: "in political conflict in Nigeria, ethnicity retains primacy over class. Under any party political system, because of the nature of Nigerian social structure, this will remain so for some time to come."[238] Those views were, of course, aired by Obasanjo before he came back to rule Nigeria for the second time as from 1999—this time, as an elected civilian president. It's doubtful that his thinking on this matter has changed.

Diamond's discussion of the issue of ethnicity and its role in Nigerian politics falls in line with my contention that ethnicity, as it is played out in Nigeria's multi-ethnic society, is more of a political instrument than a genuine reflection of what or how ordinary Nigerians feel about one another or their ethnicity. By and large, Nigerians seem to embrace rather than object to cultural diversity. Like other African societies, the Nigerian psyche seems to be in harmony with cultural pluralism. In his analysis of the forces that brought down the First Republic, Diamond refuses to accord much weight to ethnicity. And, contrary to what conventional wisdom would suggest, Diamond believes that neither the absence of "national unity" nor the lack of "national integration" was to blame for the demise of the First Republic.[239] This is where I differ with him, as I shall demonstrate in Chapter Six. As I see it, there is an escapable symbiotic relationship between the very forces that Diamond identified as the causes of the fall of the First Republic and the lack of effective political integration in Nigeria. Since those causes of the collapse of the first republic also constitute an integral part of the explanation for the mal-integration of the polity, Diamond erred in his conclusion that the collapse of the Republic had nothing to do with political mal-integration.

Arguing like Basil Davidson that tribalism is not intrinsic to the Nigerian character, Diamond contends that tribal consciousness, which was fostered by colonial policies, assumed potency in the course of "modernization" [that is, social transformation] in Nigeria as people began to compete for scarce resources, including political power. What we know of the pre-colonial life of the groups that now constitute Nigeria appears to bear him out on this point, for, as he points out, that pre-colonial life not only demonstrates that various ethnic groups traded goods amicably more often than they warred, it also shows that the majority of ordinary folk were not even aware of the existence of peoples in distant locations.[240] Besides, pre-colonial states of Africa, such as Ghana, Mali, Songhai and Mutapa (Monomotapa) empires were multi-ethnic states—an indication that African groups have historically demonstrated that they can reasonably share common political space across ethnic lines.

Alaba Ogunsanwo's *The Transformation of Nigeria: Scenarios and Metaphors* represents a stinging evaluation of the performance of post-independence political leadership. The country, he argues, had started on the wrong foot in terms of the orientation of the civilians who inherited power from the British. By this, he means that the British had manipulated the transition to African rule in a manner designed to ensure the ascendancy of a segment of the indigenous elite, which did not threaten British economic interests in Nigeria. As a result, "genuinely democratic and patriotic forces who were easily described as demagogues and rabble rousers"[241] were pushed aside. Ogunsanwo laments that the succeeding political leaderships have tended to view public service as a means for personal aggrandizement and for manipulating ethnic sentiments for selfish ends.[242]

Castigating British colonial rule for laying the foundation for some of the ills that bedevil Nigeria, Ogunsanwo pin-points the following as legacies of colonialism that now impede the political development of the nation: structural anomalies in the federal system, the integration of the country into the world's capitalist economy, which reduced her to a dependent economy, and a defective political culture, including intolerance of political opposition—a vice that he characterizes as "the hallmark of colonialism."[243]

Ogunsanwo laments that post-colonial political leaderships have not been able to reverse Nigeria's dependent economic arrangement because such a course of action calls for a kind of leadership that Nigeria has never had—a leadership imbued with imagination, selflessness and courage. Mental colonization of the elite has forestalled the emergence of such a leadership—a mental colonization that makes the elite anything but patriotic and selfless.[244] He observes that the elite manifests a value orientation that is alien to the Nigerian traditional culture. Here is how he explains it:

> Traditional cultural values in all parts of Nigeria placed premium on hard work, tolerance, good neighborliness and honesty. Misappropriation or stealing of community property would lead to ostracism as it was greatly frowned upon. Up till today many a rural folk still cherish this old time honesty and approbation of stealing communal property.[245]

Ogunsanwo is critical of both civilian and military leaderships in Nigeria, pointing out that they manifested class interests that have proven detrimental to the interests of the masses. Evoking an argument similar to Diamond's class action hypothesis, Ogunsanwo contends:

> It may well be argued that objectively, the country's multidimensional elite has since independence represented a particular social category whose class character has held it together in the determination to hold on to power and that it is only divided by the nature of and struggle over the accumulation process.[246]

The roots of the preceding phenomenon, he goes on to argue, were laid by a colonial system, which "created a bifurcation in values in which gradually public property was seen to belong to the alien government and therefore not really subject to the rules and norms of 'thou shall not steal.'"[247] The resultant accumulation process, he notes, has cost the nation dearly as evidenced by a report, among others, that Nigerian financial records could not account for a sum of 17.1 billion dollars which was part of the foreign exchanges that Nigeria earned from exports between 1979 and 1983. This time period refers to the infamous civilian government of Shehu Shagari—a regime, which as Ogunsanwo puts it, produced billionaires and millionaires out of nothing but their membership of the ruling political parties.[248]

Unlike Joseph, Ogunsanwo does not think much of the military administrations of Nigeria or their overall impact on the well-being of Nigerians. He laments that despite what he sees as the unenviable record of military rulership in Nigeria, the rank and file of Nigerians saw the military as an antidote to poor civilian leadership. He argues that such an error of judgment on the part of some Nigerians is attributable to the fact that the services of the civilian partners of the military have helped to mask the fundamental weakness of soldiers as political leaders.[249] On this question, Ogunsanwo differs from Richard A. Joseph's rather positive view of the record of Nigeria's military's political leadership. While both of them have provided powerful support for their divergent positions, there is no doubt that the records of Nigerian soldiers as political leaders demonstrate that soldiers are not immune to the temptation to use public office for personal gains.

A logical conclusion from the findings and analysis of the preceding chapter is that since the factors that militate against effective leadership and political integration Nigeria are internally and externally derived, the ultimate remedies to the problem must reflect both sides of the equation. The chapter revealed or shed light on a number of variables pertinent to national leadership and political integration in Africa in general and Nigeria in particular. Several external and internal factors constrain effective leadership on the continent and consequently impede efforts at political integration. Incessant military interventions in the governments of African countries obstruct the evolution and maturation of a political culture along with the political institutions necessary for the achievement of political integration. Even in the case of Nigeria where military governments received a mixture of positive and negative reviews in the literature, the fact that soldiers occupied the political stage for twenty-nine of the country's forty-five years of independence from British colonial rule (1960–2005) means that Nigerian politicians—despite their profligate leadership during their periods in government—have had a relatively short chance to construct and nourish an enduring political system for Nigeria. The chapter also demonstrated that the military regimes on the continent, including Nigeria's, have not been immune to profligacy.

While the personalized leadership, which, up until the 1990s, characterized the political scene on the continent, produced unpleasant results here and there, the lack of institutionalized leadership was/is compounded by the all-powerful force of neo-colonialism. IMF's Structural Adjustment Programs have weakened the capacity of the affected nation-states to pursue programs of social mobilization—programs which are a sina quo non for political integration. Even in those exceptional cases, like Thomas Sankara's, where political leadership manifested a good-faith effort, they found that imperialism limits the extent to which they can implement nationalist aspirations. Davidson has observed that situations such as Sankara's were inevitable; colonialism had turned Africa into "sub-systems of sub-capitalist dependency"[250] and the efforts of African leaders to turn the situation around were doomed to fail in the face of the monopoly and oligopoly, which infest the present world economic order to which Africa was tied through colonialism—ties that have only gotten worse through the instrumentalities of the world trade organization, the international monetary fund and the world bank, along with the plethora of conditionalties that come with various multilateral and even bilateral aid programs of the contemporary era. In a sense, the problem is not capitalism per se; for as Davidson correctly stated, African countries are simply sub-capitalist dependencies. The debilitating problem of corruption is, in many respects, a function of this sub-capitalist system. As Davidson puts it, "no system of capitalism can possibly be built without a large and even dominant element of corruption."[251] The United States, leader of the "free market" world, can testify to this.

Chapter Four
State Creation: A Tool for Political Integration in Nigeria

Post-colonial societies like Nigeria are characterized by teething problems, such as low levels of political integration, which substantially account for their perennial state of instability. This is because, for the most part, the post-colonial nations are artificial states that were put together for the economic interests of Western European colonial powers. The colonial powers did not, and it was not in their interest, to build or lay the groundwork for genuinely-integrated nations out of those economic patch-works. Thus, the political leaderships of the post-colonial states have devoted substantial attention and resources to the task of forging national cohesion—sometimes described as nation-building. Political scientists describe this as a process of political integration. Chapter Three defines political integration as the problem of cultivating a political culture and of inducing commitment to it[1] For political leadership, this involves two broad challenges: "(a) how to elicit from subjects deference and devotion to the claims of the state, and (b) how to increase normative consensus governing political behavior among members of the political system."[2]

How have successive post-independence Nigerian political leaderships handled this task? Apart from assorted political and educational programs (like requiring school children to memorize and recite the national anthem) designed to increase national consciousness in Nigeria, various Nigerian political leaderships have sought to forge national cohesion in Nigeria in a round-about manner—that is, by fragmenting the component groups of the nation while at the same time promoting allegiance to the center. This has meant the creation of more and more administrative centers known as states, which have governments of their own. It appears that the more centers that are so carved out, the stronger the central government becomes.

This chapter examines state-creation as a tool for political integration or what is more commonly referred to as national unity in Nigeria. It discusses how Nigeria's post-independence political leadership applied the tool of state-creation in its drive for political integration, popularly known as nation-building. In using this tool, a succession of Nigerian governments transformed Nigeria from a country that consisted of three regions by the time that it became independent of British colonial rule in 1960 to one that is now composed of thirty-six states. It was a gradual transformation. Under British rule, the country was turned into three regions in 1955; in 1963, it was changed to four regions; in 1967, it was broken up into twelve

Table 4.1. Nigeria's Evolution to Thirty-six States

1955	**Three Regions:** Eastern Region, Northern Region, and Western Region
1963	**Four Regions:** Eastern Region, Northern Region, Western Region and Mid-Western Region
1967	**Twelve States:** Benue-Plateau State, East-Central State, Kano State, Kwara State, Lagos State, Mid-Western State, North-Central State, North-Eastern State, North-Western State, South-*Eastern State, Rivers State and Western States*
1976	**Nineteen States:** Anambra State, Bauchi State, Bendel State, Benue State, Borno State, Cross-River State, Gongola State, Imo State, Kaduna State, Kano State, Kwara State, Lagos State, Niger State, Ogun State, Ondo State, Oyo State, Plateau State, Sokoto State, and Rivers State
1989	**Twenty-one States:** Akwa-Ibom State, Anambra State, Bauchi State, Bendel State, Benue State, Borno State, Cross-River State, Gongola State, Imo State, Kaduna State, Kano State, Katsina State, Kwara State, Lagos State, Niger State, Ogun State, Plateau State, Sokoto State, *and Rivers State*
1992	**Thirty States:** Abia State, Adamawa State, Akwa-Ibom State, Anambra State, Bauchi State, Benue State, Borno State, Cross-River State, Delta State, Edo State, Enugu State, Imo State, Jigawa State, Kaduna State, Kano State, Katsina State, Kebbi State, Kogi State, Kwara State, Lagos State, Niger State, Ogun State, Ondo State, Osun State, Oyo State, Plateau State, *Rivers State, Taraba State, Sokoto State, and Yobe State*
1996	**Thirty-six States:** Abia State, Adamawa State, Akwa-Ibom State, Anambra State, Bauchi State, Bayelsa State, Benue State, Borno State, Cross-River State, Delta State, Edo State, Ebony State, Ekiti State, Enugu State, Gombe State, Imo State, Jigawa State, Kaduna State, Kano State, Katsina State, Kebbi State, Kogi State, Kwara State, Lagos State, Nasarawa State, Niger State, Ogun State, Ondo State, Osun State, Oyo State, Plateau State, Rivers State, Taraba State, Sokoto *State, and Yobe State, Zamfara State*

states; in 1976, it was further divided into nineteen states; then in 1989, it was changed to a twenty-one state structure; in 1992, it became a nation of thirty states; and then, in 1996, Nigeria achieved its current status as a nation of thirty-six states. Table 4.1 shows this progression of Nigeria from three regions to thirty-six states.

The chapter also assesses the success or failure of state creation in furthering this grand objective of national/political integration. In addressing the latter issue, two questions are critical. One, has the creation of more states strengthened allegiance to the nation state? Two, has it furthered the evolution of a national normative consensus for political conduct?

The politics of the First Republic (1960 to 1966) serves as a background for a comprehensive analysis and understanding of both the root causes of the movement for new states and the attitudes and actions of succeeding political leaderships towards the issue. Hence this chapter contains a detailed examination of that period of Nigeria's political history.

As it would be recalled, the 1946 British Colonial Constitutional Reform in Nigeria institutionalized the concept of regionalism in Nigeria—a move that Nigerian nationalists like Azikiwe and student unions had condemned as a seed of disunity. Indeed, that action was part of a conscious British divide and rule policy to foster broad ethnic consciousness and conflict[3] Despite the criticism and condemnation, the British went on to seal that policy through the 1954 Constitutional Reform. The reform formally established Nigeria as a federation of three regions (the Northern region, the Eastern region and the Western region) with a central government situated in Lagos. The reform laid the foundation of what Alaba Ogunsanwo described as structural deformation in Nigeria[4] By this, he refers to the fact that the Northern Region, one of those three regions thus enacted by British colonialism, was twice as big and populous as the other two regions put together.

This structural imbalance constituted a major source of political irritation for the First Republic. Needless to say, this factor, along with other defects in the political culture, led ultimately to the collapse of that republic. The structural imbalance was compounded by the fact that the three regions also happened to be the locations of Nigeria's three major ethnic groups—the Hausa/Fulani in the North, the Igbo in the East and the Yoruba in the West. The tri-polar regional structure skewed the federal system in favor of the Northern region, which is dominated by the Hausa/Fulani ethnic group and a conservative semi-feudal Islamic oligarchy. "In the Muslim emirates of the North, electoral politics and socioeconomic change challenged the dominance of . . . 'an integrated Muslim ruling class,' which had developed over centuries."[5] The lop-sided federal structure gave the North a 53.8 percent share of the national population, while the East (25.6 percent) and the West (20.5 percent) were roughly equal. In addition, the Northern region occupied more than three quarters of Nigeria's physical territory[6]

Since the politics of the day centered more on ethnicity rather than ideology, as our studies have shown, the coincidence of region and ethnicity in a lop-sided federal structure only made a bad situation worse. Against this backdrop was the fact that the key political parties of the day—the Northern Peoples Congress (NPC) of the North, the National Council of Nigeria and the Cameroons (later renamed the National Convention of Nigerian Citizens) of the East and the Action Group of the West had arisen from ethnic unions (with the slight exception of the NCNC, which had a self-professed nationalistic vision).[7] In addition to being founded upon ethnic grounds, these parties had relentlessly and successfully employed ethnicity (that is, appeals to deep-seated ethnic prejudices and fears) as a tool for galvanizing electoral support. Such practice dates back to the first major election of 1951 and extended to the fraudulent and brutal federal and regional polls of 1964 and 1965, respectively.[8] This type of conduct of the political leadership prompted Diamond to suggest that Nigerian political attitudes and behavior accounted in large part, for the death of Nigeria's elected civilian administrations.[9]

In decrying the behavior of Nigerian politicians during the First Republic, a Nigerian commentator of that era adopted a more severe tone: "Bad workmen blame their tools. Bad politicians blame their constitution. There is not much wrong with the Nigerian Constitution. What is wrong is that there is not much will to make it work."[10] While the preceding assessment suffers from that fallacy of reasoning known as over-generalization (for it glosses over the defects in the structural provisions of the 1963 Constitution of the First Republic, including the structural imbalances in the federal system), it accurately portrays the conduct of the generality of Nigerian politicians of that time.

Thus, the roots of the problem are deeper than the shortcomings of the political culture as identified in the preceding paragraph. To illustrate this point, it is imperative to return to British colonial policies. The size and population of the North, which became a nightmare for Southern politicians as time went on, might not have proved as threatening as they did but for the fact that Britain had created and nurtured a North-South divide in the Nigerian political psyche before she quit the scene with her colonial bag of tricks. Note that before the 1914 amalgamation of Northern and Southern Nigeria, Britain had ruled the North as a separate protectorate from the South. But the amalgamation did not bring about substantive changes in the way Britain ruled Nigeria. As Diamond puts it (Ake had stressed this point as well), "colonial rule . . . failed to develop institutions that could have integrated Nigeria around common cultural, social and political symbols and structures."[11] At the risk of stating the obvious, one should point out that it would not have been in the imperial British interest to create symbols of national unity for Nigeria, for imperialism is interested only in the institutions and symbols that could further its objectives. What Britain did instead was to promote policies that had the effect of deepening the cleavages between the North and the South.[12] These policies include the practice whereby Southerners who moved to the North were not only consigned to segregated housing and education but were also denied freehold to land. While Britain shielded the North from Western education but actively encouraged it in the South, she [implicitly] discouraged Northern Muslims from associating with the 'pagans and infidels' in the South[13] Besides, the curriculum of the "Western" education excluded lessons in national consciousness, national integration and national allegiance[14] Diamond reports that "this separate administration of North and South not only profoundly hindered the development of a common national identity but also generated an immense development gap."[15]

The results were profoundly tragic for the nation. As of 1947, the North accounted for only 2.5 percent of Nigeria's primary school enrolment; by independence in 1960 the number had reached only 10 percent. These figures in turn led to more "imbalances" in other areas of Nigeria's national life. For instance, due mainly to its educational edge, the South soon became dominant not only in the federal public service but also in the Northern Region's public service as well—a factor that became a source of northern resentment against the south, particularly the Igbos[16] Matters were not helped by the vitriolic pronouncements of Northern conservative, political leadership during the First Republic. "In fact, the political instability of the time stemmed significantly from [the] determination of the Northern ruling class to establish firm control over the federal, state and its resources, and so to secure its dominance over the political classes of the Eastern and Western regions."[17]

While education suffered from the North-South bi-polar policies of colonial administration, the economy also developed along regional rather than national lines, thus forestalling the emergence of a national economic class based on trans-ethnic consciousness and social coherence. Regional and ethnic coordinates polarized the emerging economic class[18] In addition to this phenomenon, the state was the chief source of the wherewithal of this growing economic/political class for the simple reason that prior to and after independence Nigeria has had a paltry private sector, based largely on foreign-controlled economic institutions and activities; the public sector dominated the economy. Political power and material wealth, and consequently membership of the privileged socio-economic class, derived from access to the state rather than economic productivity[19] This class had acquired sumptuous tastes which reflected its internalization of Western capitalist materialistic and elitist standards of consumption. (This is against the backdrop of a traditional culture that did not cherish accumulation of personal wealth.)[20]

It is for the preceding reasons that elections in Nigeria became life or death struggles both before, and much worse, after independence, including the First Republic (1960–1966), the Second Republic (1979–1983), and to a great extent, the ongoing Third Republic that began with Nigeria's return to civilian rule in 1999. Political office seekers did not hesitate to flout the rules of political competition and to resort to desperate tactics such as crass appeals to real or imagined ethnic fears and prejudices and outright political repression, thuggery, violence and election rigging.[21] In this state of affairs, the north-south polarity, the regional divides, the ethnic divides and the religious divides became handy weapons of the political warlords.

Writing about the dastardly nature of the fraudulent and brutal elections of the First Republic,[22] Eme Ekekwe forthrightly notes that "Nigerian politics in the First Republic could be quite adequately described as approaching a Hobbesian state of nature . . . For the politicians, especially during periods of regional or national elections, life was indeed 'solitary, poor, nasty, brutish and short.'"[23] As for the 1983 general elections of the Second Republic, which Falola and Ihonvbere reported, in their book, as the most rigged elections in Nigeria's history, none of the parties which participated in them hardly escaped charges and counter-charges of fraudulent practices[24] Nwabueze's candid assessment of the 1983 polls reports that "a large part of [the rigging] . . . is . . . attributable to illegal voting, particularly multiple voting and dumping of ballot papers, which was practiced by nearly all the political parties to a greater or less extent."[25] As for the National Party of Nigeria, (NPN), which controlled the federal government at this time, Nwabueze has wondered whether the party would have won the elections with a landslide without rigging.[26]

Not surprisingly, Ogunsanwo (1991), Diamond (1988) and Ekekwe (1986) have characterized Nigerian politics as mere class action, which in the words of Diamond means the struggle by the elite for power, prestige, security and challenge. In this sense, the Nigerian political leadership, in general, is seen as one that has not been dedicated to the pursuit of the public good. Hence its view of elections as life or death struggles. However, as the preceding and subsequent discussions have/will show, there is more to Nigerian politics than class action.

In similar fashion, the head count of the number of people who inhabit the territory of Nigeria, which ordinarily might be viewed as a mere mechanical and administrative exercise, has proved, throughout Nigeria's history, to be a hard-nut to crack. Like the elections, the First Republic's two census counts of 1962 and 1963 became life or death issues. This is because the census determines the basis for the distribution of government amenities, including party political representation, and in effect, each region's share of "access to the state." As Ekekwe would put it, such access merely furthered the class action objectives of the socio-political/economic elite. In the nation's first and second attempts to conduct its own national census in 1962 and 1963, the politicians manipulated the returns, just as they had padded election results, in order to obtain a favorable share of the national population count. Due to the controversy it generated, particularly between Northern and Southern politicians, the 1962 census result was never officially published. But before it was finally cancelled by the Prime Minister, two versions of the result had been unofficially released. One version released by the Federal ministry of information, placed the country's population at forty-two, broken down as: twenty-two million for the North; twelve million for the East and eight million for the West, including the Midwest. The other version placed the overall figure at fifty-two million, broken down as thirty million for the North; twelve million for the East and ten million for the West.[27] One of the charges and counter-charges provoked by these contradictory figures was that both the North and the East had inflated their census figures.

The ensuing rancor and bitterness deepened the nation's north-south cleavages and became the gun-power that inflamed and compounded future conflicts. As the *Daily Times* of Nigeria observed at that time, "the history of the 1962 census is a long process of confusion, bitterness, mistrust and violent exchange of words."[28]

A second census was, therefore, conducted in November 1963. This gave the country a total population of 55.6 million, representing a questionable increase of 83 percent in ten years. This was broken down as 29.78 million for the North; 12.39 million for the East; 10.28 million for the West; 2.53 million for the Mid-West; and six hundred and seventy-five thousand for Lagos. The results of the second count provoked as much controversy between Northern and Southern politicians as the previous ones, but this time, they were accepted by the Federal Government. The Eastern region in particular remained bitterly opposed to the results and carried its protest all the way to the Supreme Court but to no avail.[29]

In 1973, under the leadership of General Yakubu Gowon, Nigeria once more tried to conduct a national census but, like the First Republic's experiences, the results did not meet national acceptance[30] One of the reasons that the 1973 census results proved controversial was the fact that their figures worsened the North-South imbalance; in fact, the Western states actually experienced a decline below their 1952 levels[31] Therefore, the results were cancelled. As Aluko put it rather prophetically back in his 1965 publication, "it is . . . obvious that no census of Nigeria has really enjoyed widespread acceptance, right back to 1901."[32] Although the federal officers in-charge of the discredited census of 1973 had tried to blame the failure of the exercise on the field workers, they did acknowledge that the process had fallen victim to the same forces that had frustrated previous head counts in Nigeria. So, to a large degree, the 1973 census report bears out Aluko's historical perspective: "a good head count in this country is hardly possible as long as allocation of revenue and the representation in parliament are tied to census figures."[33] But Nigeria cannot afford to surrender itself to this blackmail. The fact that census results carry far-reaching economic implications should not mean that Nigeria cannot muster enough integrity to do an honest head-count. Development is/ought to be centered on people; the nation has no choice but use demographic information in its planning. The nation cannot avoid it. The nation cannot run away from the fact that Nigerians themselves have been responsible for the fraud associated with the nation's head-counts. Nigeria cannot copout by blaming the problem on the fact that demographic information is important to revenue sharing and representative democracy. To do so would be tantamount to suggesting that examination frauds occur not because of a character flaw on the part of the examinees and examiners but because examinations do affect the life chances of individuals! On a positive note, though, it would appear that the nation is beginning to over-come its census challenge, for the national census of 1991, which placed Nigeria's population at 88.9 million, turned out better than previous exercises. One analyst recalls it euphorically:

> It is however salutary to note that the phenomenon now appears to be a thing of the past, especially with the successful conduct of the 1991 census. The 1991 census, conducted by the National Population Commission, was preceded by the kind of elaborate preparation that would be expected of a scientifically conducted census, by international standards[34]

At the time that this publication was being finalized, the nation went through another head count in March 2006, whose results were still being awaited.

Nonetheless, the roots of the Nigerian census difficulties date back to British colonial administration's commissions and omissions. During colonial times, the British never really conducted a thorough census of Nigeria but instead relied on hap-hazard estimates. This remained the state of affairs from 1900 to 1931. Under British colonial rule, the first painstaking attempt to conduct the head count of Nigerians took place in 1950–3.[35] Besides the administrative shortcomings of British colonial administration, there were other reasons this effort did not yield satisfactory results. Aluko recalls that "there was still a lot of suspicion about the motives for the census, as many Nigerians were reluctant to have their wives and children counted. Many regarded the census as a plot to enable the tax-gatherers to collect heavier taxes."[36]

However, the most critical problem with the colonially-conducted census of 1950–3 was a charge by Southern politicians that the results had been manipulated by the British in order to give the North (which the colonial establishment perceived, rightly or wrongly, as a dependable ally) a political edge in Nigerian politics. In fact, the 1950–3 census resulted in the allocation of fifty percent of the representation in the federal legislature to the Northern region.[37] This was the polluted background against which the 1962 and 1963 censuses were held. Aluko recalls that the outcome of the 1962 census was a disappointment for some Nigerians who had nursed a hope that the head-count would serve as the first accurate census in the nation's history as well as a model for other developing nations. But colonialism had sowed the seed of distrust between Northern and Southern politicians over population distribution in Nigeria; thus, it was little wonder that a post-colonial government of Nigeria could not produce a reliable census. This particular colonial legacy has had the effect of compounding other imbalances in the federal structure which colonialism had bequeathed upon Nigeria. It is almost as if British colonial policy had set booby traps that would inevitably derail an independent Nigerian state! But can't supposedly independent Nigeria find a way to outgrow whatever legacies that it inherited from colonialism?

As would be expected, the controversy generated by the second census of 1963 exerted a ripple effect on the young nation. It brought about an across-the-board party realignment along the north-south divide as the leading parties of the South joined forces. A political commentator vividly captured the political condition of the First Republic when he observed: "the centrifugal forces tossing our ship of state are by far more powerful than the centripetal forces."[38] In the ensuing political realignment, the NCNC of the East and the Action Group of the West—formed the United Progressive Grand Alliance (UPGA).[39] The alliance included two minor opposition parties based in the North: the Northern Elements Progressive Union (NEPU) and the United Middle Belt Congress (UMBC). On the other hand, a break-away party of the West, the Nigerian National Democratic Party (NNDP), teamed up with the NPC of the North to form the Nigerian National Alliance (NNA). In addition, there was an upsurge in anti-Igbo sentiments in the North.[40] The stage was thus set for a show down as shown by subsequent crises. The explosive general election of 1964 and its highly disputed results (the election was boycotted by UPGA), and the ill-fated and fraudulent 1965 Western Regional Election, which remains the most violent in Nigeria's history, had been foreshadowed by simmering resentment and frustration arising from the census disappointments and rancors. The culmination of all these was the January 15, 1966 coup d'etat which expelled the rather disorderly crop of political leaders from the stage. Those crises mirrored much more than what Ekekwe would prefer to label as class action. There were genuine concerns on the part of Southern politicians in particular about the federal structure and its implications for the well-being of segments of the populace. As Diamond acknowledges,

> The crisis . . . crystallized feelings about the unfairness and hence illegitimacy of the federal system. Their defeat on the census left NCNC leaders with the same feeling as the defeated Action Group politicians before them—that there was something fundamentally wrong with a system that seemed rigged to guarantee perpetual domination by a particular region and party.[41]

But in addition to that factor, it is self-evident that Nigerian political leadership as a whole (including the federal and regional governments of that time period) had mishandled both the census exercises and the elections. It is also equally true that the census impasse was the out-growth of a seed of disunity and distrust implanted by colonial policy. Nonetheless, the census and election crises represent sad commentaries on the behavior of the political elite. It's a behavioral style which does not show a commitment on the part of the political leaders to democratic principles and procedures. Rather, it reflects what Nwabueze has fittingly characterized as a disgraceful penchant for arbitrariness and perversion on the part of Nigerian leaders[42] As Diamond puts it, "Goals tended to overtake and define the means, and when one party to a conflict violated legal procedures and a basic sense of fair play its opposition was pressed to respond in like fashion."[43] Diamond goes on to comment that "these acts fed upon each other in escalating fashion until there were no rules of the game at all—except the basic law that raw force triumphs in a normative vacuum."[44]

My postulation is that in as much as Ekekwe's, Diamond's and Ogun-sanwo's theory of class action bears relevance to the politics of the First Republic and of the Second Republic as well, the colonially-originated structural anomalies (complicated by shortcomings in the political culture such as the behavioral and normative aberrations richly acknowledged by those scholars), which were discussed in the foregoing, represent the major systemic precipitants of the clamor for new states in Nigeria. For this reason, I submit that it is necessary to draw a distinction between the motives behind political leadership's response to the agitation for new states and what might have been the personal, class or even ethnic motives of the individuals who spear-headed the movement for new states. Besides, I contend that the motives of the latter reflect not merely class-action desires but also (as I will show in the succeeding pages of this chapter), genuine fears held by both majority and minority ethnic groups of political/ethnic/cultural domination. For as the preceding events and crises of the First Republic amply demonstrate, it was not only the political culture that required change; the federal structure itself needed a significant overhaul. By creating new states as various political leaderships subsequently did at different periods in Nigerian history, they acted not merely from the standpoint of political expediency as was the case sometimes, but also from a felt and demonstrated necessity for the readjustment of a defective, colonially-created structure of federalism in Nigeria.

Even before the British departed in 1960, the leaders of minority ethnic groups clustered within the territorial boundaries of the major groups had begun to press for their own separate states where they could breathe freely, figuratively speaking. Such demands include those for a Middle-Belt state in the North, a Midwest State in the South-West and a Calabar-Ogoja-Rivers State in the South-East. Altogether, fifteen requests for new states were submitted during the constitutional conferences that preceded Nigeria's independence[45] These pressures prompted the colonial government to set up the Willink commission of 1957 to examine the issue. Although the British subsequently failed to create new states and consequently left Nigeria with the ticking time-bomb represented by the lop-sided tri-polar regional federal structure, the Willink commission reported that the requests for new states stemmed from the fears of regional domination harbored by minority ethnic groups. (Remember that each of the three regions was controlled by a "majority" ethnic group). Ekekwe contends that the expressed fear of regional domination is an "indication that the demands for the creation of states had little to do with federal balance."[46] Instead, he observes furthermore, the evidence before the Willink commission showed that the pressures for new states arose from economic and cultural insecurities.

However, I defer with the preceding viewpoint regarding this early drive for new states in Nigeria. My interpretation is that the nature of the relationship between the majority and minority ethnic groups then and now had/has serious implications for effective and peaceful federalism or what Ekekwe prefers to describe as federal balance. This is borne out by the very fact that a major source of political animosity and tension during the First Republic was inter-party competition for the support of minority ethnic groups. As it were, the three major parties, the NPC, the NCNC and Action Group, raided each other's "political territory" for a political foothold in the minority enclaves. Thus, while it was convenient for the NPC and NCNC to oppose the agitation for new states in their Northern and Eastern backyards respectively, those same parties did not hesitate to endorse the movement for a Mid-West State within the Western jurisdiction of their Action Group opponents. In like manner, while the Action Group had actively supported the movement for a COR State in NCNC's East and the movement for a Middle Belt state in NPC's North, it had given mere lukewarm support (because it was not politically correct for it not to do so) to the Midwestern state agitation within its own Western backyard.[47] This drive, on the part of the leading political parties, to under-cut each other "at the home base" partly accounted for the promptness with which the NPC-NCNC federal coalition created a Midwest state in 1963, while conveniently ignoring the burning demands for a Middle-Belt state in NPC's Northern political territory and the one for a COR state in NCNC's Eastern territory.[48] Such political insincerity generated unhealthy tension in the system. Political competition around the issue of new states was not waged principally on the basis of ideology or programs of social transformation but on appeals to deep-seated fears and prejudices which minority groups harbored against their "majority" neighbors. Had Nigerian politics of that time been conducted on the basis of ideological and policy questions and choices, this inter-party competition for the political support of minority ethnic groups would have had a less disintegrative potential. Had ideological and policy-oriented politics prevailed, the nation would, probably, have been spared of the succession of crises which characterized the life of the First Republic. Had the state issue been sincerely addressed from the standpoint of meeting the legitimate aspirations of people, there probably would not have occurred the Tiv uprisings of 1959, 1960, and 1964. As this study has demonstrated, those uprisings, in combination with the 1962 and 1963 censuses, the 1964 federal elections, the 1962 Western parliamentary Crisis and the 1965 election crisis in that region as well, contributed to the military coup d'etat of January 1966.[49] A defective federal structure lay at the roots of those crises; had political leadership sincerely addressed the associated problem of new states, the history of the First Republic might have been different.

The foregoing lends strong support to the thesis of this chapter, for it further demonstrates that the defective federal structure which Nigeria's political leadership inherited from colonial rule was inherently disintegrative for two reasons. One, it tilted the balance of politics in favor of an outsized North; two, it pocketed restless ethnic minorities within regions which did not allow them enough room to pursue their rights to life, liberty and the pursuit of happiness. Even though the creation of the Midwest region in 1963 by the NPC-NCNC ruling coalition was partly calculated to weaken the Action Group, it, nonetheless, still represents a response to a long-standing yawning for self-determination which had been neglected at the risk of regional peace. And if the peace of one region is disturbed, the nation itself is at risk as shown by the way the election crises of the West and their aftermath spilled over and unleashed a chain of events that ultimately crippled the federal government.

The defective nature of the Federal Structure of the First Republic indirectly exerted negative consequences on federal elections. The North's possession of a plurality of the seats in the federal legislature by virtue of its population supremacy meant in effect that it was guaranteed to maintain control over the political leadership of the nation. As one political scientist observes,

> There is an obvious anomaly in having one Region that is larger than all the others combined. This disparity is having the effect of polarizing opposition between two sections (North and South) of the country. National unity may not be able to stand the strain of this polarization.[50]

The disputed census results of 1962 and 1963 merely reinforced this picture and left the nation further polarized. The census dashed NCNC's hope of winning leadership of the nation. In light of the foregoing, the campaign for the nation's first post-independence general election of 1964 took on the tone of a warfare. Thuggery, violence and various forms of intimidation characterized the campaigns. Neither southern nor northern politicians could campaign freely in each other's "territory."

The language of campaign rhetoric was marked by pervasive bigotry including rank appeals to ethnic pride and prejudice. Diamond reports that as the campaign wore on, restraint further crumbled and anti-democratic behavior escalated, forcing some traditional rulers to appeal to the prime minister to introduce an emergency legislation against thuggery and hooliganism. Life itself came under serious threat so much so that the politicians could no longer appear in public without carrying weapons to protect themselves from the ghost that they had unleashed. In the Middle Belt of the North, the contest between supporters of the NPC and opposing parties left hundreds of people dead and thousands arrested, forcing the government to call in the army.[51] So deep and widespread was this crude political campaign that both Prime Minister Tafawa Balewa and President Nnamdi Azikiwe found it necessary to rebuke their fellow politicians. Decrying the gospel of tribalism being peddled by the feuding parties, the prime minister warned that tribalism threatened the survival of the nation. On his part, the president "asked how politicians could take such delight 'in beating the tom-tom of tribal hatred' in a nation whose many religions taught love, kindness and charity."[52]

In view of the preceding and apparently in recognition that the outcome of the upcoming 1964 general election was a faith accompli in favor of continued Northern control of the nation's politics, the United Progressive Grand Alliance, UPGA, (made up principally of the NCNC and the Action Group—the two leading southern parties) decided to boycott the 1964 federal election. But the boycott turned out to be an incomplete success, for it was only the Eastern Region that effectively observed it. And, it also proved counter-productive for it gave the NPC-controlled Nigerian National Alliance (NNA) a chance to win a landslide victory which gave the party 198 of the 253 seats in the federal legislature[53] Thus, Agume Opia views the decision of UPGA to boycott the election as "an error of judgment,"[54] which left the political field wide open for NNA. Since UPGA subsequently compromised its original principled position not to take part in the election—whose campaign had been conducted in an anti-democratic atmosphere of terror—by joining the "national government"[55] formed by Prime Minister Balewa after the disputed election, it appears that Opia is right in describing UPGA's ill-fated boycott decision as an error. In a well-honed analysis of the election crisis, Diamond observes that the crisis was the product of a multiplicity of polarizing factors which had been gathering momentum through consecutive conflicts of the post-independence period. These factors, he explains, include: "the gathering of forces around opposite extremes, the disappearance of moderate or mediating forces and of salient cross-cutting cleavages, the erosion of the rules of competition and of belief in the possibility of mutual benefit."[56] Of fundamental importance is an aspect of his analysis which agrees with my own interpretation of the colonially-designed federal structure: Diamond's keen observation that the roots of the 1964 election crisis extend farther to "the tensions and contradictions of the colonial period."[57]

Among those tensions and contradictions was of course the lop-sided regional tri-polar structure which, like a ghost, haunted and frustrated the hopes of southern politicians of ever winning the leadership of Nigeria through the electoral process. Since the electoral process depends on majority rule, and ethnicity governed/governs Nigeria's politics, the fact that the North contains a majority of the nation's population meant that a prime ministerial contest between a northern candidate and a southern candidate was pre-destined to result in a victory for the former. But this concern that the North would rule in perpetuity was not necessarily an exclusively southern political headache. For there exists within the North, minority, non-Islamic groups like the Tiv, which resented the rule of what, for a better choice of words, has been described as the region's conservative, Islamic Fulani/Hausa oligarchy. So, it is not surprising that a spokesman of the Tiv, Joseph Tarka, and then leader of the United Middle Belt Congress had also voiced a fear of the prospect of perpetual Northern rulership of Nigeria. Hence, his poignant and historic observation that:

> The creation of new states is the only basis on which the unity of this country is going to continue, and it is upon the creation of states that the breaking of the monopoly of all other regions by one region which constitutes an unbalanced structure in the federation will be achieved[58]

In any case, as long as such voices were those of the Tarkas of Nigeria (that is, the minorities), they remained consigned to the political Siberia of "minority concerns"—but nonetheless concerns that had been around as far back as colonial times. And as long as state creation remained the concern of "minorities," the majority groups or their parties such as the NCNC and the Action Group could afford to merely exploit the issue for electoral gains. However, as the politics of the First Republic began to unfold and the implications of an out-sized North began to dawn on everyone (the census counts had failed to redress the federal imbalance),[59] some majority groups increasingly felt marginalized. This added a new dimension to the movement for new states as the majority parties came to the realization that they could no longer exploit the quest for new states as a vote-catching issue. Thus, in the aftermath of the 1962/63 census crises which left the Eastern region politically worse off than it had ever been since independence, its premier, Dr. Michael Okpara, of the Igbo majority ethnic group, called for a break-up of the federation into 25 states[60] As it turned out, this suggestion represented much more than Okpara's personal position, for UPGA, the alliance which his party, the NCNC, had formed with the Action Group and a couple of Northern opposition parties, later included the creation of new states in its manifesto for the 1964 election.[61] Although Okpara's 25-state structure would not have altogether eliminated the north-south divide in Nigerian politics, it, at least, would have decreased the system's vulnerability to polarization along regional and ethnic lines, by allowing for the possibility of criss-cutting alliances between northern and southern states. Diamond recognizes this point but quickly recalls that the United States had fought a civil war despite the existence of a similar structure in pre-Civil war America.[62]

As Premier Okpara's proposal and Tarka's warning demonstrate, the creation of the Midwest region in 1963 had merely scratched the surface of a problem (i.e. the stringent demand by minorities for their own political space), which had become a festering sore for the young republic. It also left unresolved the bigger problem of regional imbalance caused primarily by an out-sized North. This fear of "Northern domination" lies beneath Okpara's advocacy of a 25-state structure for the nation in the hope that it would break the backbone of what he and other Southern politicians had come to perceive as northern hegemony.

This fear had also provoked anti-democratic and anti-systemic behavior during the First Republic as some segments of the nation were left to feel that "the system does not work." Two events will suffice to illustrate this point. One is Action Group's intra-party feud of 1962 which led to a split between the party leader, Chief Obafemi Awolowo and the premier, Chief Samuel Ladoke Akintola. Following a petition signed by sixty of the Region's AG's one hundred and seventeen Action Group's Regional parliamentary representatives, Governor Adesoji Aderemi dismissed Akintola as premier on May 21, 1962. Chief O.S. Adegbenro was immediately sworn-in as the new premier.[63] But Akintola remained defiant and in fact forced his way back to his office the next day. The House of Assembly was to meet on May 25 to confirm the appointment of Adegbenro as the new premier[64] However, on that day, Akintola's supporters in the state legislature, who were by far outnumbered by Awolowo's, filibustered and obstructed this and two other attempts of the house to meet in order to confirm Adegbenro's appointment. On those three occasions that the state assembly tried to meet, Akintola's supporters physically disrupted the effort, prompting the police to clear the house with tear gas. Awolowo, the Action Group's leader, appealed in vain to the prime minister to guarantee police protection for the legislators. Diamond suggests that the prime minister refused to accede to Awolowo's request for partisan reasons because his party, the NPC and its federal partner, the NCNC, had come to see the Action Group, which was the Chief Federal Opposition, as a political nuisance and were, therefore, anxious to see it sink. There were a number of reasons the ruling parties at the center harbored a fear of the Action Group as an opposition party. Among them was Awolowo's strident criticism of federal policies, his party's manipulation of regional power politics, and his party's espousal of socialist economic goals.[65] So, in a triumph of what amounted to a tyranny of the minority, Akintola's handful of supporters in the legislature were allowed to physically obstruct the legislative arm of government. In other words, by obstructing orderly constitutional governance, they took the laws into their own hands. For partisan, political calculations, the Prime Minister looked the other way while this happened; he failed to demonstrate the statesmanship required by the moment. The whole affair represents a sad commentary on the political leadership of Prime Minister Balewa whose actions and inactions left him open to charges of intolerance of Opposition. Awolowo himself had very early detected the NPC-led federal government's antipathy towards the opposition:

> Several threats have of late been issued by spokesmen of the Federal Government . . . It has been said that, after independence, if the Western Region Government does not behave itself it will be dissolved, and that the Action Group is an evil party which does not deserve to live in a free Nigeria.[66]

As if to confirm Awolowo's fears, the federal government eventually—in the wake of the political stalemate that resulted from the preceding intra-party feud in the Western Action Group—imposed a state of emergency in the region on May 29, 1962. It appointed a administrator, Senator M.A. Majekodunmi, to govern the region. Initially, this federal administrator restricted the movement of all leading politicians within the troubled region; however, within two months of the emergency rule,[67] he allowed Akintola's supporters to move about and act freely while still restricting Awolowo's—an action which did not portray him as an impartial umpire. Akintola later brought a suit challenging his dismissal as premier and was able to get a Supreme Court ruling in his favor. However, at this time, Nigeria had not yet become a republic and, therefore, decisions of its Supreme Court were subject to the final word of the British Privy Council in London to which Adegbenro appealed. The Council reversed the ruling of the Nigerian Supreme Court and thus upheld the dismissal of Premier Akintola. But in anticipation of the Privy Council's ruling, the Western Region had hurriedly amended the regional constitution to ensure that it would be of no effect. Diamond provides the details:

> Anticipating the Judicial Committee's decision by one hour, the Regional Government hastily summoned a special session of the House

and amended the Region's constitution—retroactive to October 1960—
requiring a no-confidence vote before a Premier's removal. The House
then declared no confidence in Adegbenro as premier and reaffirmed
its confidence in Akintola. On 6 June the amendment was ratified at an
emergency meeting of the Federal Parliament.[68]

This was clearly an affront to due process, to the rule of law—a blatantly
partisan abuse (with the backing of the federal government) of the regional
assembly's authority to amend the constitution. A constitutional amendment
should serve the end of making the government more effective by removing
or changing provisions that constrict its ability to serve the people. It is not
designed to serve as a tool for blatantly partisan political objectives or as a
way to circumvent the law.

The second event, which illustrates the effect of the fear of Northern
"hegemony" during the First Republic, was a follow-up to the preceding
regional crisis. One of the events that followed the declaration of emergency rule in the West was the arrest and trial of the leader of the Action
Group, Awolowo, for treasonable felony. He was charged with planning
to seize the federal government by force. And he was found guilty and sen-
tenced to ten years imprisonment in September 1963. This merely escalated
the slide of the nation toward disaster. As one political observer puts it,

> The trial did little to strengthen popular faith in Nigerian justice. The
> acknowledged contradictions and weaknesses in the evidence, the dubi-
> ousness of the motives of several key prosecution witnesses, and above
> all the inherent implausibility of a plot to capture Lagos with a few pis-
> tols, rifles and torches, with apparently no arrangements for winning
> power in the Regions, strengthened a widespread belief that Awolowo
> had somehow been betrayed, if not actually framed.[69]

Thus, those two events, the declaration of emergency rule in the West and the
trial and conviction of Awolowo for a charge of treasonable felony, which
apparently was not proven beyond all reasonable doubt, are among the
manifestations of the limitations and dangers of the bi-polar politics of the
First Republic. They also demonstrate how the north-south political schism
provoked anti-systemic and anti-democratic actions: (1) the refusal of the
prime minister to use the police to enforce order in a legislative house, (2) the
bestial conduct of Akintola's legislative supporters, and (3) Chief Awolowo's
alleged attempt to seize the federal government by non-democratic means.

Towards the end of that republic, the creation of more states increasingly became the last hope for redressing the imbalance of the federal

structure and thereby preserving the fledgling state. But before the prayers of the champions of new states could be answered, the military swept the politicians off the stage on January 15, 1966. And in an ironic twist of events, the soldiers themselves performed the first major act in the dismantling of the troublesome regional structure. Given NPC's political dominance in the First Republic and its reticence toward the idea of new states, the political leadership of the time could not have established new states by a democratic process, for that would have amounted to a political suicide on the part of the Northern ruling class, which saw the preservation of "one north" as vital to what Premier Ahmadu Bello had described as northerners' goal of gaining 'control of everything in the country.'[70] But given the military's autocratic style of leadership—leadership by decree—the succeeding government of General Yakubu Gowon (who became Head of State as a result of the counter-coup of July 1966), was able to do, in one fell swoop, what the civilians could not do during six years of tongue-twisting on the issue. It is pertinent to mention here that the civilian leaders of the First Republic were not necessarily devoid of brilliant ideas about how to govern the nation; their chief handicap was lack of political will and their failure, as a group, to place the national interests of Nigeria above partisan/regional political considerations when a situation so dictated. Both Prime Minister Balewa and President Azikiwe did acknowledge this lack of commitment to the national interest by their admonition of their colleagues who had engaged in ethnic bashing and cheer-leading. The fact that their pleas fell on deaf ears and exerted little effect on the political climate of the day, demonstrates that political leadership requires much more than the sole efforts of the man/woman at the top; it also requires the efforts of subordinate players on the stage of political power. In short, the job of providing effective political leadership in a polity is the collective responsibility of the political elite. That is why, as Ake stressed in Chapter Three, a normative consensus is an essential ingredient for both effective political leadership and effective political integration, as the two work hand in hand.

On May 27, 1967, General Gowon made the most popular announcement of his nine-year rulership of Nigeria (1966–75) when he informed an agitated nation (the polity was in the grips of rapidly escalating crises) that Nigeria had been broken up into twelve states. Though political expediency was the immediate precipitant of that move (but a political expediency of a different nature from the vote-catching calculus of the NPC-NCNC coalition which created the Midwest region in 1963), no one doubts that it broke the backbone of the monstrous regions. The twelve states were created on the eve of Nigeria's civil war (1967–70), and in a sense, it was part of Gowon's attempt to stop the drift of the injured Eastern region toward secession. The region, brimming with the pain and anger arising from the mass slaughters of Igbo army officers (including the Head of State, General Aguiyi-Ironsi) and civilians living in the North during and after the July 29, 1966 counter-coup, was on the verge of seceding from Nigeria when Gowon announced the twelve-state structure. (About thirty thousand Igbos were massacred during this crisis.)[71] The action was indeed a political blow to the East, for it excised from the region two minority ethnic groups and gave them their own states. In effect, it answered the age-old dream of the COR state movement. As General Olusegun Obasanjo, who years later became Nigeria's military Head of State, observes in his account of his stewardship as a war commander during the Nigerian Civil War, "short of military action at that time, creation of states by decree was the only weapon ready in hand. At first, states were to be created only in the Eastern Region. Such action was considered impolitic and fraught with danger."[72] But the civil war eventually broke out anyway. For the Eastern Region made good its threat of secession. The region had lost faith in the ability of the federal government to protect the lives and property of Igbos in other parts of Nigeria, particularly the North where majority of the massacres of Igbos had taken place. This loss of faith in the central government is reflected in Colonel Odumegwu Ojukwu's proclamation of the now defunct nation of "Biafra."[73] But the secession was short-lived, for it crumbled in January 1970 after nearly three years of blood-letting. While Obasanjo contends that Gowon's action was designed to under-cut Ojukwu, Gowon himself has portrayed his act differently. Had he created states only in the East as Obasanjo reveals he might have done, then he surely would have deserved condemnation for short-sighted and blatantly partisan political leadership. If the North had been left in tact, such an act would have put fears in the minds of the Yoruba whose support Gowon sorely needed for a successful prosecution of the civil war. No doubt, it would have served as a splendid political ammunition for the East.

In his national broadcast of the new states, Gowon states that he believed that 'the main obstacle to future stability . . . is the present imbalance in the Nigerian Federation.'[74] He points out that no nation would survive if a section of it (an indirect reference to the Northern region) was in a position to hold the rest of the country to ransom. Gowon expressed satisfaction 'that the creation of new states is the only possible basis for stability and equality'[75] and that he believed that most Nigerians shared that opinion. While there is some merit to the contention that Gowon's action was primarily designed to forestall the secession of the East probably because the rest of Nigeria coveted the petroleum reserves located therein, it cannot be denied that since the act was meant to keep Nigeria intact, it qualifies as a contribution toward political integration in the nation. Even before Gowon, his predecessor, General J.T.U. Aguiyi Ironsi, who was assassinated in the July 29 counter-coup that brought the former to office, did recognize the peril posed by the regional structure of the First Republic. Hence, his ill-timed and perhaps ill-conceived but otherwise patriotic decision to abolish the regions and turn the country into a unitary system of government based on provinces and a unified civil service.

It was ill-conceived for two reasons. One, it was insensitive to Northern fear of southern domination of the civil services—a fear that had arisen from the overwhelming educational superiority of the latter over the former. As earlier noted, this gap in education was a legacy of colonial rule which had discouraged Western education in the North. Two, Ironsi announced the change to a unitary system without first clearing a major political obstacle of that time, namely the question of what to do with the detained plotters of the January 15 coup. The North, which lost its premier, the prime minister and a brigadier to the coup, had been anxious to see the coup plotters brought to trial. But given the national acclaim that greeted that coup, Ironsi would have offended a cross-section of Nigerian public opinion if he had subjected the men to trial. So, he equivocated. But the fact remained that the coup, which left predominantly non-Igbo army officers and politicians dead, had provoked suspicions, particularly in the North, of an attempt by the Igbos to dominate the country. Thus, Ironsi's unitary system, well-intentioned as it was in the national interest to clip the wings of the regions, remains one of the most ill-timed and counterproductive actions of political leadership in Nigeria's history. Ironsi acted on the issue with the dispatch of military discipline, but it was a problem that required the calm and measured judgment of political wizardry. As Obasanjo puts it, "if Ironsi had displayed a greater sensitivity to Northern thinking, he could have capitalized on the relief that immediately followed the coup."[76] Opia put it less diplomatically. Pointing out that General Ironsi found himself at the head of a military government which had been brought about by a coup plotted, led and executed by someone else (namely, Major Chukwuma Kaduna Nzeogwu), who, regrettably, never had a chance to implement his patriotic dreams, Opia portrays Ironsi as a politically naive general who nonetheless "was an honest man . . . who tried to run an honest regime."[77] For while almost every historian of this period agrees that the January 15 1966 coup had to happen, and indeed, it was initially nationally acclaimed as a welcome relief from the political warfare of the First Republic,[78] Obasanjo was correct in his observation that the aims of the coup plotters "were not borne out by [their] method, style and results."[79]

Gowon's twelve state structure closely resembles a model proposed by Nnamdi Azikiwe as far back as 1943,[80] long before the three regions of Nigeria were institutionalized in 1954. Azikiwe had proposed that Nigeria should be established as a federation of eight states based on geographical rather than cultural considerations. It is instructive that Azikiwe had observed, in that proposal, that Nigeria's Constitutional framework should accommodate geographical configuration rather than cultural diversity, for he did not believe, as I pointed out in Chapter Three, that there are fundamental cultural differences among African ethnic groups.[81]

Be that as it may, most political analysts would agree that Gowon's twelve-state structure weakened the power of the former regions. By making the regions weaker, the twelve state-structure created by Gowon had the effect of making the center stronger. By weakening the political base of each major ethnic group, the act took away from each group its de facto ability to hold the nation to ransom implicit in the size and constitutional powers of the regional structures of the First Republic. In fact, one can extend the analysis by suggesting that by giving the Eastern "minorities" states of their own, Gowon pulled the rug from Ojukwu's feet and thus ensured the failure of the secession even before it got off the ground by robbing the Igbos of the badly-needed loyalty and support of those minority groups. The fact that some people from the new Eastern minority states subsequently enlisted in the federal army and joined in fighting against the secession proves my point[82] In addition, Gowon's action represents a contribution to political integration because by breaking up the regions, it tilted the balance of centrifugal and centripetal forces in Nigerian politics in favor of the latter. For I submit that since part of the two-prong challenge of political integration is how to elicit from subjects deference and devotion to the claims of the state, the tipping of the political balance in favor of the centripetal forces should, in turn, give citizens reason to devote more attention and possibly deference to the center. One of course recognizes that several other factors related to political leadership are critical to the deference and devotion of citizens to the state. These include questions such as "does the leadership lead in a manner that induces citizens to respect and be loyal to the state?" These and other questions will be tackled in Chapter Five which contains an analysis of six Nigerian political leaderships, using my Afrocentric/Africa-centered theory of political integration as the analytical framework.

Gowon's historic act of May 27, 1967 did not put an end to the clamor for new states in Nigeria. Ekekwe opines that renewed demands for states during the 1970s was driven by the increased revenue from petroleum during that period. The resultant federal disbursements to the states, he observes, had spawned a new and visible nouveau riches. The new demands arose from groups which felt left-out in the sharing of this 'national cake.'[83] But there is more to this than Ekekwe would concede. The fact is that one of the unintended consequences of the creation of twelve states was the emergence of "statism" as a substitution for "regionalism" in Nigerian life. The only difference between the two vices is that the former did not pose as much threat to the existence of the country as a corporate body as regionalism did in its heyday. But statism as a form of discrimination in Nigerian life, eroded/erode the rights of citizens who were so victimized not any less than regionalism had done during the first republic. There are two types of statism, which I have labeled as inter-statism and intra-statism. In the case of inter-statism, a member of an ethnic group could find himself or herself victimized (through denial of economic and political opportunities) by a state that belongs to the same ethnic group as his/hers. Intra-statism, on the other hand, occurs within the same state, where a person from one sector or segment of a state is denied access to state resources simply because he/she comes from an area of the state which has little or no political clout. This latter factor (that is, intra-statism) emerged as a new basis for demands for new states both during and after Gowon's time. Gowon refused to bow to those demands. He was overthrown on July 29, 1975, but his historic act of 1967 had already left almost an indelible impression on the minds of Nigerians.

Although upon his overthrow newspapers roundly condemned Gowon for several commissions and omissions of his regime, they did not fail to give him credit for what he did in 1967. Writing in the wake of Gowon's overthrow, one national newspaper described the creation of twelve states as 'the greatest achievement for which [Gowon] will be remembered.'[84] In the opinion of that newspaper, the twelve-state structure 'has removed for all time the main obstacle to lasting unity'[85] in Nigeria. While the newspaper may be guilty of excessive optimism in respect of the impact of Gowon's twelve-state structure—for there are loose ends in the Nigerian political culture which must be tied before the nation can enjoy true and lasting peace, unity and progress—there is no doubt that the chances of Nigeria's survival as a nation were enhanced by that structure. In this regard, Gowon's political leadership, albeit a military one, deserves to be ranked together with the African military leaderships which Harbeson have credited with neutralizing and subduing "residual ethnic tensions and conflict."[86]

Another keen assessment of Gowon's stewardship holds that the twelve-state structure not only made the federal government stronger, it also made "the far-flung federation governable."[87] But as I hinted earlier, had Gowon been the head of an elected civilian government, he probably would not have been able to pull off that political miracle. As Joseph notes in his study of Nigerian military regimes, the military government had an advantage in this matter due to a number of political assets not available to a democratic, elected government. Besides the fact that the military regime controls the preponderance of the forces of terror by which it can easily enforce its will, it has, in addition, self-servingly made political leadership less cumbersome by suspending constitutional strictures, checks and balances of governance. It also enacted an edict which shielded its decrees from judicial review[88] As the experience of the Shagari civilian administration (1979–83) demonstrated when it tried to create new states (the 1979 Constitution's guidelines and criteria for the creation of new states are simply daunting),[89] a civilian government which governs through an elected legislature with its slow and circumlocutious process, would not have "decreed" twelve states into existence without contending with a multitude of "interest groups" and perhaps court litigations and counter-litigations[90] Whether a nation, such as Nigeria, ultimately benefits or suffers from the authoritarian nature of military governance is a different but major question altogether.

Long before the return of civilian rule, however, Gowon's successor, Brigadier Murtala Muhammed, did not hesitate to take advantage of the systemic flexibility of military rulership in taking action toward the goal of national integration. Thus, he made the creation of new states an important item on the agenda of his short-lived administration when he assumed office in July 1975. In fact, less than six months after coming to power, Muhammed created seven additional states, bringing the number to nineteen by 1976. Joseph is of the view that this act further strengthened centripetal forces in the Nigerian nation. As he phrased it, Murtala's creation of seven additional states weakened the backbone of "the intense demands for political power by sectional groups."[91] And I believe that by simultaneously weakening and multiplying the political and economic capacities of the states vis-à-vis the center, Mohammed's creation of seven additional states increased the potential for criss-cutting cleavages (as opposed to coinciding cleavages) in the Nigerian state—cleavages that were inadequate during the First Republic. The theory of cross-cutting cleavages holds that "when individuals are cross-pressured by the simultaneous pull of competing and more or less equally salient loyalties, the resulting conflict is less intense, hence less politically destabilizing."[92] The flip side of the coin holds that "coinciding cleavages . . . tend to polarize and inflame conflict."[93] As Diamond puts it, "polarization will be minimized if the bases of conflict are constantly changing and the alignments continually shifting, uniting previous antagonists and dividing previous allies."[94] The United States of America typifies this situation of cross-cutting cleavages.

It must be pointed out, however, that the Nigerian state and its people cannot derive maximum benefit from the calculations premised upon these structural readjustments without the right political leadership—an imaginative, Africa-centered leadership that places the national interests above state, personal or party partisan interests.

Thus, there should be little surprise that the Ayo Irikefe panel on new states appointed by Mohammed's administration in 1975 later reported that state creation had had a limited effect on national unity and national integration.[95] For as we have seen, the creation of new states has not brought about the transformation of Nigeria's political culture (it was not necessarily a direct objective of the creation of new states), which is a necessity for Nigeria's political peace and political integration. As Ogunsanwo has forcefully argued, Nigeria's political and economic environment needs to be transformed before Nigerians can hope for longevity and stability in the polity. He notes that several decades after political independence, Nigeria remains a dependent capitalist economy (in the late 80's and 90's the economy was in the doldrums), while the political elite continues to resort to ethnicity, statism and religion to "fan embers of hatred and intolerance."[96]

Thus, the 1975 Irikefe panel on new states reported that despite the creation of twelve states in 1967, "tribalism is . . . very much still alive with us."[97] The report confirmed the reality of statism in Nigeria by noting that the new demands had arisen from claims of discrimination in the citing and distribution of state amenities, projects and scholarships. There were also allegations of cultural degradations[98] But Ekekwe is quick to point out that those concerns were akin to those identified by a colonial commission in 1958[99] My own view is that the problem is partly a reflection of poor political leadership—a leadership that failed to implant bureaucratic ethos in the nation. For had political leadership at the states done its job properly (that is, ruled in a manner that gave every section of a state a sense of belonging), probably no section of a given state would have felt left out. Despite Irikefe panel's finding that the creation of twelve states had not put an end to tribalism, it still considered state-creation an important tool for political integration as shown by the panel's recommendation that the Muhammed administration should create new states. This, to me, reflects an underlying assumption that the creation of additional states, like a new dose of medicine for a sick patient, was viewed as something that could indirectly cure Nigeria's disease of tribalism. In other words, by lessening the incidence of tribalism, the creation of additional states was expected to foster allegiance to the Nigerian state and thereby enhance the nation's progress toward political integration. This was why the Irikefe panel recommended that ethnic grouping ought not be used as a criterion for new states[100] By accepting the Irikefe panel's recommendation, the Muhammed administration essentially concurred with this assumption.

Murtala Muhammed was killed in an abortive coup in 1976, but his administration was continued by General Olusegun Obasanjo. Although demands for additional states persisted during Obasanjo's reign, his government retained the 19-state structure until 1979 when it handed over power to an elected civilian government. If the stringent pre-conditions[101] for new states set out in the 1979 Constitution are anything to go by, one could surmise that the Obasanjo administration, which supervised the drafting of that constitution, did not harbor a wish for new states in Nigeria. As I indicated earlier, the civilian administration of Shehu Shagari, along with other political parties, actually promised to create new states in the country but Segun Gbadegesin has suggested that the promise had nothing to do with a desire to foster political integration; the parties simply exploited the yawning for new states for the sake of electoral votes[102] Ekekwe mentions "desire" for "even development" in the country as the main slogan for demands for new states during the Second Republic. There were up to fifty-three such demands during that period[103] Given the austere criteria required by the 1979 Constitution for the creation of new states, it is not surprising that the politicians of the Second Republic could not transform their electoral promises of new states into reality before they were sacked by the military in December 1983.

The military government of General Ibrahim Babangida, which came to office in 1985, projected a more liberal attitude toward the question of new states than Obasanjo's. In 1989, Babangida created two new states, bringing the total of states in Nigeria to twenty-one. He added nine new states in 1992, thereby making Nigeria a federation of thirty states. In 1996, his successor, General Sanni Abacha created six more states, bringing the total to thirty-six states. (See Figure 4.1 for a map showing the thirty-six states of Nigeria.)

Like their predecessors, what apparently impelled Babangida's and Abacha's additional state-creation exercises, which in effect multiplied centripetal forces within the body politic and made the federal government even stronger, is still the desire to achieve political integration.

In a sense, Gowon, Muhammed, Babangida and Abacha more than fulfilled Premier Okpara's First Republic's dream of having Nigeria broken up into 25 states—a dream based on the premise that the fragmentation of Nigeria's ethnic groups would remove from the shoulders of the nation the prospect of a single ethnic group holding the country to ransom. Hopefully, the end result would be a more integrated Nigerian nation. The extent to which this becomes a reality will depend, however, on the stature and sub-

Figure 4.1. Map showing thirty-six states of Nigeria. In 1996, General Abacha's Federal Military Government created six new states in Nigeria to bring the number to the present total of thirty-six states.

stance of both political leadership and the political culture. The voting pattern of Nigerians during the presidential election of June 12, 1993 (the results were nullified by General Babangida) indicates that Nigerians have become, marginally at least, more Nigerian than ethnic in their political outlook. Results published by the National Electoral Commission (NEC) before Babangida cancelled the process showed that Mudaseru Abiola, a Southerner, recorded victories across ethnic lines, including a key Northern state like Kano.[104] *Africa Confidential* reports that figures "leaked from the National Electoral Commission showed" that Abiola, of the Social Democratic Party, (SDP) received 58 percent of the vote as opposed to 32 percent for Bashir Tofa, of the National Republican Convention (NRC).[105] Does this indicate that the Nigerians are becoming more issue-oriented in their voting choices? This question cannot be determined without a scientific opinion survey of a sample of Nigerian voters. For now, one can only postulate that the creation of states, which weakened ethnic and regional strongholds and thus shifted the allegiance of the citizens to the center, must have had a lot to do with the voting pattern of the ill-fated June 12, 1993 presidential election. As one Nigerian college student in the United States aptly puts it, "it appears that our people in Nigeria have come to trust one another." As one scholar puts it, "the creation of states in Nigeria as a means of building a nation out of a multitude of ethnic groups, each with different languages and traditions, seems to be proving a success."[106] Another scholar, Adebayo Adedeji, observes that the June 12, 1993 election punctured a number of myths about the attitudes of Nigerian voters, particularly the notion that Nigerians are more apt to vote along ethnic or religious lines. He explains:

> The SDP presidential candidate, M.K.O. Abiola, with his vice-presidential flag-bearer Baba Kingibe, qualified under our electoral law in 28 out of the 30 states. That is unheard of. It has never happened. For the first time, in fact, nine northern states gave the SDP candidate the majority of their votes. Nine! I thought it was a great day for Nigeria.[107]

Adedeji goes on to assert that the presidential votes indicated that what Nigerians care much more about is good governance. However, Adegboyega Somide holds a different view about the impact of the manner in which state creation has been executed. As he puts it, "by creating states along ethnic lines, federalism in Nigeria has tended to reinforce ethnic identity thus negating the stability sought in federalism in the first place."[108]

What is not clear, however, is whether Somide's assessment was rather provoked by certain events that have occurred since the breaking up of Nigeria's regionalism. A case in point is the unfortunate chapter in Nigeria's political development, involving Babangida's fiddling with the electoral process for his government's promised transfer of power to civilians. His arrogant fiddling with that process had the potential to wipe out whatever modest psychological gains that Nigeria had made toward political integration from such political reforms as the creation of states and from painful national tragedies like the bloody Civil War of 1967–70. (The hand-over was originally scheduled for 1990, but was post-poned three times.) As Adedeji comments: "it was really a pity that Babangida annulled the presidential elections, because it would have been a solid foundation for the unity and development of Nigeria."[109] By canceling the results of the June 12, 1993 presidential contest between Abiola and Tofa in which the former, a Southerner, was alleged to have emerged victorious, Babangida rekindled memories of the troubled First Republic of Nigeria. His action has had the unfortunate consequence of resurrecting north-south polaristic thinking, which marred the politics of the First Republic. Thus, Wole Soyinka was right on target when he warned that Babangida was "toying with the future of our nation."[110]

A recap of the events that culminated in the cancellation of the June 1993 presidential election will help to buttress my conviction that unprincipled and self-seeking political leadership remains the bane of African politics. First, Babangida should have allowed the democratic process to take its due course so as to give all segments of Nigeria a feeling that the system works. Note that one of the factors that wrecked the First Republic was a growing realization or suspicion by southern politicians that the Nigerian system was designed to keep them out of power at the center. By denying Abiola the chance to rule despite his alleged electoral victory, Babangida touched on a very sensitive political nerve.

Second, when citizens perceive that their leaders do not obey the laws of the land, they are less likely to remain loyal, law-abiding and patriotic. The democratic process of selecting candidates for public service must not only be free and fair, it must be seen to be so. But Babandiga undermined the legitimacy of elections as a means of changing governments in Nigeria when he brazenly interrupted NEC's processing of the June 1993 presidential election results. In fact, his conduct (i.e. the violation of the rules of the electoral process) amounts to an anti-systemic behavior. For even though Babangida, like his military predecessors, had ruled by decree, the fact remains that the survival of the Nigerian polity calls for a set of rules-of-the-game (i.e., a bureaucratic order) and a determination on the part of leadership to play by those rules and be seen to do so.

Three, NEC's suspension of the announcement of the results of the election on June 16, 1993,[111] was contrary to a decree[112] which forbid courts from interfering with the electoral process. Four, the aftermath of the election had brought ridicule to the Nigerian judiciary, for in their struggle to force NEC to publish or not publish the results of the election, politicians got various courts to issue injunctions and counter-injunctions which turned out as mere nullity. In fact, Babangida had claimed that one of the reasons his government cancelled the election results was to save the Nigerian judiciary from further ridicule.[113] But that explanation could not have dignified his conduct, for had he allowed the electoral process to run its natural course, he would have averted the court charade. The consequent affront to the Nigerian judiciary is a blow to the rule of law which does not augur well for Nigeria's effort to curb its huge social problem of indiscipline. The post-election impasse, including Babangida's conduct, lends credence to my theory that effective, patriotic and selfless political leadership must necessarily be an integral part of the drive for political integration. It demonstrates that the behavior of key Nigerian political actors has proven to be as significant as structural/systemic factors in determining the destiny of the nation. Nwabueze was quite right when he observed that while it is true that ethnicity constitutes a hitch to Nigeria's march toward progress, "the deeper, more pervasive problem is simply the absence of a national ethic."[114] A national ethic, he explains, "involves the question of our attitude, as Nigerians, to the state and its Constitution."[115] (The issue of a national ethic will be discussed in detail in the next chapter.)

Babangida's conduct violated a cardinal pre-requisite for effective political leadership which requires that solutions to national crises should be such that could be viewed as legitimate and fair by each major competitor.[116] Nigeria's multifarious population makes such an approach to crisis-resolution all the more necessary. Babangida's prevention of Abiola, a Yoruba, from taking office cannot possibly be viewed as legitimate and fair by the Yoruba of Nigeria in particular and all fair-minded Nigerians in general. If an election cannot serve Nigeria as a legitimate and fair means of determining who wields political power, what else could?

The foregoing discussion and analysis suggest that no matter how far political leadership goes in splintering Nigeria into feeble administrative centers labeled as states, without a commitment on its part to an appropriate normative consensus and democratic principles (as reflected in the behavior of the political actors), political stability will continue to elude her, and the distance between the nation and genuine political integration will continue to widen.

Chapter Five
An Afrocentric[1]/Africa-centered Theory of Leadership and Political Integration

Chapter F-ive accomplishes a two-prong objective: 1) On the basis of the preceding review of the record of leadership and political integration in Nigeria in particular and Africa in general, it declares *an Afrocentric*/Africa-centered theory of Leadership and Political Integration, and 2) it uses the theory as the prism for assessing the performances of six Nigerian political leaderships on political integration. The chapter consists of four parts. Part one introduces the Afrocentric/Africa-centered theory of leadership and political integration; part two explains the rationale for situating the theory in the Afrocentric/Africa-centered mold; part three describes the constructs of the Afrocentric/Africa-centered theory of political and integrative leadership; and part four analyzes six Nigerian political leaderships on the basis of the Afrocentric/Africa-centered theory of political and integrative leadership. The theory is rooted in and driven by the facts, observations, and findings of this study. That is, it is a research-based theory.

For this theory, I define political integration as a process of developing a Maatic political culture and of inducing the commitment of the citizenry, particularly the political elite, to it, in order to accomplish two major objectives: (1) political stability and (2) a sense of cohesion in the nation-state. Political culture, as defined earlier, is a system of empirical beliefs, expressive symbols and values which denotes the contours of political action. The task of political integration rests principally on the shoulders of the political leadership; but, broadly-speaking, the responsibility is shared by the political elite as a whole. Political stability means the existence of a durable, systematic and constitutional mode of governance based on effective institutions and the mandate of the citizens. This implies institutionalized governance based on legitimate rules and regulations derived from law and convention and from equitable and humane cultural norms. Such a political dispensation is essential for sociopolitical peace and national development. Political elite refers to the cross-section of opinion leaders in the social, economic, religious, professional and ethnic spheres of national life.

Using the constructs of the theory, the chapter answers the following questions. To what extent did the political leadership of each of the six governments lead to or further the goal of political integration in Nigeria? How integrative or disintegrative were their philosophical outlook, policies, actions and results? The governments are those of Prime Minister Tafawa Balewa (1960–1966), General J.T.U. Aguiyi-Ironsi (January 1966 to July 1966), General Yakubu Gowon (1966–1975), Brigadier Murtala Muhammed (July 1975 to February 1976), General Olusegun Obasanjo (1976–1979), and President Shehu Shagari (1979–1983).

PART I: INTRODUCTION TO AN AFROCENTRIC/ AFRICA-CENTERED THEORY OF LEADERSHIP AND POLITICAL INTEGRATION

The Afrocentric/Africa-centered theory of political leadership and political integration holds that a purposeful, benevolent, communicative, concordant, populistic, *Maatic* and historically-conscious African political system is capable of effective and integrative political leadership.[2] Such a system can weather the disruptive consequences of the social mobilization necessary for political integration. The seven constructs are essential but not exhaustive ingredients of an African political system capable of effective political and integrative leadership. In other words, this theory holds that a politically integrated African political system is one that manifests seven structural characteristics as follows: (1) the system is purposeful; (2) the system is benevolent; (3) the system is communicative; (4) the system is concordant; (5) the system is populistic, (6) the underlying political culture is *Maatic*; and (7) the political elite is historically-conscious.

Notice that a critical component of this theory of political leadership and political integration holds that the political culture that lies beneath the political system must be *Maatic*. Political Culture, which refers to 'the system of empirical beliefs, expressive symbols and values which defines the situation in which political action takes place, is crucial to the task of political integration.[3] For the individual, the political culture regulates political behavior. The political culture furnishes the political system with 'a systematic structure of values and rational considerations which ensures coherence in the performance of institutions and organizations.'[4] An integrated political system depends upon a consensus among individual political actors over the norms of political behavior, as well as a commitment on their part to the patterns of political actions legitimized by those norms.

PART II: RATIONALE FOR THE AFROCENTRIC/ AFRICA-CENTERED PARADIGM

But before going deeper into the preceding subjects, the question of what makes a theory Afrocentric or Africa-centered needs to be clarified. Why is Afrocentric/Africa-centered philosophy applicable to the situation on the African continent in general and Nigeria in particular? As was indicated in the introductory chapter, Afrocentric philosophy is the idea that African ideals and values should constitute the core of any analysis involving African culture and behavior. This is an ideology of liberation, a philosophical outlook derived from African historical and cultural experiences.[5]

Africology, a human science devoted to exploring how Africans have historically and contemporaneously used their physical, social and cultural milieu to advance harmony, utilizes three protocols in its research—the functional, the etymological and the categal. It is imperative to emphasize that Africology is neither purely social science nor humanities but an integration of both branches of knowledge, as well as the application of approaches to phenomena based on the Afrocentric/Africa-centered paradigm. In this endeavor, Africology emphasizes cultural immersion as a prerequisite tool of critical scholarship. Thus, as Asante puts it, "unlike most social sciences [Africology] does not examine from a distance in order to predict behavior."[6]

The three paradigmatic instruments, which are based on the "assumptions of the Afrocentric approach to human knowledge,"[7] are defined as follows: "The functional paradigm represents needs, policy, and action. In the categal paradigm are issues of schemes, gender, class, themes, and files. The etymological paradigm deals with language, particularly in terms of word and concept origin."[8] This unfolding theory of African political and integrative leadership falls within the umbrella of the functional dimension of Africological research.

As the literature review has demonstrated, the African political elite is, by and large, still entrapped by mental colonization—a factor which Ogunsanwo identified as an obstacle to economic transformation in Nigeria.[9] The African mind has been under various types of assault from Western Imperialists' propaganda and indoctrination for the greater part of the last five hundred years of the Western ascendancy. The foundation for this assault was laid through colonial education. For the most part, colonial education was not meant to instill pride and confidence in young people as members of the African community. Rather, it was designed to inculcate "a sense of deference towards all that was European."[10] Cultural and biological degradation were among the tools that imperialism/racism employed to justify the enslavement, colonization and neo-colonization of Africans. Wa Thiong'O pin-points this phenomenon as it continues to manifest itself in the contemporary era:

> The maintenance, management, manipulation, and mobilization of the entire system of education, language and language use, literature, religion, the media, have always ensured for the oppressor nation power over the transmission of a certain ideology, set of values, outlook, attitudes, feelings, etc, and hence power over the whole area of consciousness.[11]

As part of this onslaught, the African world has been historically painted "as an insolvent debtor"[12] to the rest of humanity. The cumulative impact of this trans-generationally disseminated psychological warfare on Africans has not been washed away. The relics continue to haunt the African world either in the form of "colonial mentality" on the continent or in the form of "slave mentality" in the African Diaspora, so much so that as Diop has argued, the knowledge that the African world originated "the 'Western' Civilization flaunted before our eyes today" would amaze the "incredulous . . . African reader."[13] He/she would be surprised to "discover that most of the ideas used today to domesticate, atrophy, dissolve, or steal his 'soul,' were conceived by his own ancestors."[14]

Since Afrocentric or Africa-centered epistemology is designed to regenerate African peoples "culturally and politically,"[15] it can serve as a liberating mechanism for "re-centering" African political leadership. Afrocentric or the Africa-centered paradigm has as its foundation the Ancient Egyptian philosophical frame of reference. Linda James Myers writes that the conceptual system of ancient Africa 'orders one's thoughts, perceptions, feelings, and actions so as to yield maximum positivity in experience.'[16] One of the works, which have demonstrated that Ancient Egyptian culture was an extension of African culture is Lancinay Keita's brilliant work: "The African Philosophical Tradition." This work primarily establishes that Africa boosts of a "sufficiently firm literate philosophical tradition,"[17] which dates back to ancient times, namely the Egyptian epoch. Keita explains that this philosophical tradition consists of a classical period, a medieval period and a modern period. The classical period of African philosophy covers the thoughts of ancient Egyptians. These thoughts not only influenced the rest of Africa, but also the Greek world and European Renaissance.

Keita is part of a rather long list of Diopian scholars who have written about the Kemetic impact on what is generally referred to as Western civilization. From them, we have also come to know, among other things, that the ancient Egyptians belonged to the Black race; that they, in fact, introduced writing as a human skill; and that they were the first philosophers and scientists of the known world. Among other things,

> The thought systems of the Ancient Egyptians represent the most literate expression of the African in ancient history. These thought systems were based on the essentially African view of the world as being both subject to empirical and metaphysical interpretation.[18]

Diop, in *The African Origin of Civilization: Myth or Reality* adds to this evidence by recording that the first set of Black people to live in Egypt was called by the name of Anu. The Anu were the people who created the essentials of Egyptian civilization. The Anu were the first to engage in farming, irrigation, to build dams, invent sciences, arts, writing, and the calendar. The Anu were the authors of such ancient books of wisdom as the *Coming Forth By Day* (which had been otherwise labeled as *the Book of the Dead*), and the texts of the pyramids.[19] Diop's other seminal work, *Civilization or Barbarism* sheds additional light on linkages between ancient Egyptian philosophical tradition and those of Africa in general.

Such linkages between Ancient Egypt and the rest of Black Africa extend to the arena of political systems. Among the commonalities is the matrilineal line of succession to the throne which in general characterized African political systems.[20] Belief in and adherence to the concept of vital force is another common feature of traditional African political systems which was shared with Ancient Egypt. "Vital Force" comes from a belief that a set of hierarchical forces governs the universe. This ontology posits that:

> Every being, animate or inanimate, could occupy only a specific place according to his or its potential. These forces were cumulative: thus, a living being who had as talisman the fang or claw of a lion, in which the vital force of the animal was concentrated, increased his own power by that much. In order to overcome him in battle, one had to have a sum of forces greater than his own plus the lion's.[21]

Thus, were two kings to engage in some kind of rivalry, their initial combat would be at the vital force level before a physical engagement. Far from being an isolated practice, this metaphysics was a predominant trait of African political society, including Kemet, the Yoruba, Dagomba, Tchamba, Djukon, Igara, Songhai, Wuadai, Haussa of Gobir, Katsina and Daoura, the Shillucks, the Mbum in Uganda-Burundi, and ancient Meroe.[22] The king represented the repository of the greatest vital force in his kingdom. Herein lies the main significance of the vital force metaphysics, for as the bearer of the greatest vital force, the King performed the role of mediator between his kingdom and the superior universe. So sacrosanct was this kingly role that it partly determined the legitimacy of his office. Legitimacy of political office holders was highly priced in traditional society. As Diop explains, African society believed that if the king was not legitimate, (that is, if he did not come to office according to the rites of tradition, and if he did not observe the sacredness of his office), "all of nature will be sterile, drought will overtake the fields, women will not longer bear children, epidemics will strike the people."[23] Vital force being an integral component of the legitimacy of a king, if there was a reduction in his vital force (which is critical to the very survival of his society), he would be put to actual or ritualistic death in order to reinforce his vital force. Thus, for the African traditional society, the king was the guarantor of the "ontological, and therefore the terrestrial and social order."[24]

Further testimony of the Africannes of the Egyptian civilization comes from Frank Willet's work on African sculpture. In it, Willet provides sculptural evidence for the cultural semblances between Kemet and the rest of Africa. "Egypt was basically an African culture, with intrusions of Asian culture," he writes.[25] Willet reports common characteristics between the art of pre-Dynastic Egypt and those of other African societies. For example, the function of Egyptian statues as a repository of supernatural force, was the same as ancestor figures from many parts of Africa. These ancestor figures serve in the two sister cultures as the home for all eternity of the "spiritual essence of the man represented."[26] Willet observes:

> The naturalistic form which Egyptian art often took, and the high degree of technical skill with which it was fashioned should not blind us to the fact that the ideas underlying it are nearer to . . . Africa than they are to Periclean Athens or to Renaissance Italy.[27]

Egyptian art, he reaffirms, firmly belongs to the family of African art and should be seen as a "local manifestation of a widespread African tradition."[28]

Despite the fact that the ancient Africans achieved literacy long before the Europeans did, a notion exists that African philosophy is oral in nature. In some cases, it is argued that African philosophy itself does not even exist. What is this so? Keita, along with other Diopian scholars, offers a number of reasons for this. One was/is the systematic attempt of hegemonic Eurocentric historiography and its emulators to divorce ancient Egypt, the mother of written philosophy, from the rest of Africa. Egypt was then conceptually, but not geographically, made a part of the Oriental world—a classic case, in my view, of how reality depends on the angle of your perception. "The aim . . . was to create a world in which civilization was the patrimony solely of the Western and Eastern peoples with the African world being the receptacle of all that was uncivilized or 'primitive.'"[29] But was this just meant to suit the fancy of those hegemonic Eurocentric historians, or to make them "feel good" about themselves? Keita and other Diopian scholars have noted that the motives were: (1) to foster the myth of White supremacy, and 2) to justify the enslavement and colonization of Africans. As Diop puts it, Egyptologists, had been stunned by the greatness of ancient Egypt when Champollion the Younger deciphered hieroglyphics in 1822. Egypt came to be seen as the cradle of civilization.

> But imperialism being what it is, it became increasingly 'inadmissible' to continue to accept the theory—evident until then—of a Negro Egypt. The birth of [hegemonic Eurocentric] Egyptology was thus marked by the need to destroy the memory of a Negro Egypt at any cost and in all minds.[30]

In order to rationalize colonialism—a process by which the colonized was economically, politically, and culturally exploited for the benefit of Western Europeans—the victims had to be made to look less human than the Europeans. Thus, an oppressive and inhuman project was interpreted as a mechanism for bringing the victims into contact with Western European civilization.[31] Exploitation became a "civilizing mission," carried out by the benevolent Europeans, the "do-gooders of the world." Similarly, the enslavement of Africans by this same benevolent and God-fearing Western European enslavers and colonizers had to be "morally" justified by casting Africans as a people without a history . . . as a people who had contributed "nothing" to humankind and who were merely "the White man's burden." Having thus been portrayed as liabilities who were less than the truly human Europeans, there no longer existed any moral inhibition against the Great Enslavement (by the way the Arabs had also engaged in the enslavement of Africans). This was one of the early manifestations of the "blame the victim syndrome" which pervades the Western psyche.

Another factor that reinforces the notion of the orality or non-existence of African philosophy is Africa's loss of the memory of ancient Egypt—a process that began during the medieval period of African philosophy with the intrusion of Arabic into the Sudanic empires as the language of intellectual expression in-place of the Kemetic language. On the other hand, the Europeans were able to remain "within the Greco-Roman intellectual ambit by using Latin as the language of the philosopher, and by maintaining the memory of the Greeks in the terms and concepts of science and mathematics."[32]

For Africa, slavery and colonization only made matters worse. Keita observes:

> The result of these two phenomena has been a cultural anomie of the African transplanted to the New World and a state of amnesia of the contemporary African whose knowledge of history and philosophy is limited to European thought systems. That pre-colonial Africa witnessed a classical and medieval period is not common knowledge among modern day African thinkers.[33]

Continuing, Keita points out a factor, which from all intents and purposes, is an unpopular truth: "In a world in which the African thinker is made to perceive himself as a tyro among the so-called civilized, he is forced to justify his existence only by defending those traits imposed on him by the colonizer."[34] The upshot of all this is that the contemporary African has found himself as one of the propagators of the misleading notion that "European culture was literate, logical, and scientific [, while] the African culture is oral, superstitious, and aphilosophical."[35]

Functionally-speaking, the Afrocentric emphasis on African ideals and values can help nudge de-centered African politics toward the right path. (In Africological terms, centrism means situating observation and behavior in the person's historical experiences.)[36] Witness Diamond's persuasive contention in the preceding chapter that the politics of Nigeria's First Republic, and I would include those of the Second Republic, and to an extent, those of the ongoing Third Republic, suffered from a 'normative vacuum.'[37]

In Africological terms, the politics of the First and Second Republics were de-centered. It was this de-centering that prompted Ogunsanwo's castigation of contemporary Nigerian elite as being the very anti-thesis of its predecessor in traditional society. The details of his observation are worthy of a recapture here:

> Traditional cultural values in all parts of Nigeria placed premium on hard work, tolerance, good neighborliness and honesty. Misappropriation or stealing of community property would lead to ostracism as it was greatly frowned upon. Up till today many a rural folk still cherish this old time honesty and approbation of stealing communal property.[38]

In contrast, colonialism distorted values in such a manner that public property came to be seen as the property of 'the alien government and therefore not really subject to the rules and norms of 'thou shall not steal.'[39] Ogunsanwo continues by pointing out that urbanization and a massive rural-to-urban migration brought about 'pressures and counter-pressures' upon individuals and groups. Without the restraining influence of the social codes of rural life, these pressures on individuals and groups led to 'normlessness and consequent readiness to misappropriate public property.'[40]

It must be pointed out that African ideals and values are not fixed in the stars. Given the dynamic nature of society, African ideals and values have changed over time and space; they are relativistic and situational. African ideals and values exist in an inter-connected world—in an age of cultural diffusionism and cultural synchronization engineered by rapidly-advancing technology that has rendered instantaneous a great deal of the interaction and inter-cultural communication between peoples, nations and continents.

Given this backdrop, Asante was right in suggesting that "we are seriously in battle for the future of our culture."[41] The centrality of culture to the life of a people cannot be over-stressed, for it provides "patterns for interpreting reality that give people a general design for living."[42] Ultimately, "the cultural factor,"[43] as Ngugi Wa Thiong'O puts it, is the engine that drives economics and politics. Thus, it follows that if a culture is undermined by exogenous factors or retains some anachronistic traditions, it cannot adequately fertilize the socio-economic and political life of the people. Afrocentric or the Africa-centered paradigm is not a glorification of the African past; similarly, it does not believe that African culture, whose dynamism it recognizes, should be a prisoner of traditionalism—that is, traditionalism for the sake of it even where a given tradition no longer serves a worthwhile human purpose. Hence Asante's shrewd postulation that "Afrocentricity seeks to modify African traditions where necessary to meet the demands of modern society."[44] His subsequent work, *Kemet, Afrocentricity and Knowledge* indirectly reaffirms this enlightened position when he recognizes that all cultures are transitional, and that there is a trend in the African world toward cosmocultural understanding. However, it is necessary, Asante contends (and rightly so), that:

> Meaning in the contemporary context must be derived from the most centered aspects of the African's being. When this is not the case, psychological dislocation creates automatons who are unable to fully capture the historical moment because they are living on someone else's terms.[45]

This is a profound and progressive stand; in the emerging global village, the African must stand side by side with others—not as a subordinate as he/she is portrayed in the present scheme of things.

In making necessary modifications to African cultural traditions, I submit that Afrocentrists should not reject every idea or technique that cannot be traced to African roots unless the value assumptions of such an idea or technique cannot be Africanized. This is why I find problematic and contradictory (i.e., contradictory of the preceding position) Asante's suggestion that "the Afrocentrist studies every thought, action, behavior, and value, and if it cannot be found in our culture or in our history, it is dispensed with quickly."[46] For, it seems that a pro-human value, which is not necessarily resident in the African culture or history, may prove beneficial where an Afrocentrist identifies an African tradition that requires modification. Keto's argument in this regard proves handy. As I noted earlier, he contends that while the African centers of learning ought to become 'the academic nurseries for the re-emergence of . . . Africa centered intellectual flame . . . [they ought to keep their doors] open to perspectives, methodologies, and view-points from other parts of the world.'[47] It is as imperative to African culture as it would be to other cultures to keep their minds open, for no culture of the world has a monopoly of wisdom. African culture itself has exerted enormous influence upon the world at large as documented by the works of the late Cheikh Anta Diop and several others.[48]

In like fashion, African culture has not been an island onto itself. As Ohaegbulam artfully puts it, African people not only share a common humanity with other members of the human family, they have naturally inter-mingled with them "throughout the ages of recorded and unrecorded history."[49] In addition, African people "share some common values, aspirations, hopes, pain, suffering, death and thoughts of life after death with other human inhabitants of the planet earth."[50]

Despite these threads that bind African people with other human societies, there are events and facts in the African past and present which make the African experience unique and distinguishable from those of other peoples. Ohaegbulam observes, with characteristic keenness, that this "uniqueness which is more than a product of environmental forces explains our stress on the black experience rather than on the entire human experience."[51] He, therefore, defines the African Experience as:

> The whole gamut of facts and events observed and observable in the various facets of the lives of black people in the development of human civilization, in arts, culture, education, economics, politics, literature, religion and in human or world affairs.[52]

One of the implications of Ohaegbulam's expansive articulation of the African Experience is that African ideals and values have crystallized in an environment impacted upon by both endogenous and exogenous forces. As we have demonstrated, some of these forces, like the Great Enslavement and Colonialism, exerted a negative impact. But there have been mutually beneficial interactions between Africans and other human groups, particularly in the area of modern technology although as the works of Cheikh Anta Diop, Chancellor Williams, John G. Jackson, Ivan Van Sertima, Martin Bernal, Herodotus, Strabo,[53] etc have shown, the foundation for science and technology was laid in ancient Africa.

African ideals and values evolved in the context of the preceding milieu and will continue to metamophorize that way. Thus, when I argue that African politics should be centered upon African ideals and values, I recognize that those ideals and values, in their constantly evolving context, are not exclusive, and need not be exclusive of positive ideas and techniques from other human experiences. But most critically, where a set of ideals and values are borrowed, they must be Africanized—that is, they must be reshaped to reflect the African Experience in order to ensure that they can serve the African Interest. *(The African interest refers to the welfare, progress and peace of African peoples.)* For as Keto points out, "ideologies that do not effectively Africanize their value assumptions have tended to enjoy short life spans in the African . . . cultural world."[54]

The African Interest must be the guide-post of African politics. The philosophical outlook, policies and actions of African political leaders and policy-makers should primarily seek, pursue and advance the African interest. Political leadership in Africa and Nigeria should generate and promote *victorious consciousness* in the people. As Asante eloquently articulates it, victorious consciousness means: 'The overwhelming power of a group of people thinking in the same direction. It is not unity in the traditional sense of a group of people coming together to achieve a single purpose; it is a full spiritual and intellectual commitment to a vision."[55]

Since governance is a two-way traffic, the commitment of both sides of the coin—the leadership and the led—to a vision like national/political integration cannot be over-stressed. But it remains the duty of political leadership to employ whatever means necessary for bringing about popular participation in public affairs. Any social, political or economic change, which is not based on popular participation, can only last as long as the ivory-tower class that brought it into being as demonstrated by the eventual collapse of Soviet Socialism—a failed experiment in top-down democracy. Long-lasting change would require "the overwhelming power of a group of people thinking in the same direction"—to use Asante's phraseology.

PART III: CONSTRUCTS OF THE AFROCENTRIC/AFRICA-CENTERED THEORY OF LEADERSHIP & POLITICAL INTEGRATION

Since the foregoing analysis establishes the rationale for wrapping my theory of leadership and political integration with the philosophical garment of the Afrocentric or Africa-centered paradigm, my next task is to explain and analyze the "structural characteristics" or seven constructs embedded in the theory.

They are as follows:

(a) **Purposeful**: A purposeful African political system may be operationalized as a legitimately instituted (this means that it is a mandated system), cross-sectionally representative government, which has a clear sense of mission in the national interest as well as the capacity and willingness to give life to its policies and programs. *Capacity* refers to five factors: 1. the regard which the citizens feel for the government; 2. the economic resources at the disposal of the government; 3. the information available to the government; 4. the rights which the Constitution conferred upon the government;[56] and 5. the Africa-centered philosophical outlook and nationalistic vision of the leadership. The instruments by which the government exercises its capacity include the public service (the bureaucracy), the media of mass communication, the armed forces, the police force,[57] and the intelligence service.

(b) **Benevolent**: The second construct of the Afrocentric/Africa-centered theory of political and integrative leadership holds that a **benevolent** political system is essential for political integration. A benevolent political system may be operationalized as one whose political elite (which is defined as a "coalition of the leaders of the major social, religious, professional, and ethnic groups"[58]) is not only willing and able to lead, but is also dedicated to pursuing the general welfare of the nation. According to Ake, the political elite is responsible for destroying or changing 'certain habits of mind' and destroying 'certain traditional symbols of collective identity.'[59] The political elite also strives to re-direct the general population along the path of new norms, new goals, new motivations—a new life. While I agree that it is desirable to destroy habits of mind, such as ethnocentric thinking and fatalism, ethnic and religious bigotry, nepotism and sexism, which impede progress and undermine efforts designed to bring about or accelerate political integration in the nation-state, I see things differently in the case of traditional symbols of collective identity. Rather than seek to undermine those symbols of collective identity, the political elite should strive to emphasize the common ethnic symbols of collective identity across the nation-state. I suspect, however, that Ake's suggestion was motivated by a concern about the disintegrative potentials of a manipulative stress on ethnic particularism in a heterogeneous society. This is because he writes later on in favor of 'cultural symbols and historical experiences that can be exploited for reinforcing social solidarity.'[60]

As previous chapters demonstrated, the chief problem with ethnic consciousness as it has evolved in Africa is that it was deliberately promoted by colonialism as a means of dividing the people and thus keeping them in check. The colonialists and victims of colonial education automatically assumed that linguistic differences translated into cultural differences despite the fact that in the case of Nigeria for instance, its four hundred or so indigenous languages[61] share a high level of "structural similarity."[62] Cultural Anthropology in particular, which is an imperial project, has aided and abetted this mind-set.

The dominant impulse of "African Studies" has been to assume and then to seek to identify or even "discover" and magnify the factors that make one African ethnic group different from another—an approach that facilitates imperialism and neo-colonialism. As Asante puts it,

> What many scholars who participate in African Studies do is not properly African Studies but European Studies of Africa. This has little to do with the racial background of the scholar but rather with the perspective from which the person examines data.[63]

We have seen that some elements of post-colonial leadership have followed the foot-steps of the colonists by fanning embers of ethnicity or sheer ethnic bigotry in order to further their own political ambitions. Thus, the assumption that deep cultural differences separate African ethnic groups has permeated both academia and the political intelligentsia—"differences" that selfish political leaders have exploited in an *Aminian*[64] fashion for their own political ends. In view of this history, symbols of collective identity have become something to be dreaded rather than cherished because of the apriori assumption that the symbols which, for instance, unify the Igbo ethnic group in Nigeria are somewhat and fundamentally distinct from the symbols that unify the Yoruba or Hausa ethnic group. I contend that when stripped of their exogenous religious and linguistic affiliations, the elements that denote the Igbo culture are, in principle, similar to the elements that denote the Yoruba, Hausa or Igala culture. Earlier, I cited an analogous observation by Azikiwe, who in a 1937 publication, stated that colonialism had intensified insignificant 'cultural differences' among African ethnic groups.[65] Diop's *Cultural Unity of Black Africa* is a seminal work which has helped to transform this "traditional" way of looking at African culture. Due to this and other works,[66] academic research has provided rich evidentiary support for the commonalities that bind African cultural centers. An aspect of African cultural life that exemplifies such commonalities is what is popularly referred to as African traditional Religion, which, itself, constitutes an integral component of African traditional way of life[67] (that is, African culture itself). As John S. Mbiti's *African Religions and Philosophy* establishes, African religion represents:

> An Ontological phenomenon; it pertains to the question of existence or being. Within traditional life, the individual is immersed in a religious participation which starts before birth and continues after his death. For him, therefore, and for the larger community of which he is part, to live is to be caught up in a religious drama.[68]

Mbiti's study also underscores the cultural unity of Africa, for it points out that the continent's "religious beliefs and practices show . . . more similarities than differences."[69]

The point of all this is that far from being divisive factors, when correctly studied and interpreted,[70] traditional symbols of collective identity can serve as symbols for the promotion of national/political integration, which the political elite should venerate and propagate to the general population as opposed to Ake's suggestion that those symbols ought to be destroyed.

(c) **Communicative:** An African political system is communicative if the political elite and the ordinary folk are in touch with each other—that is, if there is a free and adequate flow of intercourse between the political elite and the general population.[71] This means that the system guards against a perilous gap between the political elite and the masses. It is necessary that the elite employ a language and an ideological frame of reference intelligible to the masses. Secondly, the political code should be of such philosophical orientation that it can be embraced by the masses. Political code, which Ake describes as political formula, consists of the principles—moral, constitutional, legal, and philosophical—upon which political leadership rests its claims to political power. Therefore, a communicative government can be operationalized as one which keeps the general population adequately informed about its intentions, policies, and programs in a language that is intelligible to the average citizen.

Interestingly, Ake holds that ethnic particularism fosters 'segmentary political alignments'[72] which help to bridge elite-mass gap. This stands in contradiction to his earlier stance that traditional symbols of collective identity deserve to the demolished. Thirdly, a communicative political system is able to convince the governed that the actions of the political leadership are in the best interest of the nation-state. "Here, it is the belief rather than the reality that counts. It may be that in reality, the government may not be serving the interest of the governed."[73] In the final analysis, however, no amount of government propaganda can create this "belief" if government policies and actions inflict pain rather than succor on the populace.

(d) **Concordant:** A concordant African political system is one with a cohesive governing elite capable of forging consensual politics. Concordance can be operationalized on the basis of three factors: (1) the ability of the governing elite to forge a consensus for policy formulation and implementation; (2) the existence of an effective apparatus for resolving conflict and enforcing discipline within the ranks of the political elite; (3) the elite's consciousness of the collective nature of its civic responsibilities.[74] The governing elite may not muster a consensus on every issue, but it is necessary that it at least commands the support of a majority of its members over a policy initiative if such a policy is ever to succeed.

Ake notes that the governing elite faces a possibility of being challenged by a counter-elite and suggests cooptation of influential citizens as a check against it. As an additional means of safeguarding its solidarity, the governing elite needs to contain the influence of social differences on the body politic and to discourage misuse of such differences.[75]

(e) **Populistic:** While political elite's solidarity is critical in this theory, there is a recognition that popular participation in policy-formulation and implementation is vital for long-lasting social transformation. For, it would ensure that political leadership carries the masses with it as it plugs along the path of social transformation. Decision-making ought to be democratized in a manner that would encompass the national, local and grass-roots levels. So, a populistic African political system can be operationalized as one which conducts policy formulation and implementation through cross-sectionally-representative organs and grassroots involvement.

In fact, the "African Charter for Popular Participation in Development and Transformation," which was adopted in Arusha, Tanzania in 1990, underscores the imperative nature of people's participation in socio-economic and political transformation, otherwise known as development. The charter decries the inadequacy of popular initiatives and self-reliant efforts in the development strategies of African governments. It reads in part:

> The political context of socio-economic development has been characterized, in many instances, by an over-centralization of power and

impediments to the effective participation of the overwhelming majority of the people in social, political, and economic development.[76]

Thus, there is no gain-saying that without popular support and full participation of all segments of the populace, political leadership's efforts at
political integration are unlikely to permeate the veins of the body politic.

A critical aspect of popular participation in governance relates to the
place of women in society. No African political system can integrate its
society fully without equal rights for women. The issue of equal rights for
women is critical to popular participation, for without equal rights, women
cannot participate fully in the process of social transformation. In fact, the
charter advocates that "the attainment of equal rights by women in social,
economic, and political spheres must become a central feature of a democratic and participatory pattern of development."[77]

All barriers to women's full participation in the socio-economic and
political life of Nigerian society, rooted in both traditional beliefs and/or
exogenous religions like Islam, must be torn down. Whenever and where-
ever, society restricts, either by law or convention, the full participation of
any segment of its population in its socio-economic and political life, that
society consequently dissipates human resources that would have enhanced
its productivity. Such a society cannot attain its potentials.

It is significant to note that traditional African political leadership
manifested an element of populism. For instance, a typical African king
would take time off to go around his kingdom (accompanied by his assistants) to listen to and attend to complaints and concerns of his subjects. As
Diop reports: "These kings were sometimes so conscious of their role that
they tried in every way to maintain contact with the people, to investigate
grievances directly, so as to feel its political and social pulse."[78]

This level of populism contrasts sharply with the elitism that characterizes contemporary African political leadership—a leadership which tends
to keep as much distance as conceivable from the very people whom they
are supposed to serve.

(f) **Maatic:** As a construct of this theory of leadership and political
integration, Maatic is derived from the term *Maat*, which refers to the set
of principles enshrined in ancient Egypt's (kemet's) Code of Conduct for a
humanistic society. A Maatic African government can be operationalized
as one that manifests an effective level of accountability by emphasizing
and running a clean government through active preventive and punitive
anti-corruption programs. Maat is the codification of the Kemetes' view
of human relations. It covers their conception of correct human conduct,
correct societal norms and values. Maat was central to the Egyptian

philosophy of life. Its efficacy as an ointment for human relations is evidenced by the fact that the five thousand year, Kemetic civilization remains the most durable in world history. Maat stands for truth, justice, propriety, harmony, balance, reciprocity, and order.[79] Maulana Karenga, in the *Selections From the Husia*, interprets Maat as "the foundation of both nature and righteousness in human society."[80] Pointing out that "traditional Egyptologists [had] translated Maat mostly as justice,"[81] he states that its true meaning is righteousness. Karenga explains: "righteousness seems to me to be the most comprehensive and inclusive term and suggests and necessitates both truth and justice."[82] Maat was the Kemetes' "spirit and method of organizing and conducting the relations of human society."[83]

Maat holds that life is a system based on order, and in turn order is the harbinger of creation. Nevertheless, Egyptian philosophers recognized that life is characterized by both constructive and destructive forces.[84] Thus, in the Egyptian "Wisdom Literature,"[85] Maat was translated as rules of morality and ethics. As Egytologist Siegfried Morenz notes, Maat is "both the task which man sets himself and, as righteousness, the promise and reward which await him on fulfilling it."[86] According to Egyptian legend, Maat had been brought to life by the primordial god at the time of creation. Egyptian pharaohs had the responsibility of operationalizing Maat.

Maat encompasses the concept of an ideal human being. It views the ideal human being as a silent, moderate, and sensible person who respects society's norms and values. The ideal person, also known as the "Silent One," is characterized by self-control, modesty, kindness, generosity, discretion, truthfulness, and serenity. In contrast to the silent one is "the fool or the Hothead"—a person who is controlled by "his emotions and instincts which lead to a behavior disapproved by society."[87] The hothead is given to gluttony, greed, arrogance, bad temper, and vindictiveness. The hothead is typified by "egoism and . . . aggressivity and the fact that he follows his emotions and instincts without resistance [,] whereas the Silent One is disciplined and altruistic."[88]

However, as Gertie Englund notes, the Egyptians recognized the fallibility of human nature and thus acknowledged, particularly toward the dying years of the civilization, that the Wise one (the Silent one) could falter under certain conditions. At the earlier stage of the civilization, the wise one had been conceived as an irreconcilable opposite of the Hothead so much so that the Silent One was expected to stay away, even physically, from the Hothead.[89] Ancient Egyptian philosophers believed that for order to prevail in the state, a balance should be maintained between the Hotheads and the Silent Ones. Thus, during the few times, like "the so-called intermediary periods" in ancient Egyptian history when this balance was upset, the state faltered.[90]

Indeed, various scholars, ancient and modern, have written about the Maatic philosophical under-pinnings of traditional African society. Pre-colonial society is noted for its abhorrence of official corruption and respect for community property. Ogunsanwo pointed this out earlier. A good illustration of the revulsion that traditional society felt toward official corruption was the fate that befell a corrupt Ghanaian dynasty that reigned between the sixth and eight centuries. The masses so despised this dynasty that they systematically killed off its members. Even then, the masses did not stop there. They made sure that the lineage of this dynasty was effectively ended by extracting "fetuses from the wombs of women of the royal family."[91] Additional evidence of pre-colonial society's stress on probity comes from the records of Ibn Battuta's travels through the Medieval Sudanic empires of Africa. He wrote that he was struck by the people's and their leaders' sense of justice as exemplified by the swiftness with which their leaders punished those who transgressed against justice. The medieval itinerant scholar also wrote that African society of that era—the continent's proverbial age of innocence—was marked by safety and respect for life and hospitality toward strangers.[92]

Since this study has already established clearly that ancient Egypt was an African culture, the idea of using Maatic values and ideals to strengthen Nigeria's political culture is a logical one. The social code of an African society remarkable for both its longevity, stability and original contributions to the development of human society itself, deserves to be adapted by those societies of today which are still in search of not only political stability but also integrity and balance in their national lives. Recall Nwabueze's decry (in Chapter Three) of the lack of a national ethic in Nigeria's body politic. A National Ethic, Nwabueze holds, incorporates (1) respect for the constitution, (2) a spirit of fair play, (3) a tradition against abuse of power, (4) a commitment to the national interest, (5) public probity, (6) respect for individual liberty, (7) obedience to the law, (8) self-reliance, and (9) a limited role for the armed forces. These are extra-constitutional values necessary for a successful operation of a constitutional democracy. Nwabueze explains:

> What this means is that the question of a national ethic is essentially not one to be solved by constitutional prescription. Habit or tradition or a moral sense is not automatically created by stipulations in a constitution; they are formed from actual social behavior over a period of time.[93]

I submit that the infusion of Maatic values into the training and education of Africans from childhood to adulthood is a pre-requisite for the germination of a political culture oiled and nourished by a code of ethics reflective of the preceding. Maat encompasses the concept of an ideal human being. African children should be molded like the Silent one: a human being characterized by self-control, modesty, kindness, generosity, discretion, truthfulness, serenity and altruism. African educational systems, including the mass media, particularly television, should utilize images of the hothead as the "bad guy." The hothead typifies gluttony, greed, arrogance, bad temper, vindictiveness, egoism, aggressivity and emotionalism. Through this type of foundation, there can emerge an African political culture that could fulfill Nwabueze's dream of "national ethic" for Nigeria.

(g) **Historically-Conscious:** A historically conscious Nigerian/African political elite can be operationalized as one which, in its philosophical outlook, policies and actions, manifests consciousness of not only its national and continental history, but also of the role of Africa in world history, as well as the place of the African world in the contemporary global scheme of things. A historically conscious government conducts itself (on both national and international issues) in a manner which shows that it takes cognizance of the mistakes and lessons of the past. It is an elite that possesses an acute consciousness that African political leadership has no choice but to succeed. A political elite that lacks such consciousness faces the risk of repeating the mistakes of history. Consciousness of African history is necessary for a continental belief in self which was undermined by a long period of colonially-instituted, educationally-disseminated doses of anti-Africanism. Historical consciousness is a pre-requisite for a vision of a self-reliant approach to development. For, as we have shown, African approaches to development continue to be predicated upon a slavish mentality that Africa cannot forge ahead without external assistance. This mentality is an apparent bi-product of what the African learned from a Western academy that taught her that her world is a liability to human history. In sum, a basic message of the Western academy was and has been one that says: "whatever came from Europe was good or useful, and whatever came from Africa was either the reverse or not worth studying."[94] The impact of the Anti-Africanism that underlies Western epistemology has been so enduring that in 1993, despite the so-called Age of Information Explosion, a multi-national corporation like AT&T published a cartoon portraying Africans as monkeys. As I observed in a critique published by the *Philadelphia Tribune*, "the AT&T cartoon, like the green monkey hypothesis on AIDS, symbolizes the anti-African tendency inherent in the [Western] educational system."[95] I went on to suggest that were Carter G. Woodson alive, he would gladly "testify that we are dealing with a system which is designed to produce such cartoonists, irrespective of the color of their skin."[96]

Another aspect of the impact of this education is its alienating effect on the African mind. As Diop argued earlier in this chapter, the knowledge that the African world originated 'the 'Western' Civilization flaunted before our eyes today' would amaze the 'incredulous . . . African reader.'[97] He/she would be surprised to 'discover that most of the ideas used today to domesticate, atrophy, dissolve, or steal his 'soul,' were conceived by his own ancestors.'[98] Belief in self could enable Africans to look inward rather than outward for answers to the perennial economic and political headaches that have been the bane of the African world since the Western intervention in its civilization, starting from the fifteenth century.

Historical consciousness would prevent Nigerian/African political leaders from ignoring the lessons of this history in their national and global contexts. Were Nigeria's ex-military Head of State, General Ibrahim Babangida,[99] conscious of Nigeria's political history, he probably would not have threatened the political peace of the country as he did when he interfered with the June 12, 1993 still-born presidential election. He would have realized that mishandled elections had bred mistrust, fear, animosity and instability in the life of Nigeria. The ethnic anxiety, fear, and suspicion rekindled by Babangida's scuttling of the June 12 presidential election left the nation's ethnic centrifugal forces stronger than they have been since the Civil War of 1967 to 1970. The resultant political climate was such that the likelihood of "a North versus South West confrontation in the army"[100] was even broached.

In fact, succeeding Nigerian political leaderships have been accused of lacking consciousness of critical lessons from their national history. As Nwankwo puts it, "Nigerian leaders believe that they could afford to forget the past, without making efforts to remember what should not be forgotten in the interest of the nation."[101] Nwankwo is correct. No nation could afford to ignore its past, for the memories of the past are critical to shaping the present and the future. Nwankwo goes on to state that "historical imagination demands, not only that one remembers"[102] the sources of the mistakes and tragedies of the past, "but also that we reassess the extent of damage inflicted on our unity by past failures to tackle the problem at its roots."[103] He declares:

> Without an adequate assessment of the history of our failure, especially the mode of mutation and evolution in its essence overtime, it will permanently remain difficult, if not impossible, for us to reach new frontiers of national development.[104]

Nwankwo's articulation of the significance of correct historical consciousness to the life of a people is as poignant as it can be. I contend that such consciousness is a necessary ingredient for effective political and integrative leadership.

Theoretical Postulation

My postulation, based on the preceding theory, is that if an Afrocentric/Africacentered philosophy of leadership (which promotes, among other factors, **the African Interest and African consciousness** as opposed to ethnic or clannish consciousness), becomes dominant on the Continent, it could facilitate the evolution of an Africa-centered political culture (that is, a Maatic political culture), which is necessary for effective leadership and political integration in African states. An Afrocentric philosophical outlook is under girded by the Africa-centered paradigm. As formulated by Asante, its foremost proponent, Afrocentric philosophy, which is rooted in African history and culture, holds that it is legitimate to view phenomena from the African standpoint, in the context of constantly evolving African ideals and values.[105]

PART IV: AN AFROCENTRIC/AFRICA-CENTERED ANALYSIS OF SIX NIGERIAN POLITICAL LEADERSHIPS

This book focuses on Nigeria's post-independence political leadership and its impact on political integration. It covers the period of 1960 to 1983, but it includes relevant antebellum and postbellum developments.[106] This means that the study concentrates on the First Republic (1960 to 1966), the Second Republic (1979 to 1983), and intervening military governments of Nigeria. The study, therefore, involves mainly six civilian and military governments. The following is an analysis of each of those governments designed to ascertain the extent to which their political leaderships reflected the ingredients of the seven constructs of the Afrocentic/Africa-centered theory of political and integrative leadership.

The Civilian Administration of Prime Minister Tafawa Balewa, 1960 to 1966

In 1960, Britain handed over political power to an elected civilian government headed by Prime Minister Abubakar Tafawa Balewa. This was a parliamentary system of government modeled after the British system. While the prime minister was the chief executive and head of the federal government, there was a ceremonial president whose functions resembled those of Britain's ceremonial monarchy. This ceremonial office was occupied by Dr. Nnamdi Azikiwe, the late Owelle of Onitsha.

There was a bicameral legislature—the Senate and the House of Representatives. During the First Republic, Nigeria had four regions: the Northern Region, the Eastern Region, the Western Region and the Midwest (which was created post-factum in 1963). Each of the regional governments had its own premier and ceremonial governor and its own legislature consisting of a House of Assembly and a ceremonial House of Chiefs. A federal judiciary existed side by side with regional judiciaries, followed by customary or sharia courts (in the north).

The military coup of January 15, 1966 ended this experiment in parliamentary democracy. As preceding chapters have shown, this experiment, which was conducted against the backdrop of constricting colonial legacies, was quite a rocky one. Among those who were assassinated during the 1966 coup d'etat was Prime Minister Balewa. Prime Minister Balewa, a moslem from the northern section of Nigeria, was a man whose formal education had terminated at the secondary school level. He became Nigeria's first Prime Minister because he was the head of his political party, the Northern Peoples Congress (NPC), which won the largest federal legislative seats in the independence election of 1959. Next in ranking were two other political parties: the National Council of Nigerian Citizens (NCNC) (originally known as the National Convention of Nigeria and the Cameroons) and the Action Group (AG). But there were several smaller parties, including the Northern Peoples Progressive Union (NEPU) and the United Middle Belt Party (UMBP). As preceding chapters have shown, each of these political parties, including the three major parties, was regionally and ethnically based. Prime Minister Balewa's NPC was dominated by the Hausa/Fulani ethnic twins—the two largest ethnic groups in the Northern Region.

This chapter highlights and analyzes major policies, programs, actions and pronouncements of Prime Minister Balewa (as well as applicable actions and pronouncements of his cabinet, President Azikiwe, federal legislators and regional premiers (in so far as the actions and pronouncements of those premiers impacted upon federal-state relations)), in an attempt to determine how they reflected or did not reflect the Afrocentric/Africa-centered theory of political and integrative leadership. This approach is based on my conviction that leadership is a collective responsibility. The analysis also touches upon the achievements/or crises of the First Republic's political leadership.

To what extent was this leadership purposeful, benevolent, communicative, concordant, populistic, maatic, and historically-conscious? A purposeful African political system is one based on a legitimately instituted, cross-sectionally representative government which has a clear sense of mission in the national interest as well as the capacity and willingness to give life to its policies and programs.

Balewa's government was duly elected to office through the 1959 independence election in accordance with the 1960 federal constitution of Nigeria. Thus, it was legitimately instituted although, as the following discussion will demonstrate, eyebrows were raised at the time of the election by the rather hasty invitation which the departing British colonial administrator extended to Balewa to form the national government.[107] Additional information is provided on this incident later in this chapter.

Constitutional or dejure legitimacy is one thing; defacto legitimacy is another. Government must conduct itself not only in accordance with the rule of law, but also in harmony with natural justice and basic fairness. It must conduct itself in a manner that could command and preserve the continued loyalty and respect of citizens. One inherited problem of Balewa's government, which haunted it like a ghost, was the lopsidedness of the federal structure—a structure that compounded the problems and crises of the First Republic. Even though this structure was constitutionally sanctioned, it and its effects served to dilute the legitimacy of the system in the eyes of Southern politicians. As already noted, several other consequences of the North-South divide in the politics of this era posed structural obstacles to Balewa's leadership. Diamond articulates this problem rather remarkably well in the following passage:

> Southern political leaders clearly perceived the NPC's determination to dominate the Federation and, they felt, to usurp resources and positions that rightfully belonged to Southerners. As the Federal Government's economic power and initiative expanded, the prospect of this dominance became steadily more disturbing.[108]

These, however, were not the only constraints on Balewa's government. A fundamental constraint was the fact that the independence which Britain granted Nigeria in 1960 was merely a limited, neo-colonial independence. It was an independence with in-built limits on the "degree to which new nations were really free to govern themselves and settle their own affairs in their own way."[109] This neo-colonial scheme was, as Davidson puts it, "a many-sided attempt by outside powers to tie the new nations closely to the interests and needs of those outside powers."[110] These many-sided attempts were/are overt and covert, he adds. Richard Drayton was more specific in his indictment of neo-colonialism. He puts it in blunt terms:

> There are many who like to blame Africa's weak governments and economies, famines and disease on its post-1960 leadership. But the fragility of contemporary Africa is a direct consequence of two

centuries of slaving, followed by another of colonial despotism. Nor
was 'decolonization' all it seemed: both Britain and France attempted
to corrupt the whole project of political sovereignty.[111]

And why was it in the self-interest of the colonial overloads to corrupt the
"project of political sovereignty" for African countries? The answer is simple: they wanted to perpetuate their economic exploitation of the continent.

Drayton follows in the footsteps of the Davidson's of African historiography. Shedding further light on the shady ways and dirty tricks of neo-
colonialism, Drayton, once again, hits the nail in the head:

> It is remarkable that none of those in Britain who talk about African
> dictatorship and kleptocracy seem aware that Idi Amin came to power
> in Uganda through British covert action, and that Nigeria's generals
> were supported and manipulated from 1960 onwards in support of
> Britain's oil interests.[112]

In addition to neo-colonial apron strings, Balewa also faced a constraint
that arose from the fact that for much of the period of the First Republic,
the central government remained a weak institution manipulated by potent
regions. Ekwueme Felix Okoli views this as a situation in which the federal
government could not enforce its constitutional authority without the backing of regional governments or a combination of regional governments.[113]

No doubt, the presence of these institutional obstacles constituted a
square peg in the round hole of political leadership, but as Ogunsanwo,
Diamond, as well as Jackson and Rosberg's studies show, the actions or
inactions of African leaders (like Balewa's) have proven to be as significant
as the inherited obstacles, in molding the fortunes or misfortunes of post-
independence Africa. In the particular case of Nigeria, even if the politics
of the First Republic had been fought on the basis of issues rather than
ethnicity, that condition alone would not have turned Nigeria into a stable
democracy.[114] For, as foregoing chapters have demonstrated, the behavior
of the political leaders of the day leaves much to be desired.

Therefore, one needs to ask the question: did Balewa's leadership
exacerbate or ameliorate the inherited problems? Did it have the vision and
did it take necessary steps to tear down the shackles of neo-colonial independence? More specifically, did Balewa's political leadership attenuate or
enhance his government's defacto legitimacy?

Among other vices, the election malpractices that featured prominently
during this regime, as well as reported governmental corruption (which
was not punished by Prime Minister Balewa) as evidenced by ostentatious

living and wealth display by top government functionaries even in the face of unenviable labor conditions in the country that prompted a 13-day General Strike in 1964,[115] could not have strengthened the legitimacy of the government in the eyes of the governed. Prime Minister Balewa's "unwillingness (or inability)"[116] to remove corrupt ministers has been cited as one of the reasons for the demise of his government, despite Balewa's "personal reputation for honesty and moderation."[117]

Granted that the prime minister's party was not the only culprit in the election frauds of the First Republic, particularly those of the 1964 General Election, Balewa might have strengthened the chances for peace in the country if he had "subordinated" his personal ambition for office by calling for a fresh election. His formation of a "government of national unity"[118] after the rather disastrous first national post-independence election of 1964—partly designed to restore a sense of balance to a nation which had been deeply fractionalized by divisive politics—did not and could not have strengthened the legitimacy of the government of the day in the eyes of the general public. In fact, it had the effect of eliminating the role of the Opposition from the central government.[119]

In addition, Balewa could have acted to forestall the electoral disaster of 1964 by rejecting the highly-disputed 1963 census returns (which set the stage for the electoral catastrophe of 1964). His government's acceptance of the disputed census results did a major harm to the legitimacy of the system itself. Such was this harm that the NCNC went as far as declaring "that they would regard as illegitimate the NPC majority which the [federal] election seems certain to produce."[120] Here is a case where a national problem was "solved" with a "band-aid;" beneath this band-aid, the problem decayed like a festering sore. Overtime, the residue of unresolved problems complicated and compounded evolving national crises. Thus, the explosion that followed the 1965 Regional Crisis in the West drew quite a bit of energy from the frustrations of the past.

In fact, Balewa's leadership during the First regional crisis of 1962 in the West is best described as bad leadership. Prior to the crisis, Western politicians had voiced concerns about alleged diabolical designs of the central government. But Balewa did not allay this long-held fear that the federal government was bent on fomenting trouble in the West because of its disapproval of Chief Awolowo's role as the Leader of Opposition at the center. In fact, Ekwueme Felix Okoli (1980) and Diamond (1988) did not mince words in charging Balewa's government with precipitating the Western Crisis. Diamond writes: "The disruption in the House and subsequent declaration of Emergency . . . were part of a premeditated plan by the Federal Coalition partners, working in collusion with the Akintola faction."[121]

Okoli reports that Prime Minister Balewa had assured the Akintola Group that the federal government would intervene 'if a sufficient row was made in the Western House.'[122] Recall that eventually, Awolowo, the Action Group Leader, was tried, convicted and jailed for treasonable felony—a culmination of the 1962 Western Regional Crisis. Balewa should have cared more about the national interest than whatever narrow partisan benefits that his party derived or stood to gain from the weakening of Action Group's regional influence at the center. Balewa did not show statesmanship when he refused Chief Awolowo's repeated appeals for police protection of the Regional Legislature from the thuggery of Akintola's faction. Instead, he turned a deaf ear and allowed a handful of legislators to flagrantly violate the law which they had sworn to uphold. Certainly, Balewa's inaction could not have enhanced the legitimacy of the federal government in the eyes of the Nigerian public at large.

Being cross-sectionally representational is another ingredient of a purposeful government. To what extent was Balewa's government cross-representational, or to put it in the parlance of later-day Nigerian politics, to what extent did his government reflect the "federal character"[123] of the Nigerian nation in appointments and allocations of federal projects?

First, although the NPC-NCNC alliance which formed the federal government in 1960, represented a bridge across the dangerous North-South bipolar politics of that era, it did not go far enough, for it left the Action Group (hence, the West) in a state of isolation and frustration. Could the East have been isolated as well? Okoli observes that Southern politicians had no choice but to form an alliance with the Northern People's Congress[124] because even before decisive returns of the 1959 independence election had come in (note that eventually, the NPC fell short, by nine seats, of the simple majority of federal parliamentary seats required for a party to form the government),[125] the departing British Colonial Administrator, Sir James Robertson, "upset the democratic process of post-election coalition formation by appointing Sir Abubakar Tafawa Balewa as Prime Minister."[126] He laments that this irregularity "set the tone for post independence election practices."[127] Given this circumstance, Balewa ought to have laid emphasis on ways of working with the Opposition (particularly the Action Group which was not part of the alliance). Instead, his NPC-NCNC alliance took steps to eliminate the Opposition altogether. This partisan political leadership proved disastrous for the nation. Okoli reports:

> Once the Western Region was eliminated as a powerful element in the competition, the struggle for dominance became the main preoccupation

of the Eastern and Northern Regions. It was this struggle that led to the eventual collapse of the Federation of Nigeria.[128]

Had Balewa exhibited a greater ability to manage politics of pluralism, which is what the Nigerian state calls for, maybe the regions would have felt a lesser temptation to engage in that fatal struggle for political dominance.

Despite the existence of the NPC-NCNC alliance, the composition of Balewa's cabinet left the North with the key ministerial positions. Since the NPC (i.e. the Northern party) had won a majority of the national legislative seats—the party later formed the alliance with the NCNC because it fell short of the required simple majority by nine votes—it could be reasonably argued that Balewa was justified in assigning key ministerial positions to Northern candidates. This appears to be the nature of party politics. But in the context of Nigerian politics, ever haunted by a Southern fear of "Northern domination," the fact that northerners held strategic positions in Balewa's government worsened this anxiety. Matters were not helped by the fact that the 1962–68 development plan of Nigeria allotted most of the ear-marked expenditures to the Northern Region. Diamond describes this preferential appropriation as an irony because the South, with its higher rates of school graduation and employment needs, needed more matching funds for social transformation.[129]

Did Balewa's leadership possess a clear sense of mission in the national interest? One way to answer this question is through the major policy undertaking of Balewa's government, namely the 1962–68 development plan. First, it is pertinent to note that the colonial development plan which preceded it, namely the 1946 ten year plan for development and welfare, was mainly aimed at instituting and legitimizing measures to enhance the profit that colonialism reaped from the Nigerian, British-controlled economy.[130] But was Balewa's post-independence development plan of 1962–68 conceived to re-direct and re-orient the Nigerian national economy in the national interest? In their work, *Towards A Political Economy of Nigeria*, Julius O. Ihonvbere and Timothy M. Shaw contend that Balewa's plan simply preserved the status-quo: "The post-colonial regime saw no urgent reason for change. The neo-colonial economy was preserved with all its distortions and mechanisms of administration and exploitation."[131] There is evidence, however, that Balewa's administration was aware of the need for change, but apparently was too timid to take the necessary steps. His Minister of Economic Development, Ibrahim Waziri, had this to say:

> If we want to really set about improving the economy of our country in a particular way they say we are communists. They can make our

countrymen suspect our every move. If they do not succeed by false propaganda, by calling us all sorts of names, if they fail to make us unpopular in order to win their case, they can arrange assassination. They can do it by poison or by setting our own people against us.[132]

Thus, it can be deduced from the foregoing that the political leadership lacked the courage necessary for a head-on assault on neo-colonialism. Ekekwe opines that there was more to it than mere lack of courage. He suggests that the governing class was also "beholden to . . . the foreign bourgeoisie."[133] In addition, the politicians of the First Republic made a mockery of economic development by turning loans boards into conduit pipes for largesse to their political cronies, friends and families. These loans, ostensibly appropriated for economic development, were turned into means of sustenance for the political parties.[134]

Another major act of Balewa's leadership, which not only was at variance with the national interest of Nigeria, but also portrayed Balewa as either unpatriotic or a leader with little or no understanding or awareness of the phenomenon of neo-colonialism was his government's complicity in a British overt attempt to strengthen its control over Nigerian affairs through the back-door. This is the so-called Anglo-Nigeria Defense Treaty of 1960. Thanks to the sharp protest mounted by a coalition of Nigerian professional, labor and student leaders, Balewa was forced to cancel the treaty.[135] It is both shocking and disappointing that Balewa could countenance such a British ploy to strengthen its exploitative ties with Nigeria.[136] At the international level, Balewa also demonstrated a similar level of accommodation with neo-colonialism. He led Nigeria, along with Liberia and Togo, in opposition to Kwame Nkrumah's proposition to turn post-independence Africa into a Commonwealth of States with one parliament. Balewa was part of the so-called Monrovia group which, instead, favored a gradualist approach to African unity that resulted in the ineffable body known as the Organization of African Unity (OAU).[137] Thus, Nkrumah, unlike Balewa, recognized that immediate unification was the more effective means of safeguarding Africa's independence and facilitating its social, economic and political progress.[138] In addition to these, Nigeria's foreign policy under Balewa is best described as "made in Britain" foreign policy.

Did Balewa's government show a willingness and possess the capacity to give life to its policies and programs? Although the federal government under Balewa was essentially a weak government partly because of the overbearing nature of regional politics, it did exhibit a will to give life to its policies and programs. This is despite the fact, as Okoli has contended, that the extent to which the government could enforce its constitutional authority depended very much on the cooperation of the regions. Unfortunately, this will was sometimes exerted toward a negative purpose like Balewa's encouragement of insurrection in the West to justify emergency rule.

The government took steps to implement its national development plan of 1962–68 although in this regard, it was hamstrung by the partisanship of the politics of the day, among other factors. As Ladipo Ademolekun puts it, "the unhealthy rivalry among the three major groupings made rational plan administration in Lagos impossible." [139] A classic illustration of this was a dispute about where the nation would cite an iron and steel complex which was part of the 1962–68 development plan. The eventual, politically-motivated decision was to cite the complex in three locations in Nigeria—in the North, the East and the West, and as Adamolekun observes, "in such moments of national survival through the art of compromise, economic considerations did not seem to matter." [140]

The government did not possess sufficient capacity for the enforcement of its policies and programs. A good example of such incapacity is the poor managerial capacity that plagued the young nation at that time. Thus, a 1966 assessment of the progress of the six development plan laments: "The simple truth is that we do not have machinery at present for the proper formulation and execution of comprehensive national development programs as a strategy of continuous social progress." [141] The government also had a weak capacity for law-enforcement. By 1965, the country had a federal police force of 15,500. Given Nigeria's estimated population of about 55 million at this time, this means that there were 3,548.4 Nigerian inhabitants per federal police officer.

The next task of this analysis is to determine whether the political system under which Balewa governed was benevolent. As earlier stated, a benevolent political system is one with a political elite (which is defined as a 'coalition of the leaders of the major social, religious, professional, and ethnic groups' [142]) that is not only willing and able to lead, but is also dedicated to pursuing the general welfare of the nation. According to Ake, the political elite is responsible for destroying or changing 'certain habits of mind' and destroying 'certain traditional symbols of collective identity.' [143] There is no doubt that Prime Minister Balewa was willing to lead; so was President Azikiwe, but he had no executive powers. Balewa's very interest in continuing as prime minister eloquently speaks for his willingness to lead. But was he able to lead? Even though the neo-colonial status of Nigeria and the country's centrifugal forces circumscribed his ability to lead, we have seen that some of his judgments, like those related to the 1962 Regional Crisis, did not augur well for the nation. Similarly, while the rank and file of the elected politicians were obviously willing to lead within their various jurisdictions, the corruption, election fraud, and tribal politics of that era cast a shadow over their ability to lead in the interest of the nation. In short, even though the period had its share of true patriots, the failure of the First Republic is, unavoidably, the collective guilt of that generation of Nigeria's political elite. Their flagrant violation of the rules of political competition did a lot to undermine the political system, for systems stability requires a commitment to the rules "even in times of stress, and at the expense of substantive political goals."[144] For the most part, the political leaders of the day placed their personal political ambitions above the general welfare of the people.

If the political elite of the First Republic was not benevolent, was it communicative? An African political system is communicative if the political elite and the ordinary folk are in touch with each other—that is, if there is a free and adequate flow of intercourse between the political elite and the general population. There were three major political parties during this republic and several minor ones. Through these instruments, the political leaders endeavored to mobilize the general population but mainly for electoral purposes. In fact, these politicians left no stone unturned—including the stone of ethnic hatred—in their desire to win grassroots favor. However, this did not necessarily ameliorate the elite-mass gap of the time, for several factors differentiated the elite from the masses, including education, income and the Western consciousness of the former. Furthermore, the political leaders of this time stimulated not a positive nationalistic energy in the masses but a negative centrifugal tendency.

A concordant African political system is one with a cohesive governing elite capable of forging consensual politics. Three factors determine whether the political elite is solidary. (1) The ability of the governing elite to forge a consensus for policy formulation and implementation; (2) the existence of an effective apparatus for resolving conflict and enforcing discipline within the ranks of the political elite; (3) the elite's consciousness of the collective nature of its civic responsibilities. There is no question that the governing elite of the First Republic was hardly concordant. Even though a growing solidarity of economic interests among the top echelon of the governing elite was in evidence at this time,[145] the passion of tribalism keep them disunited. And as Diamond contends in the preceding chapter, a true national economic class had not come into being at this time partly because economic class formation, like politics, had progressed vertically along regional/ethnic lines instead of horizontally across those divides. In addition, the fact that bi-partisanship was rather hardly a feature of the politics of this day meant that the politicians failed to close ranks in the national interest during critical periods. Hence, the crises-ridden nature of the Republic. At the end of the day, the potent forces of regionalism-ethnicity not only overwhelmed whatever common economic interests the elite might have developed, they also drove the nation into a bloody three-year civil war.

While the elite lacked concordance, popular participation in policy-formulation and implementation was hardly a feature of this era. A populistic African political system is one in which popular participation constitutes an integral part of policy making and execution. Popular participation in policy-formulation and implementation is vital for long-lasting social transformation. For, it would ensure that political leadership carries the masses with it as it plugs along the path of social transformation. The regime's major policy undertaking, namely the six-year development plan was an ivory-tower project in every sense of the word. That plan was, indeed, the handiwork of top-regional power groups; its overall objective was to promote economic growth rather than true social development.[146] In fact, politicians or administrators dominated the policy-making process during the First Republic.[147]

A maatic political culture is one whose code of conduct is reflective of the Kemetic code of conduct for a humanistic society. The Kemetic code known as Maat stands for truth, justice, propriety, harmony, balance, reciprocity, and order. Maat encompasses the concept of an ideal human being. It views the ideal human being as a silent, moderate, and sensible person who respects society's norms and values. The ideal person, also known as the "Silent One," is characterized by self-control, modesty, kindness, generosity, discretion, truthfulness, and serenity. In contrast to the silent one is "the fool or the Hothead"—a person who is controlled by 'his emotions and instincts which lead to a behavior disapproved by society.'[148] The hothead is given to gluttony, greed, arrogance, bad temper, and vindictiveness. The hothead is typified by 'egoism and . . . aggressivity and the fact that he follows his emotions and instincts without resistance whereas the Silent One is disciplined and altruistic.'[149] Ancient Egyptians believed that society needed a balance between the silent ones and the hotheads in order to enjoy stability and tranquility.

To what extent did order, harmony, balance, justice, and truth prevail during Balewa's leadership? If anything, the first republic was characterized by disorder, disharmony, imbalance, injustice and official dishonesty. It was like a ship which eventually sank after a tumultuous sail. Democratic politics is contentious in its procedure, but the process ought to lead to answers, answers acceptable to the various segments of the body politic. During the first republic, the procedure almost became both a means and an end in itself as the political leadership failed to provide real solutions to emerging problems. The census controversy was never resolved; elections never produced acceptable winners because the rules of the competition were flouted! The alleged falsifications of census returns as well as electoral manipulations, whose epitome was the 1965 Western Regional elections, reflected a fundamental problem: a crisis of ethics! For the political leaders of the first republic, the means surely justified the end. It is also evident that the politics of the day hardly came close to anything resembling a balance. The imbalance between the silent ones and the hotheads, in favor of the latter, was much reflected in the schism between the North and the South. There was a southern perception that national issues were resolved to the advantage of the North rather than by balancing out Northern and Southern interests so that the solution to a given national problem would not amount to a loss or victory for one segment of the nation. The head counts of 1962 and 1963, the General Election of 1964 and the Regional Election of 1965 were consequences of the "imbalances" in the body politic. But the grand imbalance of them all was the overbearing reported population of the north versus that of the south. Furthermore, the politicians of the day as well as the press did not, generally-speaking, exhibit a sense of balance in their rhetoric. Diamond comments:

> In a context in which so much was at stake in an election and in which the largely rural and illiterate electorate lacked the sophistication and breath of exposure to dismiss . . . fantastic charges as mere rhetorical excess, venomous rhetoric bred violence and repression.[150]

As for justice, the conviction of Chief Awolowo, the Action Group leader, despite 'acknowledged contradictions and weaknesses in the evidence,'[151] epitomized the injustices that occurred during this regime. Awolowo's imprisonment could not have inspired public confidence in the system of justice.

The political elite at this time behaved in a manner which pretty much betrayed a lack of historical consciousness. While some of the leaders, like Azikiwe and Balewa, did urge the warring politicians to temper their tribalistic and divisive rhetoric, the actions of the latter, such as his complicity in the events that necessitated emergency rule in the West, did not demonstrate a consciousness of the fragile foundation of the nation. Azikiwe's attempt (through a radio appeal to the nation on December 10, 1964)[152] to ward off the impending collapse of the Republic by raising the specter of the post-independence national disintegration of Patrice Lumumba's Congo (in Central Africa) apparently did not make much of an impression on the generality of the political leaders of the day. Thus, events continued to slide down the precipice until the military intervention of January 1966.

The foregoing analysis shows that Balewa's political leadership fell short of the expectations of the constructs of the Afrocentric/Africa-centered theory of political and integrative leadership by very wide margins. Though the succeeding administration of General J.T.U. Aguiyi-Ironsi lasted barely six months as it fell victim to the hydra-headed forces unleashed by pre-coup and post-coup developments, his government's rather historic actions and/or inactions deserve being subjected to the Afrocentric litmus test.

Major General J.T.U. Aguiyi-Ironsi (January 1966–July 1966)

Major General J.T.U. Aguiyi-Ironsi was a career soldier who had risen through the ranks to the leadership of the Nigerian armed forces. In fact, he was the first Nigerian head of the armed forces. General Ironsi became Nigeria's Head of State in January 1966 following the overthrow and assassination of Prime Minister Balewa. It is significant to note that Ironsi was not a member of the group of soldiers who planned and executed the January 15th coup d'etat.[153] In fact, Ironsi himself had narrowly escaped assassination by the coup leaders. It has been reported that the group of soldiers who had been sent to execute Ironsi were frightened off by his "thundering reprimand."[154] Indeed, it was Ironsi's counter-operation that prevented the actual coup leaders from completing their mission. It was from the Lagos Headquarters of the Nigerian Armed Forces that Ironsi led his counter-offensive against the coup plotters led by Major Chukwuma Kaduna Nzeogwu from his Northern base in Kaduna. But Ironsi's effort could not save Balewa's government. For, the prime minister, two regional governors, a federal minister and a number civilian and military functionaries of state had been slain by the coup leaders before they were over-powered.

Having over-ran the forces of Major Nzeogwu, General Ironsi then assumed the leadership of the nation by virtue of being the Supreme Commander of the Nigerian Armed Forces at this time. Although the military take-over was greeted with a nation-wide acclaim, it must be noted that it represented a seizure of political power. Therefore, it did not have Constitutional legitimacy. Whether the popular acclaim that the military take-over received can be construed as de facto legitimacy is another question altogether. In any case, the new government's first act was to suspend provisions of the 1963 Constitution of Nigeria as they related to the offices of the president, governors, prime ministers, premiers, executive councils, and parliaments.[155] It then proceeded to rule by decree. Thus, we have seen that this government did not come into being through the womb of Nigeria's Constitutional framework.

Welch points out that military governance proceeds along either of two lines: (a) a partnership with key trusted civilians while the soldiers exercise control,[156] or (b) direct rule by military personnel with minor roles for civilians.[157] Ironsi governed largely by the former method (that is, a military partnership with subordinate civilian assistants), and this modus operandi remained the format of succeeding military administrations in Nigeria until its slight variation of 1993 under which the armed forces extended their hold on political power by appointing a civilian puppet "head of state." In fact, in announcing this mutation of military control of federal political power in Nigeria, General Babangida left nothing to chance as to who was in-charge: "I want to assure our citizens . . . that the Armed Forces would in addition to its traditional roles defend the Interim National Government with all its strength to ensure its survival as by law established."[158] The political atmosphere of 1993, unpredictable as it was, was, however, a far-cry from the tumultuous situation of 1966 when Ironsi, a Christian from the South-Eastern section of Nigeria, had the misfortune of taking over the affairs of Nigeria. That period was one of the touchiest moments of Nigeria's history. The centrifugal forces in the nation's life had only become stronger, not weaker, after the first six years of independence. In the preceding chapter, Obasanjo noted that Nzeogwu's coup had good motives but was poorly executed. As a result of this poor execution, he opines, the coup "hastened Nigeria's collapse."[159] But it would appear that the troublesome manner in which the coup was executed was not the immediate factor that soured Ironsi's standing with the North in particular. For despite the bloody nature of the coup and lopsidedness of its assassinations,

> The new military government was backed by enormous popular sup-
> port. All over Nigeria people rejoiced at the end of the rule of corrupt
> politicians, and they hoped for a new dawn. Loyalty to the new regime
> was pledged by all the Nigerian political parties, [ethnic] unions, trade
> unions and students' unions.[160]

But this euphoria was short-lived due in part to the manner in which Ironsi attempted to grapple with the political ailment of the nation. Earlier, Opia credited Ironsi with a high sense of integrity but faulted him for lacking political wizardry. As he put it, "Major-General Aguiyi-Ironsi . . . tried to run an honest regime. However, he was the leader of a revolution not of his own making, and he had little political talent."[161]

Was the government of General Ironsi cross-sectionally representative? The volatile political climate under which Ironsi came into office was one that called for extreme caution and sensitivity to bruised ethnic feelings, particularly those of the North which suffered the heaviest casualties in the coup. In discussing Ironsi's administration, Joseph suggests that Ironsi had projected an image of being ethnically biased in favor of his Igbo ethnic group.[162] In politics, public perceptions of the actions of political leadership tend to carry almost as much significance as the actions themselves. This was a moment in Nigeria's checkered history which required a political leadership with perceptible respect for the nation's diversity. Even though the revolutionary zeal of Ironsi's short-lived administration indicates that he had a clear sense of mission in the national interest, Ironsi, by his methods, could NOT convince all segments of the nation that his actions were motivated by the national interest. For instance, his decision to switch the nation from federalism to unitarism was prompted by the nation's bitter experience with regional federalism. But the way Ironsi went about this change smacks of both political naivety and a lack of historical consciousness. By choosing an Igbo person (shortly after a coup which had been dubbed as an Igbo coup), to form a one-man commission that recommended the dissolution of federalism in Nigeria and its replacement with a Unitary System based on a unified Civil Service, Ironsi, an Igbo himself, played into the hands of those who were already whispering about an alleged Igbo plot to dominate the nation. Had Ironsi been adequately historically conscious, he would have handled this issue with caution and extreme diplomacy. His adoption of a unified civil service, though designed to strengthen the centripetal energy in the nation, struck at the very heart of a long-held fear by the educationally disadvantaged North of a Southern domination of the nation's public service. Inspired by the Northern deficiency in education (a deficiency which was rooted in the nature of colonial administration in Nigeria), this fear had led Northern leadership to set up the Northernization Policy of 1955, a policy that was meant to serve as a safeguard against Southern domination.[163] Furthermore, matters were not helped by Ironsi's apparent procrastination over whether the coup leaders should be put up for trial, as demanded by Northern opinion leaders. No doubt, the Northernization policy was divisive and regressive, but Ironsi moved against it with little tact and at the most inauspicious of time. Bad timing and ill-fitting methods derailed Ironsi's otherwise courageous acts of reform. As Opia puts it,

> In spite of the [ethnic] and regional overtones, the unitary idea appealed to reform-minded people in all regions of Nigeria. These were men sufficiently educated not to fear competition and were well aware of the economic and political advantages of doing away with wasteful rivalries of the regional blocs. The idea appealed to the army, which was itself the most Nigerian-minded group.[164]

Ironsi, no doubt, demonstrated a willingness to take on the forces that had tried to rip the nation apart, but the political elite at this time was neither benevolent nor concordant. Regional concerns precluded the elite from achieving a collective commitment to the general welfare of the nation. Surely, consensual politics clearly eluded the nation. Suspicions abounded; thus, it is little wonder that Joseph reports that Ironsi "had been accused of relying heavily on fellow Igbos as his civilian advisers during his brief rule."[165] Had Ironsi's government been as communicative and politically savvy as the situation necessitated to counter-act the dangerous rumors that pervaded the political scene at the time, his intentions would probably have been less misunderstood by a large segment of the population. As Clarke notes, Ironsi was a professional soldier who failed to appreciate that "it is necessary to practice politics in order to govern."[166] Similarly, A. D. Yahaya faults Ironsi for neglecting and excluding politicians "who were also power-brokers"[167] from the governing process.[168] If Ironsi could side-track politicians (arguably on the justifiable ground that they had wrecked the First Republic), might he have given some consideration to grassroots politics? Since his government was too short-lived, it is difficult to answer this question. But if his decision to let a one-man commission[169] determine an issue as fundamental and delicate as whether Nigeria should retain federalism or take to unitarism is anything to go by, then one can reasonably suggest that Ironsi was too elitist-inclined to have ever conducted a government based on a measurable degree of people's participation in policy formulation and implementation. In other words, all indications are that his administration could not have been a populistic leadership. The end result was that Ironsi could not carry the whole nation with him on his reform train. His sincere and bold attempts to integrate the nation proved counter-productive; forces who misconstrued his intentions struck in July 1966 and took his life in the process. Ironsi's six-month rule did not give much of an attention to the problem of corruption although before he was killed he had begun some work in this direction. Among other things, the administration had instituted inquiries into public corporations.[170] Ironsi himself was an above-board public officer who died a pauper.[171] Thus, to some extent, the administration exhibited Maatic tendencies, but time was not on its side. The fractured nation that Ironsi inherited by accident in January 1966 was still in the grips of the forces of disintegration when Ironsi was swept off the stage in July 1966.

However, has history vindicated Ironsi on the question of unitarism for Nigeria? In a critique of Babangida's administration, Nwankwo laments that during Babangida's tenure (1985–1993), Nigeria had progressively shifted away from federalism toward unitarism. Nwankwo accuses

Babangida's government of strengthening the powers of local governments and the ties between them and the central government at the expense of the second tier of Nigeria's three-tier governmental structure—the states. Nwankwo, who believes that this trend would hurt the nation in the long-run, condemns it:

> The gap between the local councils and the central authority is indeed wide and glaring. Without the balance which the state governments provide at the second-tier structure of federalism, a structural imbalance will be created between the capacity of the central authority to perform as it will, and the competence of the local councils to check such authority when they want.[172]

Nwankwo then goes on to explain that:

> With over 450[173] local councils in the country, and without the necessary check on over 20 state structures,[174] the political and administrative arena will be open to covert subversion and manipulation by a central authority which will claim it represents the people directly.[175]

Nwankwo presents a powerful argument that cannot be dismissed lightly, particularly the point that the whittling down of the powers of the states in relation to the local government would leave the nation more vulnerable to governmental abuse at the federal level. Nwankwo was quick to remind the nation in this critique that General Ironsi had been overthrown and killed by forces opposed to unitarism. It does not appear that Nwankwo's concerns about the growth of local governments in Nigeria impacted official thinking to any degree, for since his writing, the number of local government councils in Nigeria has risen from four hundred and fifty to seven hundred and seventy-four.

General Yakubu Gowon: July 1966–July 1975

As of the time of publishing this book, the nine-year tenure of General Yakubu Gowon, who was Nigeria's Head of State from July 1966 to July 1975, remains the longest in Nigeria's post-independence history. Gowon ruled Nigeria during its most critical period—the Civil War of 1967 to 1970. He has been described as General Ironsi's right-hand man in foiling Major Nzeogwu's coup of January 1966.[176] In fact, Ironsi, on assuming office after that coup, appointed Gowon as the Chief of Army Staff—an appointment which, unfortunately for Ironsi, did not belie the impression that he was too reliant on Igbo advisers.

Gowon, a Christian from the middle-belt area of the northern section of Nigeria, became Head of State as a result of the counter-coup of July 1966. It appears that like Ironsi, Gowon was not privy to the coup that brought him to power. Nonetheless, the counter-coup was planned and executed by fellow Northern military officers. Further evidence that the coup against Ironsi was a northern operation comes from the explanation that has been adduced for the inability of Ironsi's deputy, Brigadier Ogundipe, a Southerner, to succeed him. John D. Clarke's biography on Gowon explains why:

> Brigadier Ogundipe's position had been delicate, even dangerous. As Deputy Head of State he could see that this latest coup had been inspired by Northerners angered by General Aguiyi-Ironsi's failure to bring to trial the January conspirators who had murdered their senior officers and politicians. Ogundipe could not be blamed for feeling that he too might be their next target.[177]

Gowon, who at this time was the most senior Officer-in-Charge, thus became the head of state. So, in terms of legitimacy, Gowon, like Ironsi, was not legitimately (that is, constitutionally) installed in office.

There is, however, evidence that British officials helped to instigate the July counter-coup. General Olusegun Obasanjo, a former Nigerian military leader, reports: "The second coup was actively encouraged if not assisted by some British officials and university lecturers working and living in the North. It was no secret that to the British the North was more amenable and less radical and refractory than the South."[178] It is equally significant to note that the British authorities had been averse to Nzeogwu's coup and had promised to militarily assist General Ironsi to put it down. So, here we are with a double-dealing British posture. The same British who had promised to assist Ironsi, acted differently behind the scene. They helped to incite Northern leadership against the same Ironsi for whom they had feigned support. As Obasanjo alluded in the preceding excerpt, the British could not trust Ironsi, a southerner. Instead, they wanted a pliant northerner or southerner. In fact, such was Gowon's disposition toward the British that when he was eventually overthrown, a Nigerian newspaper rejoiced and waved him away as "that British-loved and British-praised General Yakubu Gowon."[179]

Be that as it may, how purposeful was Gowon's political leadership? Was his government cross-sectionally representative? Gowon's government could not be said to have been cross-sectionally representative at the onset and during the early years, because the South-Easterners, particularly the Igbos, who were at this time on the verge of separating from Nigeria as a result of wide-spread victimization and the slaughters of Igbos in the North, were not a part of it. In fact, as the previous chapter stated, the East eventually seceded, prompting a three-year Civil war that ended in 1970. Similarly, Gowon's most memorable and most significant act in office—the breaking up of the all-powerful regions into twelve states in 1967, was one in which the Igbos, in particular, had no say. In fact, as previously noted, an immediate objective of that exercise was to thwart the East's impending secession by dividing the Easterners and giving their "minority" populations the long-sought states of their own. Despite the foregoing, Joseph takes a different view of this question of the representational outlook of Gowon's governance. He believes that "from the time Gowon came to power in July 1966, . . . the Nigerian military could claim to have given the country governments that were highly national in representation."[180] Obviously, Joseph overlooks or fails to capture the implications of the circumstances of Gowon's early years in office.

As I have argued earlier, the fact that the state-creation act was, in part, an anti-secessionist bid, does not dilute its significance as a measure whose effects contributed toward the political integration of Nigeria. It was also a success as a tactical manoeuvre against secession, for it robbed the Igbo war effort of the vital support of the Eastern minorities. Thus, to the detriment of the Igbos, the war became largely a war between the Igbos and the rest of Nigeria. We have also seen that the twelve-state structure had the overall effect of tilting the balancing of forces in Nigerian politics from the centrifugal to the centripetal. The action also stands out as evidence of a clear sense of mission in the national interest on the part of Gowon's political leadership. It also signifies the political leadership's capacity and willingness, at least during its earlier life, to give life to its policies and programs.

The same deserves to be said about Gowon's dogged prosecution of the war to keep Nigeria one. There is no question that the Igbos were terribly victimized and in fact pushed into secession; but it is also undeniable that Gowon quashed the secession and thus preserved Nigeria as one nation. Gowon's victory did not compensate for the victimization that the Igbos had suffered, but the fact remains that it kept Nigeria one. An resolved question remains, however. Would Nigeria have achieved a solid national healing if Gowon's government had compensated the Igbos at the end of the Civil War, for the heavy economic losses that they sustained fighting a defensive war that they had to wage because of the national government's inability or unwillingness, at the critical time, to guarantee the safety of the lives of Igbos in other parts of the Nigerian nation?

It is somewhat difficult to answer the question as to whether the political elite of Nigeria for the first three years of Gowon's rule was cohesive and collectively committed to the general welfare of the country. This is so because Nigeria was divided and engaged in a civil war. With the nation thus polarized and spilling blood, one cannot write about a Nigerian elite's cohesion or commitment to this or that in the face of the existence of two warring nations within the body politic.

It is, therefore, much more logical to apply those questions to post-war Nigeria. With the war over in 1970, Gowon's government embarked on a three-legged policy of rehabilitation, reconstruction and reconciliation. Gowon's first major post-war act in the national interest was his swift move to re-integrate the Igbos into Nigeria by declaring a General Amnesty. The policy declared that there had been no victor and no vanquished as a result of the war. As Gowon put it in his broadcast to the nation soon after the war,

> We guarantee the security of life and property of all citizens in every part of Nigeria and equality in political rights. We also guarantee the right of every Nigerian to reside and work wherever he chooses in the Federation, as equal citizens of one united country. It is only right that we should all henceforth respect each other. We should all exercise civic restraint and use our freedom, taking into full account the legitimate rights and needs of the other man. There is no question of second class citizenship in Nigeria.[181]

This helped to calm the nerves of Igbos who had feared a federal government reprisal. By and large, the nation followed the preceding tone and policy with the exception of the Rivers State which, for a while, refused to allow the "returning" Igbos to reclaim their pre-War property. So, in a sense, it could be said that the political elite, by rallying behind Gowon's post-war charge, manifested benevolence and concordance. As Obasanjo puts it, "the task was honorably discharged by all Nigerians in form of relief, rehabilitation, reconstruction and reintegration . . . to the amazement of friends and foes alike."[182] The rehabilitation, reconstruction and reconciliation program could not have succeeded if the political elite and the masses had not acted in unison. That is, in this regard and as at this time period, the political system was evidently relatively communicative.

As time went on, however, things began to slide under Gowon's leadership. The purposefulness, the benevolence, the concordance, etc that characterized the political system in its intermediate, post-war life began to give way to "a deepening sense of political decay, indecisiveness and corruption."[183] In 1970, Gowon launched a nine-point program for the social transformation of the country, but this program remained mere paperwork for the duration of his administration. Allegations of corruption against prominent members of Gowon's government like Minister Joseph Tarka and against some of the state governors could not have given his regime a Maatic appearance. In the case of Tarka, Gowon acted wisely by forcing him to resign his ministerial position, but he erred when he subsequently acquitted a state governor, Joseph Deshi Gomwalk of Benue-Plateau State, of allegations of wrong doing without any known investigation.[184] Even though Gowon is believed not to be personally corrupt (he reportedly lives on a modest pension),[185] he should have acted swiftly and unequivocally against corruption. He should have remembered that Prime Minister Balewa had offended the nation by turning a deaf ear to public complaints about corruption on the part of some members of his government. Herein lies another manifestation of the effects of inadequate historical consciousness on the part of political leadership.

The leadership became less communicative to the point of being accused that he was no longer consulting members of the highest policy-making and legislative body—the Supreme Military Council. Furthermore, Gowon punctured the credibility of his administration by reneging on his promise to return power to civilians by 1974. There were even reports that the Head of State had lost control of the state military governors—his own very appointees. This only added to the sense of indiscipline and paralysis that gripped the body politic in the evening of Gowon's regime as exemplified by the near collapse of such public utilities as the national electricity production and distribution system. This period marked the beginning of Nigeria's long and continuing experience of power outage.

Because of general shortcomings in the public adherence to and enforcement of the rule of law, Nigerian military leaders saw it as a duty to instill a sense of discipline in the body politic by making "discipline" a key theme in their messages to the nation. But this theme of discipline was not characteristic of Gowon's leadership in its last years.[186] Thus, Gowon, who had started off on a right foot ended up on the wrong foot. As Joseph comments: "Gowon's evolution into an imperial, though no dictatorial, president stood in marked contrast to the modest soldier who had steered Nigeria through the perilous days of the civil war."[187] An imperial presidency, like oil, does not mix with the water of populism. Like Ironsi, Gowon's leadership did not have the markings of populism.

However, despite the decline in Gowon's leadership in its later years and despite its neo-colonial flirtations with Britain and its followership rather than leadership role in African Affairs,[188] there is no question that by 1975 the country was closer to integration and less unstable than it was when Gowon assumed the mantle of leadership in 1966. He lost power to a palace coup which took place in July 1975. This coup ushered in Brigadier Murtala Muhammed as the third military ruler of Nigeria.

Brigadier Murtala Muhammed (July 1975–February 1976)

Like General Ironsi, Brigadier Murtala Muhammed had a short but eventful (in fact, a much more eventful) tenure as Nigeria's military Head of State. The coup d'etat that removed Gowon and ushered in Muhammed was popularly received. As Bolaji A. Akinyemi notes, Gowon was charming and likeable but his policies turned Nigerians against him.[189]

In the forty-five years of Nigeria's self-rule, no Nigerian leader has projected a more purposeful political leadership than Muhammed. Being a military government that ruled by decrees and was exempt from judicial review and the long-winding scrutiny and even veto of an elected legislative body, Mohammed's administration was able to act with the kind of speed and dispatch which, perhaps, an equally motivated civilian government could not have mustered.

It is, therefore, more reasonable to compare Mohammed's leadership with a fellow military government like that of his predecessor because they possessed the same advantageous and almost unfettered capacity to rule by decree. Through such comparism, it will be seen that Mohammed's purposefulness, dedication, vision and dynamism (that is, his leadership attributes) were, by and large, the factors that made all the difference.

In fact, the initial and most discernible accomplishment of Mohammed's leadership was the restoration of a "broad sense of purpose"[190] to the nation—a factor which had served as a justification for military intervention in Nigerian political life. The sense of indiscipline that had enveloped the nation in the dying days of Gowon's administration gave way to order in the body politic when Muhammed came onto the scene. A good illustration of the disorderliness that marked Nigeria's life was the hustle and bustle that took place at public places like bus stops, post-offices, banks, etc. Rather than queue up, Nigerians would push and shove their way to the bus, post-office or bank counter. This same disorderly behavior manifested itself in different forms when Nigerians tried to secure jobs, loans or any kind of access to economic and political opportunities. In like manner, in the arena of political competition, Nigerians would not hesitate to jump the queue—that is, to flout the rules, in order to secure victory. Nigerians were, in a way, habituated to not waiting for their turn. To some extent, the political leaderships were responsible for this behavior, for too often, by their acts, they made the public believe that "connections"[191] rather than merit, determined who could get what. Indiscipline, rather than discipline, became a norm of Nigerian life. The First Republic had its share of this tendency especially in the area of political competition. Indiscipline reigned supreme in the general life of Nigerians during Gowon's time, partly as a collateral effect of the three-year Civil War and partly as a consequence of inept leadership.

But during his short spell in office, Muhammed reversed this trend. By a set of tough measures, swift punishment of acts of indiscipline and acts of corruption, and exemplary conduct,[192] Muhammed restored order to the body politic. Gowon had paid mere lip-service to his pledge to eradicate corruption from the body politic. But, like a man of action, not just words, Muhammed mounted an all-out war against corruption (although there were complaints that the process had fallen short of the standards of due process). While he did not eradicate corruption, he dealt it a stinging blow. Hundreds of public servants found to have corruptly enriched themselves or inefficient and ineffective were removed from office. Public institutions and specific government programs were investigated. These probes revealed that abuse of office or official negligence was rampant in the previous administration.[193] State Governors and other public officers under Gowon were made to return ill-gotten wealth although Alaba Ogunsanwo has observed that the exercise was not thorough enough. Mohammed's probes, he says, left the former public officers with a lot of their loot on the grounds that given Nigerian circumstances such properties acquired beyond the legitimate earnings of the officials concerned might have somehow been acquired without real malpractices.[194] The fact remains, however, that Muhammed was the first leader to make any public officials regurgitate stolen property.

Furthermore, under Muhammed, a nation which a while ago seemed ungovernable became governable almost overnight! Nigerians could feel the pulse of effective political leadership. If they had only had it as a textbook experience or a dream, Muhammed made it a real life experience for them. Nigerians began to experience uninterrupted supply of electricity, which had seemed like utopia during Gowon's time; queues formed at bus stops, post-offices, banks, etc. The water fountain at Tinubu Square, the center of Lagos City, whose stoppage symbolized the paralysis that engulfed Gowon's leadership in its last years, began once again to flourish and glow under the blazing illumination of night light. The streets began to be cleared of refuse on a regular basis. It was like a modern day miracle. The engine of the nation buzzed anew like an automobile that had received a major "tune up."

On the external front, the impact of this new government was also felt. The erstwhile British echoes in Balewa's and subsequently Gowon's foreign policies gave way to a Nigerian voice, an Africa-centered voice which reverberated across the mighty halls of the U.N. General Assembly. The nationalist struggles that were going on at that time in Angola, Mozambique, South Africa, Cape Verde, Sao Tome and Principe got a mighty "jump start" as Nigeria doubled its material and moral support for them. In Angola, in particular, Nigeria stood up (to the chagrin of Western powers, particularly the United States) and rallied the O.A.U. behind the nationalist forces of the Popular Movement for the Liberation of Angola (MPLA), which were being threatened by the Western and South Africa-backed, reactionary forces of Jonas Savimbi's National Union for the Total Independence of Angola (UNITA).[195]

It felt good to be a Nigerian at this time. Shame gave way to national pride. Despair gave way to hope. "A can-do" spirit (as opposed to the notion of "nothing works here") became to show up in the expressions of Nigerians. Those of us who were teenagers at this time had the benefit of a good role model in the person of Muhammed.

All this was accomplished in less than one year. A government which had not been legitimately instituted, in no time became legitimate in the eyes of the people. Even though Muhammed was a moslem from the city of Kano in Northern Nigeria, he captivated and earned the respect, admiration and loyalty of the generality of Nigerians across ethnic and religious lines. He achieved this by making Nigerians feel that his leadership had a clear sense of mission in the national interest. By exposing and punishing corruption swiftly, he conducted a Maatic leadership that set a good example for Nigerians. In politics, once the followership is convinced that the leadership is above board, they are most likely to follow suit. Muhammed was not only laying the foundation for an ethical, that is, Maatic political culture, he was, at the same time, inducing a commitment to it through his dynamic and exemplary leadership. In his assessment of Mohammed's administration, Joseph observes accurately:

> Muhammed had given Nigerians the kind of national leadership they had never previously known. He was dynamic, stern and projected a sense of incorruptibility. In contrast to the slack administration of Gowon's final years in power, Murtala Muhammed gave the nation a sense of direction and action, especially in carrying out the nine-point program.[196]

As a matter of fact, what Muhammed essentially did was to set in motion the actualization of the objectives of Gowon's nine-point program. In that respect, his administration (that is, Mohammed's) was a benevolent political leadership. The aims of the 1970 nine-point program were:

1. The reorganization of the armed forces;
2. The implementation of the Second National Development Plan and Repair of the damage and neglect from the war;
3. Eradication of corruption;
4. The preparation and adoption of a new constitution;
5. Introduction of a new Revenue Allocation Formula;
6. The institution of a national population census;
7. Organization of genuine national political parties;
8. The institution of elections and the installation of popularly elected governments in the states and in the center; and
9. The establishment of a new federal capital.[197]

As soon as he took office, Muhammed wasted no time in setting the implementation process in motion. His policy formulation and implementation approach was based on the report and recommendations of commissions of professional and technical experts.[198] Although this was not necessarily a populistic approach to governance, by and large, the political elite as a whole, in a display of concordance, rallied behind him with the exception of Chief Obafemi Awolowo who reacted by saying that "it would be too much of a task for it [the military] to attempt to undertake the massive and never-ending task of rebuilding or reconstructing our body politic."[199]

An early action of Mohammed's administration, which earned it the acclaim of the public, was the creation of seven additional states. This brought the number of states in Nigeria to nineteen. One of Mohammed's first acts was to set up a time table for a program of transition to civilian rule. This time-table set October 1, 1979 as the date for returning power to civilian rule. A National Committee to draft a new constitution for Nigeria was set up. In his 1975 address inaugurating the Constitution Drafting Committee, Muhammed outlined "the norms of stable and harmonious democratic order in Nigeria."[200] However, Muhammed did not live to carry this and other programs to fruition. He was assassinated during an abortive coup in February 1976. Such was the positive impression which his short span in office had made on Nigerians that his killing provoked a nation-wide outrage and condemnation. This was a radical departure from the Nigerian tradition of celebrating the demise of their national leaders. Nigeria, at the death of Muhammed, felt like a baby who had been forcibly snatched away from his/her beloved mother. Muhammed in a short spell had given them a political leadership that was considerably purposeful, benevolent, concordant, communicative, Maatic and historically consciousness. His support for MPLA demonstrated that he was conscious of the history and methods of colonialism and neo-colonialism. His assault on corruption and his own image as an incorruptible leader were Maatic and also showed him as conscious of the Nigerians' fundamental abhorrence of corruption. Although Mohammed's policies and actions received mass acclaim and his government was cross-sectionally representative, his policy-formulation process cannot be described as populistic, for it was open only to the professional and technocratic class. In sum, his leadership not only brought Nigeria closer to national integration than ever before, it induced a new respect and belief in government on the part of the citizenry.

General Olusegun Obasanjo (February 1976 to October 1979)

General Olusegun Obasanjo, who had been Mohammed's second-in-command, became Head of State after his assassination. But Obasanjo, a Christian from the southwestern section of Nigeria, was, in a way, like Ironsi and Gowon, who had been propelled to power by a coup, a counter-coup or an abortive coup in which they had not participated. Such were the circumstances that surrounded Obasanjo's ascendancy that he came to be known as the "unwilling Head of State." A parallel of sorts can be drawn between Brigadier Ogundipe and General Obasanjo. Remember that Ogundipe, Ironsi's second-in-command, did not take over the office of Head of State when Ironsi was assassinated because he was "scared." Obasanjo was also "scared," but was talked out of his fear by General Theophilus Danjuma,[201] who was the Army Chief of Staff when Muhammed was assassinated in the abortive coup of February 1976. Here is the remainder of Danjuma's account of this episode:

> When Murtala [Muhammed] was killed during the Dimka coup, Obasanjo was so terribly devastated by the death that he told me that I should take over. I declined. He said he had to go because he worked so closely with Murtala, that he couldn't see himself sitting in that office and running the affairs of the country effectively. Besides, his confidence in the loyalty of the army was so shaken that he will find it difficult to depend on the same army while being head of state.[202]

Continuing this story of how Obasanjo became Nigeria's unwillingly military leader, Danjuma adds: "I told him [Obasanjo] that there was no question as to who was going to be number one. As for the army, I told him he should leave that to me. I would take care of the army."[203]

I quoted effusively from the preceding personal interview of Danjuma in order to illustrate two points. One, Obasanjo, despite his antecedent as a war commander, was portrayed as apparently lacking the high degree of courage and fearlessness needed for the tough, if not dangerous, terrain of African leadership. To an extent, that image of not being courageous enough dogged him throughout his tenure as Nigeria's military Head of State. Two, the Nigerian Armed Forces have continued to be dominated by the North since the assassination of Ironsi and the events that followed. Hence, Danjuma's rather conceited assurance to Obasanjo of his control over the army. This domination of the armed forces by one segment of the nation has had a chilling effect on Southerners, soldiers and civilians alike. Ogundipe was "chilled" to the oblivion of an ambassadorial position by this factor. It would appear that for a while after the death of Muhammed, Obasanjo was also "chilled," but Danjuma warmed him back to life.

Thus, it was against this backdrop that Obasanjo assumed the mantle of office after the assassination of Muhammed. As time went on, however, Obasanjo exhibited more and more confidence and eventually proved to be a purposeful leader who did his utmost to carry on from where Muhammed had left off. But, there was no doubt that he not possess the fiery dynamism of Muhammed. Joseph uses a more oblique characterization. As he puts it, Obasanjo was "more genial, conciliatory and even homely"[204] than Muhammed whom he labeled as "aristocratic" and "arrogant."[205] Considering Muhammed's tough foreign policy that placed a premium upon the African interests and rejected Western imperialism, Joseph's characterization of him as arrogant comes to me as no surprise. To the typical hegemonic Western mind, an "arrogant" Black leader tends to be one who, based on principles, stands up to the West and refuses to bow to their antics and selfish designs toward Africa. Did Joseph, a Euro-American scholar, find Muhammed arrogant because he had refused to bow to Washington on the issue of Angola? Muhammed had not only rejected Washington's conservative and neo-colonial policy on Angola, he went on to mobilize the rest of Africa against it. Such a man/woman perfectly fits the hegemonic Western mind's image of an arrogant Black man/woman.

Most discussions of Mohammed's and Obasanjo's leaderships treat them together as the Muhammed/Obasanjo administration. The justification for this comes from the fact that Obasanjo's four-year leadership was one that mostly carried out the policies that had been initiated when Muhammed was still alive. In fact, when Obasanjo took over, he stated that his posture would be to carry on from where Muhammed had left off. But any analysis that presents the two leaders as one administration is a flawed one because Obasanjo was a different leader from Muhammed. Hence, my decision to treat Obasanjo's administration as a separate Nigerian political leadership.

Like the military administrations that preceded it, Obasanjo's military leadership was not legitimately constituted. As for being cross-sectionally representative, Obasanjo's leadership went to great lengths to reflect that image. Joseph was rather excessively frank in discussing this: "As a Yoruba, and thus the only non-Northerner apart from General Ironsi to serve as leader of Nigeria's central government, Obasanjo avoided the latter's fate by never appearing as a benefactor of his linguistic group."[206] It is one thing (and it is desirable) for a leader not to want to be seen as treating preferentially the ethnic group with which he is affiliated, but it is another for him to give up a prerogative as his office as head of state in an apparent effort to project himself as being "detribalized." As later revealed by General Danjuma, it would appear that Obasanjo, as a military leader, consented to a political power sharing that effectively reduced him to the status of the Head of State of Southern Nigeria rather than the Head of the entire Nigerian State. While Obasanjo was head of state, his deputy was Brigadier Shehu Musa, a moslem who hailed from the northern section of Nigeria. According to Danjuma, as mandated by a body of military leaders, known as Service Chiefs, both men worked within the framework of a political power sharing by which Obasanjo provided the list of Southern Nigerians who were to be appointed to the boards of federal government corporations, and Brigadier Musa supplied the list of the Northerners to be appointed to such boards. In Danjuma's words, "We [meaning the service chiefs] asked General Obasanjo to prepare the list of prospective members from the south and Shehu, members from the north."[207] As the Head of State, the buck stops at Obasanjo's desk. He, not the service chiefs, should have had the last word on those federal jobs. The service chiefs, along with Obasanjo's second-in-command, should have submitted their recommendations to the Head of State. The Head of State should not have submitted himself to an arrangement, which implicitly reduced him to the head of state of Southern Nigeria. He did not help the cause of national integration by so doing. Rather, he played into the hands of centrifugal forces, particularly those Nigerians who project an impression that Nigeria's leadership is their birthright.

Nonetheless, Obasanjo's military leadership was eventually highly eventful. His greatest achievement, which exemplifies Obasanjo's clear sense of purpose in the national interest, was his successful implementation and supervision of an elaborate program for the transition to civilian rule in 1979. Obasanjo kept faithfully to this program, which was launched in 1975. When compared with the subsequent performance of General Ibrahim Babangida, who ended his administration in 1993 by not completing his own program for a return to civilian rule, the magnitude and significance of Obasanjo's success in this regard become more appreciable. The transition program being of course a program designed to return the civilians to power, the political elite in general stood behind Obasanjo during the period of the transition and thus throughout his administration. So, in this sense, the political system was appreciably benevolent and concordant. The administration was also communicative, for the nation at large was mobilized behind the transition program. Obasanjo has thus been described as an adept political ruler of Nigeria who adroitly "adjusted his actions to satisfy, as well as control, the demands of Nigeria's culturally disparate peoples."[208]

Although he was also seen as above-board, Obasanjo, as a military leader, did not come across as an activist crusader against corruption. So, not much was heard on this sensitive issue during his time as a military head of the Nigerian state. This could lend itself to three possible explanations: (1) he was able to plug the loopholes in the Nigerian body politic that had allowed for large-scale corruption; (2) given his self-effacing nature, he did not dramatize his actions against corruption;[209] or (3) he simply did not make the issue of corruption a priority. In fact, it has been pointedly stated that while Obasanjo's leadership succeeded in substantially implementing the nine-point program, it could not nail the coffin of corruption. This line of reasoning holds that during this regime, corruption was practiced mainly by "public and private intermediaries"[210] rather than by army officers. Obasanjo's one visible step against corruption was his setting up of a Public Complaints Commission with headquarters in the federal capital and branches in the states. But his administration did not want to take its own medicine, for before leaving office the Obasanjo administration promulgated a decree barring the succeeding government from investigating the military for corruption.[211] What could one make of this?

Be that as it may, Obasanjo deserves credit for leaving behind a positive balance of five-point one billion dollars in the nation's account at the end of his rule in October 1979. The significance of this comes out when one recalls that the administration which succeeded him left the nation with a total of twenty six billion dollars in external and internal debts.[212] Given this fact alone, Obasanjo's political leadership could be said to have emphasized "clean governance" and accountability, which are Maatic values.

Even then, Obasanjo's leadership does not score highly on the issue of economic management. In fact, this is an area where his administration is believed to have fallen short of expectation although Obasanjo did launch massive economic projects made possible by huge surpluses from petroleum exports. The leadership also strengthened the economic indigenization program started by Gowon's administration in 1972 although some Nigerians colluded with foreign business communities to circumvent the goals of the indigenization process.[213]

Even though Obasanjo introduced an egalitarian program such as the Land Use Decree of 1978, which was designed to produce a reasonable land tenure system, check land speculation and reduce endless litigation over individual and communal property rights, his policy-formulation and implementation process was not anywhere near being described as populistic. The process reveals little or no input from the masses. The parties involved in Obasanjo's policy formulation and implementation process were the ruling military personnel, civil servants, academics, the business elite and even the foreign entrepreneurial establishment.[214]

Obasanjo was desirous to place Nigeria on the path of self-sustaining development. Hence, his agricultural revitalization scheme known as "Operation Feed the Nation." As one evaluator puts it, this program demonstrated the leadership's commitment to the 'higher national interest'[215] of Nigeria. All of these, of course, give the leadership an image of one that was benevolent.

However, one momentous objective of the nine-point program which Obasanjo did not address was that of a new national census. Given the critical importance of this subject and its impact on the evolution of Nigerian politics, Obasanjo's failure to tackle it stands out as a major omission. It, no doubt, as usual, had a ripple effect on the ebb and flow of the politics of the Second Republic.

In the foreign policy area, Obasanjo maintained a much more restrained version of the Africa-centered posture initiated by Muhammed; his approach lacked the dynamism and active personal involvement of his predecessor.[216] In fact, Ray Ofoegbu reports that under Obasanjo, Nigeria "took rapid, firm but quiet and undramatic steps to change the direction of foreign policy initiated by Murtala Mohammed."[217] Despite that, it can be argued that Obasanjo's leadership exhibited consciousness of African history and the need to liberate it from its history of colonial control. In fact, even though Obasanjo had tuned down the dynamism of the foreign policy posture initiated by Muhammed, he still steered it along the path of Africa-centeredness. Akinyemi credits Obasanjo with turning Nigeria into a Mecca of liberation fighters and making Nigeria a frontline state in the African liberation struggle.[218] Under Obasanjo, Nigeria, by a set of sticks and carrots, actively assisted the Zimbawean liberation war and also prodded Britain into a commonsensical position on Zimbabwe independence.

In 1979, Obasanjo handed the mantle of leadership over to an elected civilian administration headed by President Shehu Shagari. From all intents and purposes, Obasanjo's leadership sought to advance Nigeria toward the twin objectives of social transformation and national integration. The nation that he handed over to Shagari in 1979, despite the fact that the presidential election was not without blemish, was less prone to political instability and more amenable to political integration than what he inherited by chance in 1976. In retrospect, Ogunsanwo contends that Obasanjo's leadership is partly to blame for the failure of the civilian government that succeeded it. He faults Obasanjo's leadership for not seriously addressing "the question of what governance is for."[219] Ogunsanwo's critique seems somewhat uncharitable, considering Obasanjo's elaborate preparation, including a new Constitution with all sorts of safeguards against governmental abuse and corruption, for the transition to civilian rule. As the next discussion will demonstrate, no matter how elaborately a Constitution seeks to prevent corruption and poor governance, if it is operated by the wrong set of leaders under a near-norm less political environment, the document will not exact the effect that it was designed to bring about.

President Shehu Shagari (1979 to 1983)

Alhaji Shehu Shagari, a moslem from the northern section of Nigeria, won the military-supervised presidential election of 1979, which was contested by five candidates. He took over the reigns of government on October 1, 1979 amidst an under-current of bitterness generated by a last-minute dispute over whether he had in fact been duly elected to office. The 1979 Constitution of Nigeria required that for a candidate to become president he/she must win at least 25 percent of the votes cast in at least two-thirds of the states of Nigeria.[220] By 1979, Nigeria had nineteen states, and the Federal Electoral Commission had, in compliance with the two-thirds stipulation, required that a political organization should have offices in at least thirteen states of the federation in order to be officially registered. In the election, Shagari obtained 19.94 percent, instead of twenty-five percent of the votes in the thirteenth state. So, the runner-up party in the election, the Awolowo-led Unity Party of Nigeria (UPN) asked for a court injunction to restrain FEDECO from declaring Shagari as the winner of the election. The Supreme Court of Nigeria ruled that two-thirds of the states amounted to twelve two-thirds and thus Shagari had satisfied the Constitutional requirement for election to the office of president. The UPN could not "get over this"—to use a typical American expression. So, antagonism characterized the attitude of its federal legislators and state governors toward the president during the Second Republic.[221] In fact, Nwabueze notes that the controversy over the outcome of the 1979 election obstructed the operation of true federalism in Nigeria.[222]

In a reincarnation of the political alignments of the First Republic,[223] the president's party, the Northern (Hausa/Fulani)-dominated National

Party of Nigeria (NPN) formed an alliance with the Eastern (Igbo)-dominated Nigerian Peoples Party (NPP). Through this NPN-NPP Accord, which, as in the First Republic, left the Western (Yoruba)-dominated Unity Party of Nigeria (UPN) in political isolation,[224] the president obtained a legislative majority that enabled him to side-track what would have been a legislative deadlock during the Second Republic.

Thus, this was the background against which Shagari steered the Nigerian ship of state between 1979 and 1983. As we have seen, the government was legitimately constituted, and it was, to some extent, cross-sectionally representative. In fact, the 1979 Constitution required that the president should reflect the federal character—that is, the ethnic and religious diversity of the nation—in federal appointments. By and large, this was reflected in Shagari's ministerial appointments; he appointed at least one minister from each state. But Nwabueze holds that it was merely at this level that President Shagari met the "federal character" Constitutional stipulation. In other key federal appointments, Shagari showed little or no evidence of federal character. Strategic ministries and commissions were led by presidential appointees from the North who, in most cases, were Moslems. "The South is apt to feel alienated by this,"[225] Nwabueze suggests.

Did Shagari exhibit a clear sense of mission in the national interest? Did he have the capacity and willingness to give life to his policies and programs? In terms of intentions, Shagari, going by his pronouncements, probably meant to render valuable service to the nation, but he turned out a colossal failure. In fact, it is not an exaggeration to say that Shagari is the worst of the Nigerian leaders discussed in this chapter. One ex-military leader did not mince words about this: "It was the politicians who killed the Second Republic. Particularly, it was the inefficiency of President Shagari that killed the Second Republic. They [also] killed the economy."[226]

Despite that performance, Shagari did not hesitate to seek a second term. In any case, by seeking the presidency, even for a second time, Shagari demonstrated that he had the will to lead, but he sorely lacked the capacity for the job he coveted.

It could be argued that a certain degree of centrifugal forces worked against Shagari's leadership, but they will always do so in Nigeria's socio-political life. But if a given political leadership demonstrates the attributes contained in the Afrocentric/Africa-centered theory of political and integrative leadership, a healthy balance could be struck between the centrifugal and centripetal forces in the Nigerian body politic. Under Shagari's leadership, the political elite was almost as fractured as it was during the First Republic. The existence of five political parties, all of which were represented in the federal legislature, was itself a source of tension and conflict.

Tension and conflict are an integral part of multi-party politics, but the kind of tension and conflict which characterized the Second Republic were anti-Systemic. Incidentally, Shagari's headache did not come from the federal legislature, which did approve his bills with minimum delay.[227] The strain in the political system occurred primarily in federal-state relations. One primary source of it was the fact that in the eyes of the non-NPN politicians, Shagari had been illegitimately foisted on the presidency. But another source of the antagonism is that old Nigerian vice known as tribalism. Nwabueze opines that with the qualified exception of the National Party of Nigeria (NPN), the president's party, the other parties were ethnic in character. "Without truly integrative national parties which cut across tribal, cultural and linguistic divisions, federalism will continue to be viewed largely as 'a bargaining arrangement for interest groups." Note that the problem that Nwabueze just identified had occurred despite all the safeguards that the authors of the 1979 Constitution had put in place to prevent it. They had written provisions requiring that future political parties must be nationally based—must cut across ethnic and religious lines. In enforcing that stipulation, the federal electoral commission had registered only those political associations that were able to set up offices in at least two-thirds of the states of the federation. But poor political leadership compounded this situation. For instance, Shagari antagonized and polarized the political elite, almost across the board, by appointing Presidential Liaison Officers (PLOs) for the states. These officers were perceived as alternative governors.[228] By this administrative act, Shagari negated rather than promoted concordance in the political system. The governors resented the PLOs as a sort of encroachment on their political territories. Worse still, the president indulged in a partisan use of the Nigerian police force. In fact, this federally-controlled police force was notable for its "hostile" attitude towards the governments of non-NPN states.[229] Specific consequences of the tension between the President and the non-NPN states include on the one hand, the questionable impeachment of the governor of a non-NPN state, the federal jamming of the television station of a non-NPN state government, and on the other, a UPN governor's demolition of federal government housing units in his state.[230] In other words, the President was not the only culprit in this "cold war" between the federal government and the non-NPN state governments. In these cases, the political leadership made a mockery of the rule of law. In jamming the UPN state television station, Shagari flagrantly disobeyed a court injunction against the action.[231] There were instances where federally-appointed, state police chiefs disobeyed the orders of state courts. These and similar incidents involving the federal police and the non-NPN state governments prompted a charge that the police had been politicized and converted into a tool of intimidation and harassment against political opponents of the president.[232] This obviously had no value for national integration. Nwabueze writes:

> Any system which makes possible a situation in which a government and the primary instrument for law and order are at loggerheads, to the point of open hostility waged publicly on the pages of newspapers, holds but a gloomy prospect for the future.[233]

The police affair reflects poor political leadership more than anything else. The abuses that occurred during the First Republic when the police were decentralized,[234] had led to the centralization of the Nigerian police force in the hope that this would insulate the force from political manipulation. But alas, the hope was dashed! Thus, what could one make of it? Centralized or not centralized, the police force will continue to be manipulated as long as mischievous politicians are in charge. Had Shagari resisted the temptation to use the police to advance his political ends, federal-state relations would probably have been less tense. On the other hand, if, given the highly polarized state of politics in the Second Republic, a federal police force had existed side by side with a local government police force, there would have been a "police civil war" in the country.

Shagari also demonstrated open disrespect for the rule of law when he deported the Majority Leader of a non-NPN State Assembly on the ground that he was a foreigner and that he constituted a threat to the national security of Nigeria. The deportation was carried out with immediate effect without the deportee being given a chance to challenge the charges against him. Ultimately, the Federal Court nullified the deportation, and it turned out that the charges against the deportee were false. Nwabueze observes: "The effect of the deportation was of course to deprive Shugaba of the right guaranteed to every Nigerian citizen to move freely throughout the country and to reside in any part of it (s. 38)."[235] This case, like the abuse of the police force and flagrant disregard of court orders, left a sour taste in the mouth: it illustrates Shagari's inclination toward autocracy and arbitrariness. This inclination could not have promoted national integration in Nigeria.

The public corruption that took place during Shagari's presidency was unparalleled in Nigeria's history despite the existence of a Constitutional Code of Conduct and the machinery for its enforcement—the Code of Conduct Bureau and the Code of Conduct Tribunal.[236] Ogunsanwo reports that Shagari's four-year tenure produced multi-millionaires and billionaires whose only source of wealth was mere membership of the ruling National

Party of Nigeria. A government that had inherited a positive balance of more than five billion dollars in Nigeria's external reserves in 1979, ended up four years later, with a deficit of twenty-six billion dollars as external and internal debts. Nigeria could not trace the whereabouts of seventeen point one billion dollars, which was part of the revenue it earned from exports between 1979 and 1983.[237] Thus, Shagari's political leadership was not Maatic. In fact, despite the massive nature of the loot that occurred during his presidency, Shagari did not punish or dismiss any of his lieutenants for corruption. By this omission, Shagari exhibited a glaring lack of historical consciousness, for similar inaction on the part of Nigerian leaders had earned them the disfavor and wrath of the populace.

Even though his government was an elected one, it is doubtful that the political leadership involved the masses of Nigerians in public policy formulation and execution. Their representatives in the national legislature were supposed to reflect the wishes of their people. Populistic governance means, in part, that the political leadership must not only be accountable to the people, but must be seen to be so. Furthermore, it means that: "genuine rather than superficial and pretentious, consultations take place at every stage of policy formulation, planning and implementation with local authorities, non-governmental organizations and village and neighborhood associations."[238] Going to the people only for votes at election times or simply maintaining contacts with opinion leaders who can help the politicians win votes does not represent genuine populistic governance. So, with the level of consultations described above, even an elected civilian government cannot claim to be governing populistically.

While it is conceivable that some of the political leaders of Shagari's era were decent and patriotic, the consequences of this period's political leadership did not endear Nigerians to civilian rulership. If the 1979 elections were marginally successful, the 1983 elections were a complete disaster. Accusing all the parties of rigging in this election, Nwabueze questions the two-thirds federal legislative majority which the NPN obtained from the 1983 elections. He writes:

> Although it was generally expected that President Shagari would be re-elected, perhaps with a slightly increased majority, it is significant that he increased his total score from 5,688,857 in 1979 to 12,081,471 in 1983 . . . and the number of states in which he scored 25 percent or more of the votes cas . . . from 12 to 16 . . . He was thus able to avoid the controversy which arose in 1979 as to whether, with 19.94% in the thirteenth state, his declaration by FEDECO as winner complied with the Constitutional requirement.[239]

Had political leadership paid heed to history, the temptation to rig and cheat during this election would, perhaps, have been resisted; the lure of public office and its perquisites would have been subordinated to the higher ideal of the national interest. The fact that the election malpractices had derailed the First Republic should have caused them to act with prudence and a sense of honor. If the politicians who perpetrated the massive election frauds of 1983 were actively conscious of their national history, they probably would have not allowed history to repeat itself: this was the second time the Nigerian civilian elite demonstrated that they could not effectively and honestly supervise their own elections. But alas, honor and dignity were mostly lacking; patriotism was lacking, and there was no demonstrable commitment to the national interest. A commitment to the national interest means: "a commitment to the survival of the state as a united, stable nation, a nation in which the effective maintenance of law and order as the basis of orderly social life is accepted as the common concern of all."[240] In light of this, it is little wonder that the 1983 presidential election turned out as it did. It heightened the political tension in the country; such was the extent to which Nigerians had lost faith in the political order that they began to openly advocate a military take-over of the government. Once again, questions began to be raised about the basis of Nigeria's constitution as one country—questions which had, at least, been driven underground or rendered untenable by the thirteen years of a military interregnum that had carefully sought to cement the bonds of unity in Nigeria.

Shagari's four-year stewardship of the nation turned back the hands of the clock. By the time he was driven from office by a military coup on December 31, 1983, Shagari had left the nation more disunited, more vulnerable to instability and close to actual disintegration. Shagari's presidency is the least purposeful, the least benevolent, the least concordant, the least populistic, and the least historically conscious of the six political leaderships surveyed in this chapter. To cap it all, his political leadership was simply unMaatic. Under his leadership, the virus of corruption permeated the fabric of the nation to unprecedented levels. Hence, the following observation by Nwabueze when he assessed the state of corruption in Nigeria in his copious evaluation of Nigeria's experiment with Presidential Democracy under Shehu Shagari. Corruption, he writes, "is all-pervading, running right through the entire body politic from top to bottom, from the head of ministry or department down to the messenger."[241] Although Nwabueze is somewhat hyperbolic, his observation, to a large extent, reflects how the generality of Nigerians felt about the depth of corruption during the reign of Shagari.

The preceding analysis has demonstrated a clear fact: the failings of Shagari's administration had more to do with defects in leadership than with the system itself (despite its shortcomings)—defects that became apparent when the leadership was subjected to the litmus test of the Afrocentric/Africa-centered theory of political and integrative leadership. As Nwabueze puts it, "the human factor" is largely to blame for the failure of the Second Republic.[242]

Chapter Six
A Comparative Summary and Recommendations

This chapter presents a comparative summary, findings and recommendations of this study. Among other goals, the chapter comparatively summarizes the preceding analyses of six Nigerian political leaderships. What differences and similarities exist in their philosophical outlook, policies, actions and results? Which of them was close to effective and integrative political leadership? This chapter also provides a break-down of the overall findings of the study, and closes with a set of recommendations.

A COMPARATIVE SUMMARY

Of the six political leaderships, which I examined through the prism of the Afrocentric/Africa-centered theory of leadership and political integration in the foregoing chapter, the short-lived administration of Murtala Muhammed is the most purposeful in the sense in which purposefulness was defined in this study. This may be a source of discomfiture for those students of politics who have a basic contempt for military rule. Yet, it seems that it is through the avenue of uninterrupted constitutional governance that the nation could forge a durable political system. In fact, at each instance in the previous chapter, I made it a point of duty to draw attention to the fact that the military administrations being analyzed had not been legitimately constituted. Nonetheless, the purpose of this study was not to compare and contrast military rule with civilian rule. The study's focus was on political leadership and its impact on the task of national/political integration.

While there is no doubt that the chance to rule by decree gives a military government an operational advantage over a civilian, democratic rule (given all its strictures and encumbrances), this study demonstrated that the capacity to rule by decree does not by itself guarantee effective political leadership. Yakubu Gowon's lackluster and directionless leadership (particularly towards its dying years), in contrast to Mohammed's dynamic, action-oriented, Africa-centered and visionary leadership (both administrations ruled by decree), eloquently illustrates this point. In 1970, that is, five years before he was overthrown, Gowon had launched a nine-point program of social transformation which, for the most part (with the exception of the rehabilitation, reconciliation and reconstruction project), did not move from the stage of mere paperwork to that of execution. Although General J.T.U. Aguiyi-Ironsi's administration, which preceded Gowon's and Muhammed's, was purposeful in terms of having a clear sense of mission in the national interest, its methods proved counter-productive. Imagery is important in leadership. Ironsi's use of a one-man commission to formulate a matter as delicate and as far-reaching in consequence as the structure of the country (that is, the substitution of federalism with unitarism) was a serious political miscalculation. Even though this was a military government, with its natural inclination toward dictatorship, the unitary system's decision was one that should have reflected a cross-sectional representation and should have been preceded by cross-sectional consultations in order to make it acceptable to the various segments of the country. So, instead of the one-man commission, there should have been a multi-ethnic and multi-religious panel. In effect, while to varying degrees, Ironsi's, Gowon's and Mohammed's political leaderships demonstrated a sense of mission in the national interest, Ironsi's had the misfortune of being perceived as ethnically biased partly because of the manner in which it handled the most important decision of the administration, namely the replacement of the federal structure with a unitary system.

Olusegun Obasanjo's military leadership compared well with Mohammed's and Ironsi's in purposefulness, but Mohammed's willingness and capacity to give life to policies and programs came across as more intense. This is more likely due to the low-key leadership style (what the Americans would describe as a laid-back style) of Obasanjo's, who otherwise, did perform an elaborate and dedicated service for Nigeria. In fact, nothing could better illustrate Obasanjo's dedication to the national interest than the unflinching manner in which he steered the nation back to civilian rule in 1979. He, nonetheless, lacked the dispatch and vigor of Muhammed, or at least came across as such. In the area of foreign policy, Obasanjo and Muhammed were basically Africa-centered in their goals, but like in domestic policy, Mohammed's Africa-centeredness was much more pronounced and unequivocal than Obasanjo's. At the bottom of the scale of purposefulness were the leaderships of Tafawa Balewa and Shehu Shagari even though, ironically, they were the only two legitimately constituted leaderships in contrast with the other governments which came to power through the barrel of the gun. Balewa and Shagari ranked closely poorly on the question of a clear sense of mission in the national interest. Granted that partisan politics is inescapable in multi-party politics, these leaderships, however, expended too much energy on partisan politics rather than the leadership of the nation in a statesmanlike fashion. To put it another way, Balewa and Shagari offered partisan leadership where statesmanship was called for. Two examples will suffice. Balewa's attitude towards the 1962 parliamentary crisis in the Western Region was indisputably partisan. Shagari's antagonistic relationship with the non-NPN states stemmed partly from the partisanship of the federally-controlled police. Even though Balewa's and Shagari's were elected governments with elected legislatures, neither had the image of being cross-sectionally directed. It is an irony of sorts that these elected governments were more guilty of projecting an image of being sectional in their handling of national affairs than the unelected, military governments, with perhaps the exception of Ironsi's administration, which had a similar image problem. While Shagari's foreign policy could be characterized as somewhat, if not minimally and pretentiously, Africa-centered, Balewa's had no such orientation (his was, in fact, a neo-colonial and British-flavored foreign policy). Nonetheless, Shagari's foreign policy was less Africa-centered than Gowon's, Mohammed's and Obasanjo's. Ironsi did not articulate or pursue any discernible foreign policy worth writing about. Of course, the domestic turmoil that engulfed Nigeria during his six-month rule was so intense that he barely could have had time to shape a foreign policy.

The most difficult question to tackle in the analysis relates to the construct of benevolence in political leadership. However, it could be deduced from the analysis that Muhammed and Obasanjo were more successful than the rest in mobilizing the political elite behind issues related to the general welfare of the nation. Their years in office seemed to be the most distinctive in terms of a period during which the political elite did not allow forces of disunity to divert attention from programs designed to promote national welfare. In terms of concordance, Mohammed's and Obasanjo's periods also witnessed sustained efforts by the political elite, under the active leaderships of Muhammed and Obasanjo, to launch the nation along the path of new norms, new goals, and new motivations. These efforts led to the formulation of a new national Constitution (which took effect in 1979) that expressed the desire of the political elite to re-create the nation politically. Given the direction in which Ironsi was going before he was assassinated, it seems that his leadership would have sought to mobilize the political elite in a similar fashion. Although Ironsi's government was initially received with nation-wide cheers, he was unable to sustain the momentum of goodwill. Balewa's and Shagari's periods were the worst in the areas of benevolence and concordance. In fact, the conduct of the political elite during Balewa's and Shagari's leaderships was anti-thetical to the goal of infusing the nation with new norms and values. During Shagari's years in office in particular, the political elite made a sheer mockery of the Constitutional instruments designed to guide the nation along the path of new political norms and values.

Similarly, Balewa's and Shagari's leaderships never achieved anything close to an elite consensus on almost any given issue. The fact that their regimes ended in chaos testifies to the absence of an effective apparatus for resolving conflict and enforcing discipline within the ranks of the political elite. In general, it is also hard to pin-point evidence of the Nigerian governing elite's consciousness of the collective nature of its civic responsibilities throughout the period of this study. General Danjuma was quick to comment on this in the interview that I cited earlier. He noted that the absence of cohesion or collective consciousness on the part of the political elite was so pronounced that some Nigerian politicians would rather lose political power to the army than to their civilian, political opponents. Bi-partisanship still eludes the Nigerian political elite. Further evidence that the political elite lacks consciousness of its collective duty to the nation comes from their tendency to indulge in unrestrained self-assertiveness that sometimes takes on an overly tribalistic tone.[1] Such rhetorical excesses were so pronounced during Balewa's administration that Balewa himself and President Azikiwe could not help chiding their political colleagues.

The communicative level of each of those leaderships—that is, the extent to which the political elite, specifically the ruling group, kept in touch with the masses—is another construct whose manifestation was somewhat difficult to assess. One of the factors that were highlighted in the literature review is that new nations like Nigeria are noted for a yawning gap between the elite and ordinary folk. Factors responsible for this gap include the elite's Western education (which tends to set them ideologically apart from the masses), their proclivity to address the masses in Western languages, and their internalization of negative Western values and tastes.

It was said that the terminology of the elite is one that the masses can hardly cope with. Tanzania solved this problem by adopting Ki-Swahili as its national language. Nigeria has tried to bridge this language gap between the elite and the masses and simultaneously promote national cohesion by requiring schools to teach the three major Nigerian languages of Hausa,

Igbo and Yoruba, in addition to English. Schools, in a given linguistic zone, are also expected to teach the local language of that zone. In addition, the Constitution provides that the national legislature should employ the three major Nigerian languages and English in its deliberations. Nigerian radio and television broadcasting stations do carry local language translations of their English broadcasts, including government policies and programs.

Since this study has not carried out an empirical survey of the level of elite-mass gap in Nigeria, the most practical way to determine the extent of the problem is to use, as the unit of measurement, efforts which given political leaderships made in order to communicate their goals and intentions to the public at large. For instance, during Balewa's leadership, the political parties campaigned hard to mobilize the masses for the 1962 and 1963 censuses. During the Second Republic, when Shagari was at the helm of affairs, politicians strove to maintain ties with their electorates and constituencies. So, it can be argued that those manifest desires of political office holders to reach the electorate during the elected regimes of Balewa and Shagari must have earned those administrations higher points on the question of grassroots communication than the military governments. Nonetheless, Mohammed's public acclaim could not have materialized if his leadership had not been communicative to a significant extent. Of all those leaderships, Ironsi's is the one whose intentions were the most mis-perceived by some sections of the country. So, in this sense, the communication gap between the leadership and the led was evidently pronounced.

These leaderships also performed poorly on the question of populistic leadership. Being elected governments, Balewa's and Shagari's had the best chance to involve the grassroots in public policy formulation and implementation. However, critical issues such as their national development plans were conceived and implemented in the most elitist fashion. Ironsi's leadership was perhaps the most guilty in this regard. Notice his use of a one-man commission to determine an issue as delicate and momentous as whether the nation should stay federal or go the way of unitarism. Gowon's, Mohammed's and Obasanjo's leaderships formulated policies through commissions of experts. Nevertheless, this still represented a top-down approach to policy formulation and implementation. Noteworthy in this regard is Ekekwe's point that the predominant ideology of the masses of Nigeria emphasizes solidarity and communalism. He elaborates: "Although this class is tied to national and international markets both as food or cash crop producers, this great involvement in the wider economy has yet to be reflected in its ideological perspective."[2] In effect, Ekekwe explains, a gap exists "between the present and concrete material circumstances of the Nigerian peasantry and the dominant elements of its ideological disposition."[3] While an African society like Tanzania has taken a definite step to construct a linkage between its development strategy and the grassroots ideology of solidarity and communalism, in the form of Ujamma,[4] the dominant trend in Nigeria appears to be away from such a perspective of development even though succeeding Nigerian leaderships have professed a commitment to an egalitarian philosophy of economic development.

The fact that public policies under various Nigerian leaderships have tended to go in a direction opposite the dominant ideological orientation of the grassroots reflects the lack of meaningful grassroots participation in policy formulation, let alone, policy execution. Thus, the six leaderships under study ranked low on this score.

The analyses in Chapter Five evaluated the Maatic question by the extent to which the leaderships efficaciously addressed the problem of corruption. Mohammed's administration did the most in this regard; Balewa's, Gowon's and Shagari's did the least. Obasanjo adopted a much more systematic approach like his creation of public complaints bureaus across the nation to entertain allegations of and complaints about corruption. However, his time did not witness the kind of frontal assault which Muhammed waged on corruption. In any case, a deeper aspect of this Maatic concept is its preventive dimension. Obasanjo's leadership used the federal radio to admonish the public to resist and abstain from corruption, but subsequently he contradicted himself and projected an image of a hypocrite by ending his administration in 1979 with a decree forbidding the in-coming government from investigating military personnel for public corruption. The corruption that ravaged the country during Shagari's time shows how worse this problem had grown in the country. Shagari did not provide any discernible leadership in this regard. Corruption will remain a major blight on the nation until a generation schooled early enough with Maatic values comes about.

As for historical consciousness, Mohammed's policies and actions, in the domestic and foreign arenas, gave him the image of a leader with a deep sense of not only his nation's history but of Africa's place in the global scheme of things. His prompt and unequivocal actions against corruption were indications that Muhammed recognized not only the negative impact of this malaise on the resources available for the nation's development, but also the fate that befell his predecessors who failed to do something noticeable about it. Mohammed's desire to see a new form of politics of unity, as shown by the promptness with which he set in motion the process for building a foundation for the Second Republic, is also a reflection of his consciousness of the cleavages that rocked the Nigerian ship of state. Ironsi was on the verge of a program for cleansing the stable before he was put to death; he was also on the verge of forging ahead with a program for the re-structuring of the nation's political structure for the sake of unity. Those elements suggest that he was conscious of the country's history of divisive politics. But his consciousness of Nigeria's history was severely limited—so limited, indeed, that he either was not aware of Northern region's fear of a Southern domination of the nation's civil service or he did not care about it. While Gowon showed acute consciousness of the effect of centrifugal forces on the nation's well-being, he, as well as Balewa and Shagari, did not seem to be adequately aware of the phenomenon of neo-colonialism. In fact, Balewa did more to strengthen neo-colonial in-roads into Nigeria than to weaken them. Witness his signing of the Anglo-Nigeria Defense Pact in 1960 by which Britain wanted to make a sham of the flag independence that it had granted the country the same year. But the most sordid expression of Balewa's accommodation of or insensitivity to neo-colonialism was his opposition to Nkrumah's proposition to turn Africa into a Commonwealth of states with one parliament as the most effective way of safeguarding Africa's independence and promoting Africa's development. Balewa led the so-called Monrovia Group's opposition that killed Nkrumah's bold program for Africa. Obasanjo's program of economic indigenization (which had been half-heartedly begun by Gowon), his contributions to the development of the Economic Community of West African States (ECOWAS), and his unalloyed support for the liberation struggle in parts of Africa, showed him as appreciably conscious of his national and African history.

FINDINGS OF THE STUDY

This study reveals that post-independence political leadership in Nigeria has, generally, fallen short of the expectations of the Afrocentric/Africa-centered theory of effective political and integrative leadership. In a sense, the study confirmed the **hypothesis** of this book, namely that if an Afrocentric philosophy of leadership (which promotes, among other factors, **the African Interest and African consciousness** as opposed to ethnic or clannish consciousness), becomes dominant on the Continent, it could facilitate the evolution of an Africa-centered political culture, which is necessary for effective leadership and political integration in African states. It confirmed the hypothesis because, as the study demonstrated, the closer a leadership came towards manifesting the ingredients of an Afrocentric/Africa-centered philosophy of leadership, the closer that leadership moved toward producing good governance and a politically integrated state.

The six cases, which I analyzed in the previous chapter revealed a mixture of strengths and weaknesses in how their policies, actions and philosophical outlook weighed on the scale of the theory. In other words, the six leaderships fell on various points on the scale of purposefulness, benevolence, concordance, communication, populism, maatic values and historical consciousness. Overall, the study found that the closer those leaderships were to meeting the constructs of the theory the closer the nation came to the goal of political integration. Conversely, the farther away they were from those constructs the less stable the nation became and the more the balance of centrifugal and centripetal forces tilted in favor of the former. The leaderships of Murtala Muhammed and Tafawa Balewa are the best illustrations of those two opposite ends; the former represents the first case, while the latter represents the second case.

The study found that the Nigerian political elite in general does not have a sense of cohesion and has not evolved a consensus on norms of political behavior. So fragmented is the Nigerian political elite along ethnic, religious, north/south and to some extent class lines that it could not present a bi-partisan response to Babangida's violation of a fundamental principle of democracy by his arbitrary cancellation of a presidential election. This was an occasion when SDP and NRC should have closed ranks in defense of a cardinal principle of representative governance, in defense of the national interest. See the chapter that discusses this matter in detail.

Another notable finding of the study is that colonial legacies have been as significant as leadership omissions and commissions in shaping the politics of the nation-state. Recall the extent to which the lop-sided federal structure, based on an outsized North (coupled with the distrust, bitterness and frustrations generated by disputed censuses), ravaged and haunted the First Republic like a ghost. That north-south factor, with its hydra-headed dimensions, exerted a ripple effect on subsequent events in the country. To this day, the census controversy has not been resolved to the satisfaction of the various segments of the country. As Nwankwo pointed out, this census question really lies at the heart of the deep problems of the nation. Besides colonial legacies, external, neo-colonial forces have also impacted upon the fortunes of leadership in Nigeria. Notice the duplicitous role of the British in the coup and counter-coup of 1966. Notice Minister Waziri's (of the First Republic) explicit concern, if not fear, of potential external opposition to any initiative to steer the nation toward the path of economic nationalism. Notice the West's anti-party toward the nationalistic and bold leadership of Muhammed. This same kind of Western hostility visited Patrice Lumumba of the Congo, known for his profound sense of nationalism and Pan-Africanism. Abdel Gamel Nasser, that Egyptian ardent nationalist, experienced the same kind of Western hostility for daring to place the national interest of Egypt in the forefront.[5] The West did not take kindly to Kwame Nkrumah's enthusiastic commitment to Pan-Africanism.

As Davidson noted, neo-colonialism has visible and invisible dimensions. Ohaegbulam drew attention to the fact that external forces instigate, arm and finance insurgencies against patriotic African governments. Nzongola-Ntalaja provided a good illustration of neo-colonial intervention in African affairs by his exposition of CIA's mentorship and subsequent coronation of Mobutu Sese Seko as leader of the Democratic Republic of the Congo (formerly known as Zaire). It is equally worthy of note that African activist leaders like Muhammed and Thomas Sankara of Burkina Faso, experienced very short spans in office.

The study also found that most of the gains of independence in the area of economic nationalism have been eroded by the neo-colonial instrument of orthodox Structural Adjustment Programs. Across the continent, including Nigeria, these programs depressed local productive capacities, lowered standards of living, worsened the costs of living, and deepened the underdevelopment or dependency of the continent. The study illustrated these negative outcomes of IMF's structural surgery with the case studies of Nigeria, Zaire (now, the Democratic Republic of the Congo), Senegal and Zimbabwe. The sum total effects of these programs threatened the very stability of African society, and thereby exposed the continent to a worse state of insecurity than has ever been the case since the colonial partition of Africa in the 19th century.

It does not take a rocket scientist to recognize that the economic resources available to a government affect its ability to be purposeful. Therefore, the debilitating overall effect of IMF-sponsored Structural Adjustment Programs can only complicate the environment in which leadership is exercised on the continent. No political leadership, not matter its goodwill, can keep the loyalty of its citizenry in the face of unbearable economic conditions. So, SAP has rendered African political leadership more, not less, difficult. In fact, my evaluation appears to represent a mild assessment of the picture. Consider the following assessment provided by none other than Adebayo Adedeji, a former Executive Secretary of the United Nations Economic Commission for Africa (ECA). Adedeji believes that SAP has, in fact, wiped out the post-colonial gains of Africa. In his words,

> We have two or three generations of children whose future has been destroyed by structural adjustment programs. So this is not mere statistics, we are talking about 600 million people whose lives have been played upon by bureaucrats who don't know anything about Africa.[6]

This grim reality of contemporary Africa has noteworthy implications, including the fact that it is also difficult for people to maintain their commitment to probity, honesty and fairness in tight economic conditions. In short, economic hardship increases human temptation to contravene cherished moral codes. So, a Maatic political culture cannot flourish in the midst of economic misery. Economic scarcity also exacerbates other human vices such as ethnic or clannish discrimination. Thus, SAP threatens to weaken whatever level of concordance African political elites have achieved. Senegal stands as a good illustration of how the economic difficulties and privations brought about by SAP gave rise to separatist yearnings in an otherwise tranquil polity. We also saw how SAP sapped away the small class of African entrepreneurs that had evolved there since independence. By weakening Africa's potential for economic self-sufficiency and economic independence, SAP has, in effect, diminished African political power. Again, Adedeji's assessment is apt. Structural adjustment, he notes, has led to the collapse of African economies.

Decrying this situation, he adds ruefully:

> If you believe in the unity of humankind, people will be more serious and sorry for what has happened because of forcing those countries (because of their poverty) to undertake policies that have made their people poorer. How can you say that the only way I can help you is for you to go through a period of wretchedness and misery? How can you in clear conscience say that the best way to make you well is first of all to see you lying in your bed for days without medicine, without appropriate prescription? That is wickedness. It is indefensible.[7]

Adedeji could not be more correct. The situation is a cause for concern, for political power determines a people's ability to chart their own destiny. In this connection, it is pertinent to excerpt Walter Rodney's definition of political power:

> Power is the ultimate determinant in human society, being basic to the relations within any group and between groups. It implies the ability to defend one's interests and if necessary to impose one's will by any means available. In relations between peoples, the question of power determines maneuverability in bargaining, the extent to which one people respect the interests of another, and eventually the extent to which a people survive as a physical and cultural entity.[8]

That point is well-made, and it provides a context that illuminates the political implications of SAP's impact on African political economies.

Another notable finding of the study is that just as the North-South bi-polar politics of the First Republic of Nigeria had splintered the political class, the national economy had also evolved along regional/ethnic lines, thus forestalling the germination of a truly national economic class based on trans-ethnic consciousness and social cohesion. As it were, regional and ethnic coordinates polarized the emerging economic class. Related to this is the finding that the economic class that sprang up had owed its life to access to state resources rather than economic productivity.

The study also found that ethnicity, better known as tribalism in Nigeria, far from being a natural Nigerian instinct, is a social creation of colonialism, which, in the post-colonial era, is manipulated by self-centered and unpatriotic Nigerian political leaders. However, feelings of separateness, in the ironic midst of African cultural unity, have been nourished by linguistic differences, ethnically and religiously-based discriminations in the distribution of economic opportunities (a factor which in contemporary Nigerian parlance is sometimes described as *statism*), and the absence of visible, cultural symbols of unity due partly to a form of education that does not stress the Africanness of Nigeria's multiplicity of cultural centers.

Another significant finding of the study is that Nigerian political competition is motivated, to an appreciable degree, by class action (as opposed to the sheer desire to render national service), which this work described as the struggle by the elite for power, prestige, security and challenge. This finding holds that the nature of the interaction among four principal factors: ethnicity, class formation, a rapidly expanding state, and an electoral democracy accounted for the failures of Nigeria's First and Second Republics. In the course of this struggle, politics is reduced to a zero-sum and lawless pursuit. Constitutional injunctions are disregarded and ethnic and regional insecurities are intensified in a vicious cycle of ethnicity, violence and repression. Notice the large-scale public corruption that characterized the Second Republic despite all the safeguards against abuse of office which had been written into the 1979 Constitution.

The study also found that clashes between groups identified as Islamic fundamentalist movements and non-Moslems have become a significant contributor to the political disquiet in Nigeria and other parts of West Africa, like Senegal. In the case of Senegal, it was found that even though the Islamic fundamentalist movement receives external material support from some Arab oil-rich nations, harsh economic conditions in the affected countries like Nigeria and Senegal, created a fertile milieu for insurgency.

Another notable finding is that the Nigerian and the general African political scene is distinctively marked by the inability of the civilian establishment to control the armed forces—that is, the polity lacks the capacity to resist military usurpation of power. It was revealed that African armies were taking advantage of the security lapses in most polities in Africa. Even within this first decade of the twenty-first century, which continues an apparent flowering of democratic rule across the continent that began in the 1990s, we still witnessed the 2005 brazen action of the Togolese armed forces of installing their choice as that country's new leader (following the death of Africa's longest reigning leader, General Gnashingbe Eyadema) and the outright military take-over of power in Mauritania. In the particular case of Nigeria, this study indicated that the Nigerian political elite is so fragmented and mutually antagonistic that one faction would prefer a military take-over to losing political power to its civilian opponents. The inability of the NRC to close ranks with the SDP in support of a fundamental principle of democracy in the June 1993 ill-fated presidential election in Nigeria exemplifies this factor. By calling for a new election, instead of joining the SDP to demand that the military government should respect the judgment of the people, NRC assisted in preventing an elected civilian from taking office.

All this led to a *Vicious Circle in Nigerian politics in particular and African politics in general*: incessant military interventions in politics obstructed the maturation process of the political class. This is because the military interventions did not allow the political class enough time to mature. However, at the same time, the mistakes, omissions and commissions of civilian leaders, while in office, due partly to their political inexperience, provided what the military often cited as the reason for intervening in politics. It is like punishing a student for not passing a test for which he/she has not been given sufficient preparation time.

It was also found that one of the reasons for political corruption in Nigeria is that the political class has all but abandoned traditional cultural values which place a premium on hard work, tolerance, good neighborliness and honesty. Traditional society abhorred and punished misuse or stealing of community property. However, it was reassuringly revealed that this strict moral code still endures within the rural community.

It was found that policy formulation and implementation in Nigeria is not based on popular participation. The context of socioeconomic development has been marked by an over-centralization of power. Nonetheless, Babangida's creation of more than five hundred local administrations represented a step in the right direction of bringing about popular participation in government. Their number has since risen to more than seven hundred.

Finally, there is a question as to whether a single party system, a two-party system, as provided by the 1989 Revised Constitution of Nigeria, or a multi-party system, which exists now in Nigeria[9] with more than 30 registered political parties, stands a better chance of promoting political integration. One of the realizations of this study is that in the final analysis political integration depends more on the existence of a consensus among the political elite on the norms for political behavior and a commitment on their part to a pattern of political conduct legitimized by those norms than on the number of active political parties in the polity. In effect, the critical factor here is really the existence of a normative consensus for political behavior and an adherence to it by the political practitioners of the day, for as Adedeji puts it, "democracy is cultivating a culture, a way of life which builds into it accountability, transparency, good governance, integrity, and enables you to arrive at decisions through consultation, through consensus."[10] Without those variables, neither a single party system, a two-party system, nor a multi-party system can guarantee political integration and stability, nor what we call democracy. Democracy is not equivalent to a multiplicity of political parties. Tanzania's late visionary leader, Julius Nyerere echoed this position. In a similar tone, Adedeji adds that "democracy is not pluralism, as some people in the West tend to think."[11]

RECOMMENDATIONS

In view of the preceding findings, the following recommendations are logical.

1. Nigerian political leaderships should strive to be more purposeful. Unfortunately, the economic conditions created by IMF-sponsored Structural Adjustment Programs as from the late 1980's made it difficult for a genuinely purposeful leadership to be appreciated or seen as such by its people. However, it behooves the leadership not to permit itself to pursue an economic policy or program which, like SAP, could weaken the economic well-being of the people. The African Interest should serve as the yardstick for the decisions of African political leadership. The philosophical outlook, policies and actions of African political leaders and policy-makers should primarily seek, pursue and advance the African interest.

2. There is a need for a true commitment to the general welfare of the nation on the part of the political class. A true love for public service is needed, as opposed to what seems like the class action motivation of many a Nigerian political aspirant.

3(a). The political elite needs to find a sense of cohesion, and also needs to develop a healthy respect for the Constitution and the Law in general. Constitutional mechanisms for conflict resolution did not work well either in the First Republic or in the Second Republic because the operators of the system seemed more interested in circumventing the rules than in complying with them. Notice how population figures and the electoral procedures and instruments were deliberately manipulated during the First Republic. In the case of elections, history repeated itself during the Second Republic. Who ever said that history does not repeat itself? If that person is reading this book, he/she should pay an educational visit to Nigeria. Notice that the rules of competition have been violated, not necessarily out of ignorance, but intentionally, for selfish gains at the expense of the nation. Leadership needs to strive to be inclusive and to avoid actions and pronouncements that have the potential of making a segment or segments of the polity feel excluded from the scheme of things. The Nigerian political elite needs to cultivate a sense of bi-partisanship which could enable them to close ranks and subordinate their party partisan interests in favor of the national interest. Had SDP and NRC done this in the case of the June 12, 1993 presidential election, the outcome of the crisis might have been different; the military government might have been forced to bow to the will of the people by affirming the outcome of the June 12 presidential election.

3(b). In order to facilitate the evolution of a sense of concordance among the political elite, a National House of traditional rulers (herein after referred to as the *HOUSE OF OBEMALA*)[12] is hereby recommended. This House will fill a vacuum that exists in Nigeria's political structure—that is, the lack of a nationally-oriented cultural symbol of unity. This house will also serve as a substitute for the priest in traditional African society. In traditional society, the priest plays a key role in the investiture of the king or queen, and religion and politics are interwoven. The priest puts the king through an elaborate ceremony designed to spiritually invigorate him and to instruct him on his sacred duties and obligations to the people, including the living and ancestral populations. It is a ceremony that helps to teach the new king that he is the spiritual leader of the nation, its symbol of honor and pride, and its guardian of peace, happiness and prosperity. Note that the fact that the King in traditional society is both the spiritual and political leader of the nation means that in that society there was no formal distinction between religion and politics.[13] The establishment of a national house of traditional rulers could help reconnect, at least symbolically for a start, the national political system with the indigenous political culture, which in its various manifestations, had been subordinated and discredited by colonial rule. In other words, this house will represent a symbolic re-linkage between the contemporary political structure (which had taken off largely on the British colonial train) and the indigenous political culture. It could serve to remind political leadership of its spiritual and sacred obligations to the nation-state—a potential instrument for promoting accountability in governance. The head of the House of Obemala, who shall be known as the Obemala of Nigeria, will perform the duty of swearing-in a duly elected president.[14] Indeed, traditional African society did not separate the temporal world from the religious, and the king served as both the mediator between his kingdom and the supreme universe and the guarantor of the social order. It was the intrusion of Islam and Christianity onto the African cultural landscape that brought about the dichotomy. In consequence,

> The king, more and more symbolized the secular with its implications of coercion and administrative impositions. Under the influence of religion, he would progressively be discredited and considered the very incarnation of Satan. What had created his spiritual force, was traditional religion; that, along with the cosmogony, justified his place in society.[15]

The House of Obemala will have the role of conferring national honors on leaders—from various walks of life—who have exemplified probity, patriotism, hard work and a commitment to the maintenance of the cultural integrity of Nigeria in particular and the African world in general. The House of Obemala will select its head from amongst its membership. He will be known as the *Obemala of Nigeria* during the period of his tenure. The Obemala can serve for ONLY one-term of ten years, and will be alternately chosen from the south and north, but in a manner that is inclusive of the component zones of the North and South. Neither the North nor the South can occupy the office for two consecutive terms. However, when it's the turn of the South or the North to present an Obemala of Nigeria, the new Obemala must be chosen from a Southern or a Northern zone different from the zone from which his predecessor originated. Such a requirement is designed to ensure that the diversity of the component zones of the North and South is reflected in the selection and rotation of the office of *Obemala of Nigeria*. The chief executive of the nation will render an annual report to the House of Obemala on the state of the nation in particular and that of the African world in general. The House of Obemala will meet three times a year, or as the national situation may warrant. The state will remunerate the members for the time they spent during such meetings and for the expenses they incurred to be able to attend the meetings. Members of the House of Obemala cannot be card-carrying members of political parties. The structure and functions of the existing national legislature will not be affected by the establishment of the House of Obemala.

    3(c). The House of Obemala will swear allegiance to the African Traditional Religion, (in addition to the Constitution of the Federal Republic of Nigeria), which will be adopted as the religion of the state. In this sense, a serving OBEMALA of Nigeria will also play the role of Chief Priest of Nigeria.

3(d). Since African traditional religions share fundamental principles as this study has shown, the adoption of the African traditional religion as the *STATE RELIGION* will serve as an additional cultural symbol of unity. This should be done without prejudice to the right of individual Nigerians to sub-scribe to other forms of religion. However, the adoption of the African Tra-ditional Religion as the *religion of the state* could help to stem the nation's drift toward sectarianism due to the polarizing influence of exogenous reli-gions on the sociopolitical life of the nation. If there is one area that has not yet been decolonized in Africa; it lies in the arena of religion. Recall Sekou Toure's earlier comment that the decolonization of African minds would require what he described as 'the total reconversion of the human being who has been taught a way of thinking foreign to the real condition of his milieu.'[16] As a means of breaking this colonial stranglehold and as a means of fostering national awareness of the positive values of the African traditional religion, secondary school and university students should be encouraged to form clubs and associations devoted to the observation and promotion of positive rituals, values and ethics of the African traditional religion. Such clubs or associations must adopt and practice the seven cardinal principles of MAAT as their code of conduct. They are: truth, justice, propriety, harmony, balance, reciprocity, and order. It's instructive to point out that cultural asso-ciations, at various levels, already do observe aspects of the African tradi-tional religion, such as libations to the spirits of positive ancestors.

4. There is a need for open governance, a government that maintains regular and necessary communication with the governed. Had Ironsi been adequately communicative he probably would have been able to counter-act the negative impressions which a section of the country had formed of his government.

5. There is a need for popular participation in the formulation and execution of public policy. Nigerian leadership seems to be moving in this direction through the establishment of a large base of local government administrations, numbering up to seven hundred and seventy-four at the present time. These local units ought to be the sounding board for new policy measures. If their input is included in the shaping of national policy, chances are that they would embrace its implementation with enthusiasm. All remaining impediments to the full participation of women in every aspect of the nation's affairs should be removed, for as long as any segment of society's population is prevented, by law or custom, from participating fully in national development, the nation cannot attain its potential level of productivity.

6. A political culture rooted in Maatic principles cannot come about overnight. But those principles must be established at the foundation of society for them to ultimately influence national life. The Nigerian nation reels from a crisis of ethics. In order to contain this crisis, Nigerian schools, as from the primary school level, should seek to inculcate Maatic values in their students so that by the time they become adults, their instincts would have been conditioned against the temptation to flout the rules, against the temptation to steal public property, against the temptation to place their personal interests above the interests of the community, etc. Without such early nurturing, no amount of constitutional prescription can bring about an active sense of morality in the nation. Nigerian education should lay as much stress on "self-discipline" as other goals of education. If a society does not possess a basic revulsion against depravity, no amount of policing can check it. Maatic values, like a glue, helped to meld and hold ancient Egypt (Kemet) together for thousands of fruitful years as the Kemets plodded along in history. Kemet, no doubt, is one of the most successful societies in human history—so successful that European scholars have tried all possible means, without success, to appropriate it as a legacy of the West. Nigeria, like other African societies, is most culturally-suited to take advantage of the positive legacies of the Kemetes since, like an umbilical chord, African culture itself connects the Kemets with the rest of Africa. Nigeria needs an Africa-centered national ethic that embodies the following values: respect for the Constitution, a spirit of fair play, a tradition against abuse of power, a commitment to the national interest, public probity, respect for individual liberty, obedience to the law, and self-reliance.

7. The national political leadership should be required to either show evidence of a broad knowledge of Nigerian and African Histories in the context of World History, or to take such a course of study after taking office. Such an orientation is necessary for the emergence of a historically-conscious political leadership. Knowledge of African History in the context of World History would inculcate a sense of pride and necessary consciousness of the racial factor in World Geo-Politics and how that factor has impacted upon and impacts upon African development in general. It is absolutely necessary that Nigerian/African leaders understand the ideology of White Supremacy and how in subtle fashion it underlies the global scheme of things. It is absolutely necessary that Nigerian/African leaders understand the inequities between the Northern Hemisphere and the Southern Hemisphere in terms of access to global resources and income as well as their distribution. It is absolutely necessary that Nigerian/African leaders understand the phenomenon of underdevelopment, and how it is perpetuated. Lastly, but much more important, it is absolutely necessary

that Nigerian/African leaders should have a Pan-African consciousness that regards Diasporic Africa as an integral part of the African world. This recommendation is equally applicable to Diasporic Africans. Their leadership, at various levels, stand to benefit as much as continental African leaders from an acute sense of World History, as it affects the African world.

7(b). Nigerian education should stress the common features of Nigerian ethnic groups—that is, the common Africanness of those groups. Such education should be initiated at the primary school level and continued in various spheres up to the University levels. Nigerian governments and educational foundations should accord more importance to research proposals which seek to explore, explain and synthesize the Africanness of the component ethnic groups of the nation as far as their investment in the cultural component of Research and Development is concerned.

7(c). Nigeria should adopt Ki-Swahili as a Pan-African national language of the nation. At present, Nigeria regards English as its official language and three endogenous languages, Hausa, Igbo and Yoruba as its national languages. Given the political tension that has existed among Nigeria's three main linguistic groups—the Hausa/Fulani, the Igbo and the Yoruba—Ki-Swahili stands a good chance of being accepted as a "neutral" African language. Nigeria's adoption of Ki-Swahili as its national Pan-African language, which has become a wide-spread national language in the Eastern and Central parts of Africa, would promote two objectives: (i) It would promote the aforementioned task of fostering African consciousness in Nigerians, and (ii) it would help elevate Ki-Swahili as a Pan-African language which can be so regarded in the entire African world—Continental and Diasporic Africa.

7(d). Nigerian education should seek to infuse a liberationist, Afrocentric/Africa-centered consciousness in its recipients. This kind of consciousness would help kill the poisonous colonial legacy of black inferiority which, as this study reveals, still grips the minds of many a Nigerian. The liberationist Afrocentric consciousness would help restore *belief in self,* which has been under the assault of the anti-African propaganda that hegemonic Eurocentrism has disseminated throughout the world through its vast educational, entertainment and informational media network. Nigerian education should make its recipients fully consciousness of the reality of *Anti-Africanism* in the world's scheme of things. Nigerian and African leaders should get the United Nations to amend its Human Rights Declaration so as to place the vicious element of Anti-Africanism side by side with general racism and sexism as vices that need to be exterminated.

7(e). Nigerian political leadership should place more emphasis on Pan-African unity in politics and economics. African political and economic cooperation is a means by which the external dimension of the causes of Nigeria's internal political problems could be put in check.

Finally, and most significant, Nigerian political leadership must always strive to provide responsible, clean and effective governance. There can be no substitute for that.

Chapter Seven

Babangida's Scuttling of the June 12, 1993 Presidential Election: A Postscript

Ex-military President Ibrahim Gbadamosi Babangida's handling of the second attempt by the military interregnum in Nigeria to hand political power over to an elected civilian government exemplifies the ills that this study identified in the Nigerian political leadership and its operative political culture. In 1987, the military government of Babangida launched an elaborate program of transition to civilian rule through the "Transition to Civil Rule Political Program Decree" of that year. It was followed by a minor revision in 1989 of the 1979 presidential Constitution of Nigeria. Next, came the creation of two political parties in the country, namely the Social Democratic Party (SDP) and the National Republican Convention (NRC)—a significant departure from the Second Republic, which was based on five political parties.

Thereafter, state governors, as well as the state and national legislatures, were elected. In effect, by June 1993, the completed portion of the transition program had put civilians in charge of Nigeria's thirty state governments (at both the executive and legislative levels) and the federal legislature. However, a hitch developed over the presidential election, which was held on June 12, 1993. The June 12 presidential election was contested by two candidates, Moshood Kashimawo Olawole Abiola, 55, of the Social Democratic Party (SDP) and Bashir Tofa, 46, of the National Republican Convention (NRC). These are the two political parties, which the military government had approved for the transition program. The two-party structure was mandated by Section 220 (1) of the 1989 Constitution of Nigeria, which stipulates that only two political parties can exist in the country.[1]

Before the National Electoral Commission (NEC) could release all the results of the presidential election, the military government annulled the exercise, thus placing the nation in a political quagmire. In nullifying the election, Babangida, in a display of apparent power drunkenness, also abrogated all the laws paving the way for a return to civilian rule in the country.[2] Although the elected state political leaders and the federal legislators were spared, the nullification of the presidential election marked the end of what Oyeleye Oyediran, et al describes "one of the most ambitious, imaginative, complex, and expensive transitions from authoritarian rule that has ever been attempted anywhere."[3]

Babangida explained that he abrogated the presidential election in order to save the Nigerian judiciary, which had become involved in the election imbroglio, from further ridicule. News reports stated that the reaction of Nigerian politicians to the announcement was one of shock.[4] By "ridicule," Babangida was referring to the spate of law suits, counter law suits, court injunctions and counter-injunctions generated by the disputing politicians as they fought a "court war" over the nullified election.

However, three days after that dramatic announcement, Babangida made an about-face: he told the still bewildered nation that he would still hand over power to an elected civilian president on August 27, 1993 (as previously scheduled), but the election would be conducted through an electoral college.[5] That proposition was problematic because it did not meet the stipulation of the relevant section of the Constitution. The 1989 Constitution set up the electoral college as a kind of last resort for electing a president—where a run-off fails to produce a winner following an inconclusive first ballot.[6] But the June 12, 1993 election was not inconclusive in the real sense of it; for unofficially published results showed Abiola as the decisive winner with 58 percent of the vote as opposed to 32 percent for his NRC opponent.[7]

Babangida's post-election, confusing messages to the nation were merely part of a spate of dramatic events which took place before and after the election. Speculation was rife that Babangida nullified the election in order to cling to power. In fact, there had been a long-standing speculation about the sincerity of the military regime's commitment to its promise to return political power to elected civilians. Critics of the regime had claimed that the government "had a hidden agenda," meaning that Babangida intended to remain in office. He himself alluded to this in his last address to the national legislature (the National Assembly) in which he acknowledged that public concern about his alleged political designs had "dogged [his] administration since [its] inception."[8]

An irony of the moment was that the June 12 ballot passed off peacefully. As the nation anxiously awaited the final returns of the election, the National Electoral Commission (NEC) abruptly suspended action on the processing of the results, following a court injunction to that effect. The injunction came as a result of an action filed by a group known as the Association for a Better Nigeria. The group alleged, among other things, that the election had been tainted.[9]

It is noteworthy that this particular group, which was not a political party (SDP and NRC were the two legal political parties in Nigeria at that time), had tried to prevent the election from taking place. In fact, the association had succeeded in obtaining a court order that the election should not be held. But NEC went ahead with the election, citing, as its defense, a decree which forbade such interferences with the electoral process. This same decree stipulates that the election results had to be released within eight days of the election lest they become invalid.

As it were, the deadline for the official release of the results elapsed on June 20, 1993 as NEC maintained a stunning silence. But it broke its silence on Monday, June 21, through an announcement that it had decided to appeal against the court injunction which had compelled it to suspend the electoral process.[10] History will, of course, never cease to wonder why NEC waited until the expiration of the official time limit to appeal against that court injunction.

It is noteworthy that the self-styled Association for a Better Nigeria had campaigned for the continuation of military rule. In an interview with the British Broadcasting Corporation (BBC), a leader of the association, Arthur Nzeribe (now a Senator and still an enigmatic and maverick political actor), claimed that his group had obtained the signatures of twenty-five million Nigerians in support of the continuation in office of Babangida, the military leader.[11]

The nullification of the presidential election drew violent and non-violent protests from Nigerians of various walks of life. Nobel Laureate, Wole Soyinka, asked the federal military government to compel NEC to publish the results of the election. Abiola, the SDP candidate, who, according to a BBC report, was in the lead before NEC suspended action on the presidential election, had himself appealed to the government to intervene. On the other hand, Tofa, the NCR candidate, had been reported as calling for a new election.

Babangida's action marked the fourth time that he would delay the program of transition to civilian rule since he seized power through a reactionary military coup in 1985. What his critics meant by their charge that he had "a hidden agenda" was that he would like to cling to power although he had repeatedly denied it. In fact, no less a person than General Olusegun Obasanjo, the former Nigerian military head of state, who presided over the first and rather smooth transfer from military to civilian rule in 1979, also echoed that fear.

Two months before the still-born presidential election (March 1993), Obasanjo, known for his equanimity and self-effacement, went out of his way to release a written statement calling on Babangida to leave the stage. The statement, entitled, "Our Desperate Ways," reads in part:

> As someone who was in the battlefield during the Nigerian civil war and who unexpectedly and providentially assumed the mantle of the Commander-in-Chief of the Armed Forces of Nigeria and the leadership of the government, I beg you in the name of Allah not to mistake the silence of our people for acquiescence or weakness and the sycophancy of the greedy and opportunistic people who parade the corridors of power as representative of the true feelings of our people. Nigeria needs peace and stability. It is too fragile to face another commotion.[12]

Even though this study does not engage in an direct analysis of the politics of Nigeria's current Third Republic, one finds it irresistible to point out the historic irony that is reflected in Obasanjo's advice to Babangida. Given the current maneuverings for a constitutional amendment to allow for a third term of office for elected national and state chief executive officers in Nigeria, it seems that Obasanjo might derive some lessons by reading his own past political advice to Babangida. Although Babangida eventually proved his critics wrong (Obasanjo and other critics of his had insinuated that he harbored an ambition to self-perpetuate himself in power) (he surrendered his office on August 26, 1993 to an "interim National Government" headed by an appointed civilian, Ernest Shonekan), Obasanjo still could not be more correct in his assertion that Nigeria deserved peace and stability. Babangida himself later claimed that the spate of post-ponements in the transition program were meant to implant "corrective measures"[13] designed to preserve the nation's peace and stability.

The truth, however, is that the political predicament, which Babangida foisted upon the fragile shoulders of the nation, and in the process blemished his political record for all ages, seemed, from all intents and purposes, like a problem that could have been avoided. The question remains: why did Babangida put the nation through this agony? What was wrong with the June 12 presidential election which required a "corrective" measure? Why could he not share the "secret" with the traumatized nation during his National Assembly address on this matter?

Nigeria's political history, which was discussed in this study, shows clearly that tinkering with the electoral process inevitably produced disintegrative consequences. The First Republic in Nigeria (1960–1966) degenerated into an internecine Civil War (1967–1970) as a culmination of a number of factors, including botched federal and regional elections of 1964 and 1965, respectively. Those elections did not immediately precipitate the collapse of the First Republic; but they did set in motion a change of inexorable events, including the first and bloody military coup of January 1966. Then, there was the equally bloody counter-coup of July 1966; there was the massacre of Igbo people during that year, the declaration of Biafra in 1967; and there was the Civil War, which ended the three-year secession and re-unified Nigeria in 1970. Those cataclysmic events, in a sense, were symptoms of deep systemic and structural flaws: a host of colonial legacies, the reality of Nigeria as a neo-colonial society, and the political elite's counter-productive behavior. The colonial legacies include "colonial tribalism," cleavages between the North and the South (fueled by the North's population dominance and colonially-originated developmental imbalances between the North and the South), and what Azikiwe described earlier as the Parkistanization (that is, regionalization) of Nigerian politics. These systemic flaws were exacerbated by the mal-behavior (in some cases, the anti-systemic behavior) of the political elite with its bifurcated values.

After the Civil War, the nation formally discarded the British-style parliamentary system of government by adopting an American-style presidential Constitution in 1979, which contained all sorts of safeguards against abuse of power. The Second Republic (1979–1983) was based on this constitution. Despite the bloody path that Nigeria had threaded, the rancor that followed the not all-together unblemished election of 1979 (which was nonetheless far better than that of 1983), left a hint that the Nigerian political elite, as a whole, had not learned sufficient lessons from the nation's checkered history. The dismal performance of the Second Republic and its ultimate demise further demonstrated how little had changed in the behavior of the Nigerian political elite even though the splintering of the nation into states had appreciably check-mated the centrifugal forces. Recall that Nwankwo was quick to observe in this study that the Nigerian political class is one that has learned very little from its nation's history.

The 1983 elections were, in many respects, reminiscent of those of 1964 and 1965 in the magnitude of the rigging that characterized them. The question in 1983 was not whether any of the political parties had participated in the rigging, but who had committed the worst rigging. Not surprisingly, as I recorded in the study, historians labeled the 1983 polls as the most rigged elections in Nigeria's history.

As it turned out, the civilian government of Shehu Shagari, which had run the affairs of the nation in a lackluster manner from 1979 to 1983, as Chapter Five amply demonstrated, was re-elected to office for a second four-year term with a land-slide. A former Nigerian military leader, General T.Y. Danjuma aptly captured the mood of the nation in 1983 when he declared to the press that 'the politicians have killed democracy.'[14]

Danjuma's reference was to the political leaders of the day, for the ordinary, democratic-minded Nigerians had duly and enthusiastically performed their civic duty to vote, just as they did during the subsequent June 12, 1993 presidential election. While the political leaders failed them in 1983—forcing the military to intervene and expel Shagari from office—in 1993, it was the military leadership that killed democracy in Nigeria, to borrow Danjuma's phraseology.

It is note worthy that in nullifying the June 12 presidential election, General Babangida did not accuse the politicians of rigging the election. Instead, he pleaded that his action was designed to rescue the judiciary from a political entanglement. What he failed to realize or acknowledge is that had he allowed the electoral process to run its course, there might not have arisen a reason to get the judiciary entangled in partisan politics.

As our study clearly established, there is no doubt that the Nigerian political culture has a long way to go and that the values and behavior of the Nigerian political elite, as distinct from systemic factors, have contributed their share to Nigeria's recurrent political crises. It would amount to an overstatement to describe the political disquiet that followed the nullification of the June 12, 1993 election in Nigeria as a crisis. However, it once more reminded us that unprincipled and self-seeking political leadership, probably as much as anything else, has been the bane of African politics. This defective leadership has compounded the structural problems left behind by colonialism. The electoral scandal of 1993 also illustrates a recurring problem of political leadership in Nigeria: its tendency to apply "band-aids" rather than genuine and hard-nosed solutions to national crises. No doubt, Babangida's act of handing over national political power to an interim government represented a classic band-aid to the impasse that was caused by his nullification of the June 12, 1993 presidential election. How can Nigeria possibly wish away the fact that a duly elected president was not allowed to take office? Without solving that problem, it promised to complicate and make future crises intractable, and thus expose the nation to avoidable tension. The tragic setback in Nigerian political history also illustrated the lack of elite solidarity in Nigerian politics—a lack of elite solidarity which Danjuma so forthrightly described in the preceding chapter. For instance, in the aftermath of the botched June 12 presidential election, instead of closing ranks with the SDP against the military government, in defense of democratic principles, the defeated party, the National Republican Convention, selfishly asked for a new election.[15] This, no doubt, played into the hands of the military government, for it clearly showed that the civilians could not forge a united front on an issue as fundamental to the survival of the state as the rules for deciding who should rule.

The inability of the political elite to unite against the subversion of a cardinal principle of elective governance strengthened the hands of Babangida who had shown a lack of respect for the principles laid down for the transition program. His action did not portray him as someone who had a clear sense of purpose in the national interest although he claimed in his August National Assembly address that he had been motivated by "the higher need to serve the greater glory of our fatherland."[16] Where, however, was the evidence? What greater glory of the fatherland did he serve by obstructing a process as sacred as the election of a national president? Was this greater glory a code term for an objective that had nothing to do with the national interest, namely that there was a fear[17] that Abiola might institute a probe into alleged acts of corruption and human rights abuses on the part of Babangida's administration? In fact, Babangida's action did not serve the course of national integration. For instance, Abiola[18] was forced by his experience, to make a charge reminiscent of the dangerous rhetoric of the First Republic. In the aftermath of the still-born election, he charged that the North, which has dominated Nigeria's national leadership since independence, was trying to prevent him, a southerner, from taking national leadership.[19] In addition, there were fatal riots in the country.[20] Babangida did not serve the greater glory of Nigeria by precipitating events that psychologically drove Nigerians backwards to the North vs. South, Yoruba vs. Hausa, etc pattern of thinking that characterized the politics of the First Republic. For a while, the breaking up of the nation into a multiplicity of states had almost made that kind of attitude towards national affairs a thing to be ashamed of.

The election impasse of 1993 had required nothing short of Maatic statesmanship from Babangida. He needed to demonstrate that he truly believed, not simply preached, that the national interests of Nigeria are supreme. History would not be kind to him for obstructing the will of the people. He himself was aware of this, for as he put it in his National Assembly address, "patriotism and sense of higher values demand that I do something personally about this uncharitable perception of my person."[21] But all he did was to leave the political scene; that action was not enough to redeem his name. He should have handed political power over to the candidate who had been duly elected.

The nullification of the 1993 presidential election rekindled memories of 1975 when the then Head of State, General Yakubu Gowon, postponed indefinitely, his government's own promise to return the country to civilian rule in 1976. Soon after, Gowon, who had claimed that the conduct and utterances of Nigerian politicians had convinced him that 1976 was an "unrealistic date" for civilian rule, was toppled in a palace coup.

The nullified election was held against the backdrop of a nation that was in economic distress, coupled with political uncertainty. Nigeria, as from the late 1980s, faced a mountain of social and economic headaches. Sharply reduced earnings from petroleum (which constitutes 95 percent of Nigeria's exports), combined with the debilitating effects of an IMF-sponsored Structural Adjustment Program (SAP), hiked the cost of living, increased the rate of unemployment and slackened economic development. Capacity utilization in the production sector fell from 37.38 percent in 1991 to 34.51 percent during the first half of 1992. The fall was blamed on low consumer spending due to price inflation induced primarily by SAP,[22] incessant breakdowns of plants, shortage of working capital due to high interest rates, poor infrastructure, inadequate protection for local industries and anxieties emanating from policy instability.[23]

SAP also led to a drastic devaluation of the Naira, Nigeria's currency, while the external debt service ratio ballooned. Inflation was skyrocketing. Nigeria's reliance on the oil sector continues, however, against the backdrop of an estimate that its recoverable oil reserves (of 12.7 billion barrels of oil and 41 trillion cubic feet of gas) would be depleted in twenty-seven years, given its 1993 daily average production rate of two million barrels.[24]

It had been hoped that SAP would open the floodgate to foreign investors. While controlled foreign investment is desirable and holds the promise of jump-starting the economy, time would tell whether SAP's theoreticians were right or wrong in their calculation that structural adjustment is the key. In the meantime, the United Nations Economic Commission for Africa reports that external trade liberalization, such as that instituted by SAP, "undermines local industries"[25] which cannot compete with cheaper products from overseas. "So, African infant industries fail to take-off under extensive trade liberalization,"[26] the UN report concludes.

As would be expected, economic difficulties exacerbated ethnic, class and religious cleavages. There was, and still continues, recurrent tension between "Islamic" and "Christian" groups in pockets of Nigeria. Not surprisingly, the nation's morale hit at an all-time low, and sizeable numbers of professionals—medical doctors, professors, nurses, etc—have left the country. The political un-ease that Babangida unleashed before leaving office could not have made this dismal situation better.

Besides, Babangida's scuttling of democracy in Nigeria sent the wrong signal to African tyrants. Being the most populous nation in Africa and one of the most economically endowed countries of Africa, Nigeria, which is more than twice the size of California, tends to be regarded as a role model for, if not the leader of, the rest of Africa. Thus, Babangida's action carried the danger of emboldening the tyrants dotted across the continent in their determination to perpetuate their despotic rule. Babangida's action ran against the tide of political events, for the continent in the 1990's came under a wind of change to elected civilian governments. Ghana reverted to civilian rule in 1992. Malawi in Southern Africa, which was under a one-party dictatorship for about three decades, voted in 1993 in favor of multi-party governance although this study has shown that multi-partyism does not guarantee the reign of democracy.

General Babangida's disruption of the electoral process for a return to civilian rule also represented an unhealthy development for Nigeria herself—a real political setback—for despite the brief three-month interlude of a Shonekan civilian administration, the country later reverted to a military dictatorship of a worse kind. Military rule is never a long-term alternative to elective governance. The years that the succeeding military administration spent in office represented lost years that the nation could have used to try to evolve an enduring political system. As the events surrounding the still-born 1993 presidential election demonstrated, Nigeria's political elite has a long road to travel if it is to meet the purposeful, benevolent, concordant, communicative, populistic, Maatic and historically conscious ingredients of an effective political and integrative political leadership.

It cannot be over-emphasized that every society is entitled to the inalienable right to choose who governs it. Sovereignty resides with the people. The ultimate benefit of representative democracy is to provide a government through the will of the people. This type of representation makes a government more amenable to accountability and effective political leadership since the leaders are in power by the grace of the people and, therefore, would naturally strive to reflect their interests, needs and aspirations—at least for the sake of the desire to be re-elected.

To an extent, the Nigerian establishment has defused the destabilizing potentials of the June 12, 1993 debacle, having returned the country to an elected, civilian rule in 1999, and having thrusted the leadership of the country in the hands of Olusegun Obasanjo, a Yoruba, like Abiola, from the Southwest. That civilian rule, which is Nigeria's third experiment with representative democracy, was still in effect as at the time of this publication.

Chapter Eight
Implications for African Political Leadership

This study's findings and recommendations are of immense relevance and value to African political leadership in general. Having established that traditional African cultures share more commonalities than differences, this study hereby commends its recommendations for effective political and integrative leadership to other African countries. It was shown earlier in the study that the factors, which have constricted Nigeria's post-colonial political leadership are similar to those of other African societies. The study, however, recognizes that other African countries may, wherever necessary, modify its recommendations to suit peculiar local conditions.

Current political crisis spots in Africa, such as Somalia, Sudan, Liberia, the Democratic Republic of the Congo (formerly Zaire), and Burundi (not to mention the no-peace, no-war situation of Nigeria's) have as much to do with omissions and commissions of political leadership as they have with either colonial legacies or neo-colonial machinations. For instance, Somalia of 1993 was the result of a combination of external and internal forces. Among them were Somalia's legacies of balkanization into Italian, French, British, Ethiopian and Kenyan hands, the fractious and corrupt nature of Somalia's post-independence politics, Somalia's entrapment in the Super-power rivalry between the United States and the former Soviet Union, and Said Bare's own dictatorial leadership and overly ambitious and counter-productive attempt to reunify the Somaliland that colonialism had fragmented. By dominating Somalia's leadership between 1969 and 1990 when he was driven out of office, General Said Bare did not allow the nation to grow politically.

Had the ruling group in Sudan resisted the temptation to impose its will on the Southerners, Sudan, in all probability, would have continued to experience relative national tranquility. It probably would not have been engulfed by the continuous turmoil and blood letting that led the United States to declare in 2004 that genocide was being committed against Africans in the troubled Darfur region.

Similarly, if the so-called "native" populations of Liberia had been treated as full-fledged citizens in their own country, there perhaps would not have arisen a fertile political environment, which paved the way for a monster like the late Master Sergeant Doe and the follow-up civil war that devastated that country between 1989 and 2003, killing more than two hundred and fifty thousand people. Hopefully, Charles Taylor's exit into exile in Nigeria and subsequent trial for alleged human rights violations, as well as the recent election of Lady Ellen Johnson-Sirleaf in the country's post-war presidential election of 2005,[1] would help to preserve the uneasy peace. The new president, who also happens to be Africa's first elected female national president, cannot afford to ignore the native Liberians' feelings of marginalization that lay at the roots of all of that nation's troubles.

Had the United States not foisted its puppet in the person of Mobutu Sese Seko on Zaire (now the Democratic Republic of the Congo), that nation would, perhaps, have had a chance to embark upon a genuine, national socio-economic and political development. The country is yet to recover from the years of neglect and years of looting of its national treasury that marked the brutal reign of the late puppet of U.S. imperialism.

These four cases illustrate a thesis of this study, namely that the combination of external and internal factors account for the political and economic weakness of African states. To solve one and ignore the other would only leave the patience worse off. Besides unification and economic integration efforts on the continent, a means by which the external component of the causal factors could be checkmated is through a concerted Pan-African effort that also draws upon the largely untapped energy of the diaspora. Historically, Western Imperialism has been at its predacious and exploitative best during its moments of internal political calm and unity. Imperialism has functioned best when a balance of power prevails in the Western world. For instance, one of the factors that enabled Western Europe to solidify its colonial strangle-hold on Africa was the end of the Russo-Turkish war of 1877–1878, which ushered in an era of relative tranquility and balance of power in Europe. On the other hand, Africa at that point in history, was divided and incapacitated by the population depletion that resulted from centuries of Arab and later Western European trade in African captives. Added to this was the Berlin Treaty of 1885 through which the Western European nations agreed not to let their rivalry over African territories weaken their united front against Africa.[2]

Thus, the end of the Cold War in the 1990's has not necessarily produced the true global peace that the world in general had craved. Ironically for Africa in particular, the end of the Cold War has removed a much-needed check against the emergence of a colossus-type uni-polar regime (oh, I meant to say uni-polar bully) in world geo-politics. Even though it could be argued that the current situation in global geopolitics, which bears the look of uni-polarism might prove to be short-term in nature and that this intermediate era of international politics represents an ongoing transitional period from the Old World Order to a New World Order whose shape is still not crystal clear (there are unresolved questions about China, Germany, Japan and even Russia), the interval could spell doom for the militarily and economically less powerful nations of the world, the majority of which are located in Africa. (Africa contains twenty-nine of the forty-two nations of the world which are classified as least developed.)[3] The United Nations Human Development Index report of 2005 showed that human development increased in all regions, in the last ten years, except in Africa, south of the Sahara.

Given the upsurge, in the late 80's as well as the 90's, in ethnic uprisings around the globe, as amply exemplified by the experiences of the former Yugoslavia, Burundi, Ruwanda, Somalia (here, the social divide is primarily clannish rather than ethnic), and in some of the former states of the defunct Soviet Union like Georgia, one must ask whether smaller nations of the world are now much more vulnerable to international bullying than ever before? Would uni-polarism make the United Nations a more effective or a less effective agency for promoting and ensuring international peace, the sovereignty of individual nations and global economic and political justice? All these questions present complex challenges for political leadership in Africa. Does the 2003 United States invasion and occupation of the sovereign nation of Iraq represent merely an aberration or is it perhaps the beginning of worse things for the small and vulnerable nations of the world in this apparent transitional age of unipolarism?

It's instructive that while the European Union (EU) grows stronger and stronger, African countries, despite such rather wobbly regional attempts at economic cooperation as ECOWAS, SADC and EAEC and continental initiatives, such as the New Partnership for Africa's Development (NEPAD), are politically divided and would continue, at least in the foreseeable future, to deal individually with a unified and much more powerful Europe. The renaming in 2002 of the Organization of African Unity as the African Union has by no means brought about a sourly-needed collective African political leadership. Obviously, the odds of the bargaining process will continue to be against a balkanized continent.

Another pertinent international factor, which is continental in nature, concerns South Africa. Prior to the end of apartheid, African intelligentia nursed a great hope that the end of an oppressive white minority regime in South Africa would usher in an era of economic revivalism and political tranquility in Africa. My conjecture is that this laudable hope would materialize only through a people-oriented, Africa-centered South African government. Since the end of political apartheid, South Africa's economic reforms have proceeded rather slowly. For instance, eleven years after the emergence of black majority rule in South Africa, the land question remains unresolved. If a Mobutu-type government ever emerges in South Africa, South African Blacks might find themselves in a position similar to the conditions faced by the citizens of the geo-political entity formerly known as Zaire, while under the leadership of Mobutu Sese Seko. Under Mobutu Sese Seko, the citizens of Zaire, now known as the Democratic Republic of the Congo, experienced increasingly depressed standards of living—in fact outright economic misery—and colossal political mismanagement despite the country's mineral wealth. The Democratic Republic of the Congo leads the world in the production of industrial diamond, ranks among the world's leading copper-producers and is a leading producer of strategic ores (lithium, beryllium, tantalum, germanium, etc)—an area in which Africa dominates the world market.[4] It is evident that Mobutu Sese Seko's leadership represented the very anti-thesis of the model of political leadership, which this study has presented. What shape would Zaire had taken if Patrice Lumumba had survived as Congo's Prime Minister?

The late Kwame Nkrumah was correct when he proposed, in the 1960s, that Africa must unite in order to safeguard its independence and realize its economic potentials. Unfortunately, he could not persuade his colleagues (that is, other African leaders), that the continent should, right after independence, adopt a common parliament as a commonwealth of states. The world of the 1990s and this early decade of the twenty-first century has not only vindicated Nkrumah and proved his opponents wrong, it has brought the wisdom of his proposal to the fore. The establishment of regional economic co-operation institutions like the Economic Community of West African States (ECOWAS), the Magrib Union, and the South African Development Community (SADC), as well as continental initiatives, such as NEPAD, are steps in the right direction, but they are not sufficient to counter-act the impact of the European Union or the influence of the United States as the remaining Super power. Neither are they sufficient to ward off Japanese imperialism. Nkrumah's vision still remains of immense significance to the future of Africa and is, therefore, relevant to the question of political leadership. Unfortunately, the scope of this study did not permit me to examine the full social, political and economic ramifications of Nkrumah's unification dream. Consequently, I recommend the issue as a critical subject for further research.

Notes

NOTES TO THE PREFACE

1. For the Federal Radio Corporation of Nigeria (FRCN), in 1979, I covered the national presidential campaign tour of the late Malam Aminu Kano, who was the flagbearer of the Peoples Redemption Party (PRP). And, from 1979 to 1983, I covered the proceedings of the House of Representatives, also for the Federal Radio Corporation of Nigeria.

NOTES TO CHAPTER ONE

1. Chinua Achebe, *The Trouble With Nigeria* (London, Eng.: Heinemann, 1983) 31.
2. Robert H. Jackson & Carl G. Rosberg, *Personal Rule in Black Africa: Prince, Autocrat, Prophet, Tyrant* (Berkeley, University of California P, 1982) 7.
3. Jean Blondel, *Political Leadership* (Beverly Hills: Sage, 1987) 20.
4. Blondel 15.
5. Blondel 3.
6. Blondel 4.
7. Blondel 4.
8. Blondel 5.
9. Blondel 19.
10. Blondel 24.
11. Blondel 24.
12. Blondel 24.
13. Molefi K. Asante, *Kemet, Afrocentricity and Knowledge* (Trenton: Africa World P, 1990) 8.
14. Asante, *Kemet* 8.
15. Asante, *Kemet* 6.
16. Asante, *Kemet* 6.
17. C. Tsehloane Keto, *Vision and Time: Historical Perspective of an Africa-centered Paradigm* (Lanham: University Press of America, 2001) xvii.

18. Amended versions of the 1979 Constitution were instituted In 1989 and 1999. The amendments were minor, and the Constitution retains the presidential system. The latter version is the basis of the current civilian government of Nigeria, which has been led by President Olusegun Obasanjo since 1999.
19. Nwabueze, 294.
20. The national legislature, which is known as the National Assembly, consists of two chambers, the Senate (109 members) and House of Representatives (360 members).
21. Nwabueze 21.
22. Nwabueze 15.
23. Nwabueze 10.
24. Nwabueze 15.
25. Nwabueze 19.
26. Nwabueze 19.
27. Nwabueze 17.
28. Nwabueze 18.

NOTES TO CHAPTER TWO

1. Achebe 11.
2. M. A. Fajana. & M. A. Biggs, *Nigeria in History* (Ibadan, Nigeria: Longman, 1964) 191.
3. Kenneth B. Noble, "Nigeria Reports It Foiled a Coup By Army Rebels," *The New York Times* 23 April 1990: A1.
4. Olugbenga Ayeni, "Transition Setback?" *West Africa* Oct. 26-Nov. 1, 1992: 1820.
5. As a Radio Nigeria journalist, I covered the transitional program that brought the civilians back to power—specifically, the nation-wide election campaign tour of one of the candidates who contested the 1979 presidential election, Late Malam Aminu Kanu. I also later covered the proceedings of the national legislature of Nigeria, the National Assembly, from 1979 to 1983.
6. J. Gus Liebenow, *African Politics: Crises and Challenges* (Bloomington: Indiana University P, 1986) 257.
7. Toyin Falola and Julius Ihonvbere, *The Rise and Fall of Nigeria's Second Republic, 1979–84.* (Totowa: Ed Books, 1985) 242.
8. Falola & Ihonvbere 242.
9. Falola & Ihonvbere 242.
10. Falola & Ihonvbere 243.
11. E.C. Ndukwu, "International Financial Organizations and the NIEO," *The Future of Africa and the New International Economic Order*, eds. Ralph I. Onwuka and Olajide Aluko (London, Eng.: McMillan, 1986) 146.
12. Ken C. Kotecha, *African Politics* (Washington DC.: UP of America, 1981) 304.
13. Jackson 221.
14. Jackson 222.
15. Jackson 222.

16. K.M. Barbour, J.S. Oguntoyinbo, J.O.C. Onyemelukwe, and J.C. Nwafor *Nigeria in Maps* (London, Eng.: Hodder, 1982) 36.

17. Basil Davidson, *African Civilization Revisited: from Antiquity to Modern Times* (Trenton: Africa World P, 1991) 80.

18. Fajana & Biggs 175.

19. Fajana & Briggs 185.

20. Jackson 305.

21. Jackson 192.

22. Jackson 191.

23. Fajana & Briggs 193.

24. Fajana & Briggs 187.

25. Fajana & Briggs 188.

26. Fajana & Briggs 188.

27. Fajana & Briggs 188.

28. Fajana & Briggs 189.

29. Arthur Gavshon, *Crisis in Africa: Battleground of East and West* (Middlesex, Eng.: Penjuin, 1981) 35.

30. Isawa J. Elaigwu, "Cultural Diversity and the Federal Solution: An African Perspective," Lecture. Temple University, Philadelphia, Fall 1990.

31. Elaigwu.

32. J.F.A. Ajayi, *Milestones in Nigeria History* (Ibadan, Nigeria: Ibadan University P, 1962) 28.

33. E.A. Ijagbemi, "Historical Development I: Pre-Colonial and Colonial Nigeria," *Nigeria in Maps* (London, Eng.: Hodder, 1982) 36.

34. Ijagbemi p. 36.

35. Ijagbemi p. 37.

36. Fajana & Biggs 207.

37. Fajana & Biggs 209.

38. Fajana & Biggs 211.

39. Fajana & Biggs 212–213.

40. Fajana & Biggs 213.

41. Victor Okafor, "Afrocentric Theory & Practice: Going Beyond Facades, *The Philadelphia Tribune* 2 April 1993: 6A.

42. Fajana & Briggs 209.

43. Nnamdi Azikiwe, *Zik: A Selection From the Speeches of Nnamdi Azikiwe* (Cambridge, Gt. Brit.: The Cambridge University P, 1961) 100.

44. Austin M. Ahanotu, "The Role of Ethnic Unions in the Development of Southern Nigeria: 1916–66," *Studies in Southern Nigerian History*, ed. Boniface Obichere (London, Gt. Brit.: Frank, 1982) 163.

45. Elaigwu 11.

46. Ahanotu 155.

47. It's instructive to note that such ethnic/cultural unions still exist today, not only within Nigeria, but abroad as well. In what has become a vast Nigerian Diaspora, including the United States, Canada and Europe, ethnic/cultural associations have been forged as a means of bonding, as a means of raising funds towards homeland development projects, as a means of reifying their homeland indigenous customs and cultural practices, and as

a means of transmitting such customs and cultural practices to their Diasporic offspring who tend to be caught in the middle of the indigenous Nigerian cultural practices of their parents and the cultures of the foreign nations in which their parents reside as immigrants or naturalized citizens.

48. Ahanotu 156.
49. Ahanotu 157.
50. Ahanotu 169.
51. Ahanotu 170.
52. Ahanotu 169.
53. Ahanotu 171.
54. Ahanotu 171.
55. Mazrui 237.
56. Falola and Ihonvbere 255.
57. Obafemi Awolowo, *The Strategy and Tactics of the Peoples Republic of Nigeria* (London, Brit.: Macmillan, 1970) 75.
58. Achebe 38.
59. Achebe 38.
60. Falola & Ihonvbere 38.
61. Falola & Ihonvbere 256.
62. Falola & Ihonvbere 255.
63. Falola & Ihonvbere 256.
64. "Across the continent, Despots left Behind by Colonizers and Some Who Grabbed Power Make a Mockery of Freedom," *Emerge* April 1990: 29.
65. In November 1993, General Sanni Abacha became Nigeria's seventh military Head of State by taking over the Federal Government, following the "resignation" of Chief Ernest Shonekan, the civilian Head of the Interim Government that was empanelled by General Babangida when he ended his rule on August 26, 1993.
66. Squandermania is a Nigerian-coined political term (derived from the English Language), which stands for governmental misappropriation of public funds.
67. History is filled with great ironies, one of which is that this same Sanni Abacha that was railing against corruption in that December 1983 broadcast announcing his military junta's overthrow of President Shehu Shagari, was, years later found to have stolen and stacked away billions of Nigerian money to secret Swiss bank accounts during his own infamous military rulership of this rather unfortunate country of Nigeria. What a great irony, indeed!
68. "Across The Continent" 230.
69. Kotecha 309.
70. Falola & Ihonvbere 221.
71. Falola & Ihonvbere 219.
72. Liebenow 239.
73. Elaigwu.
74. Basil Davidson, "For a Politics of Restitution," *Africa Within the World: Beyond Dispossession and Dependence*, ed. Adebayo Adedeji (London: Zed Books, 1993) 24.
75. Kotecha 64.

76. Dorothy Dodge, *African Politics in Perspective* (London, Brit.: D. Van Nostrand, 1966) 4.

77. "Across the Continent," 29.

78. Paxton Idowu, "A Bloody Attempt," *West Africa* 30 April-May 6, 1990: 696.

79. Idowu 696.

80. Idowu 697.

81. Take note that this current civilian government does not fall within the main scope of this study.

82. Ebere Onwudiwe, "In Nigeria, Voiceless Victims of Debt," *The New York Times* 20 April 1990: A33(L).

83. Onwudiwe A33(N).

84. Idowu 696.

85. Lindsay Barrett, "Reactions to the Cabinet Changes: No Islam or Christianity," *West Africa* 22–28 Jan. 1990: 87

86. Barrett 87.

87. Elaigwu.

88. D. Chanainwa, "African Initiatives and Resistance in Southern Africa," *General History of Africa: Africa Under Colonial Domination 1880–1935*, *Vol. II*, ed. A.A. Boahen (Berkeley: Heinemann, 1985) 198.

89. Chainanwa 198.

90. C. Tsheloane Keto, *The Africa Centered Perspective of History* (Blackwood: K.A. Publications, 1989) 33.

91. Cheikh Anta Diop, *The African Origin of Civilization: Myth or Reality*, trans. Mercer Cook (Westport: Lawrence, 1974) XVII.

92. Asante, *Kemet* 9.

93. Molefi K. Asante, *Afrocentricity* (Trenton: Africa World P, 1989) 24.

94. Diop, *African Origin of Civilization* xiii.

95. Robert. T. Green. *Political Instability As a Determinant of U.S. Foreign Investment* (Austin: The University of Texas School of Business, 1972) 82.

96. Green 82.

97. Green 82.

98. Yair, Aharoni, *The Foreign Investment Decision Process* (Boston: Harvard University Graduate School of Business, 1966) 93.

99. R.S. Basi, *Determinants of United States Private Direct Investment in Foreign Countries* (Kent: Kent State University, 1963) 12.

100. National Industrial Conference Board, *Obstacles and Incentives to Private Foreign Investment*. 2 vols. (New York: National Industrial Conference Board, 1969) 3.

101. David F. Gould, "Political Risk Assessment In the Corporate Planning Environment," *Global Risk Assessments: Issues, Concepts and Applications*, ed. Jerry Rogers (Riverside: Global Risk Assessments, 1983) 16.

102. Organization For Economic Co-operation and Development, *International Direct Investment and the New Economic Environment* (Paris, France: OECD, 1989) 42.

103. Ali A. Mazrui and Michael Tidy, *Nationalism and New States in Africa* (London: Heinemann, 1984) 333.

104. Molefi K. Asante, A Six-State Continent? *African Concord* 17 Sept., 1987: 16.

105. Jackson 310.

106. Jackson 310.

107. Festus Ugboaja Ohaegbulam, *Towards An Understanding of the African Experience: From Historical and Contemporary Perspectives* (New York: University P of America, 1990) 211.

108. See Rodney, Walter. *How Europe Underdeveloped Africa.* (Washington, D.C.: Howard University P, 1982.

109. Abdur Rahman Babu, "Africa Urged to Adopt Social Economies," *West Africa* 11–17 Nov. 1991: 1983.

110. Coralie Bryant & Louise White, *Managing Development in the Third World* (Boulder: Westview Press, 1982) 3.

111. Ohaegbulam 211.

112. See Diop, Cheikh Anta. *The Cultural Unity of Black Africa: the Domains of Patriarchy and Matriarchy in Classical Antiquity.* London, Eng.: Karnak, 1989.

113. Clement T. Keto, "The Implications of an Afrocentric World-view For Africa," Lecture at an African Continental Caucus Lecture Series, Temple University, Philadelphia, Spring, 1991.

114. "Rwanda: How the Genocide Happened," *BBC NEWS,* 4 April, 2004 (http://news.bbc.co.uk/go/pr/fr//1/hi/world/africa/1288230.stm).

115. Fantu Cheru, *African Renaissance: Roadmaps to the Challenge of Globalization,*(London: Zed Books, 2002) 33.

116. Adebayo Adedeji, "Ensuring A Successful Transition," *West Africa* 11–17 Nov. 1991: 1878.

117. Adedeji 1878.

118. Ohaegbulam 214.

119. Molefi K. Asante, *Afrocentricity* (Trenton: Africa World P, 1990) 2.

120. Asante, *Afrocentricity* 2.

NOTES TO CHAPTER THREE

1. Claude Ake, *A Theory of Political Integration* (Homewood: the Dordsey P, 1967) 1.

2. Ake 1.

3. Ake 96.

4. Ake 2.

5. Ake 2.

6. Hanes Walter & Robert Smith, *American Politics and the African American Quest for Universal Freedom* (New York: Longman, 200) 41.

7. Ake 4.

8. Ake 8.

9. Ake 12.

10. Basil Davidson, *Modern Africa* (New York: Longman, 1986) 171.

11. Davidson 172.

12. *Africa Confidential*, 34.1, 8 Jan. 1993: 2.

13. Ake 19–22.

14. Ake 19–22.
15. Davidson, *Modern Africa* 171.
16. Davidson, *Modern Africa* 171.
17. Ake 27.
18. Ake 27.
19. Ake 29.
20. Ake 29.
21. Ake 31.
22. Ake 39.
23. Ake 71.
24. Ake 71.
25. Ake 71.
26. Rodney 225.
27. Ake 32.
28. F. Niyi Akinnaso, "One Nation, Four Hundred Languages: Unity and Diversity in Nigeria's Language Policy," *Language Problems and Language Planning* 13.2 Summer 1989: 137.
29. Eme O. Awa, *Federal Government in Nigeria* (Berkeley: University of California P, 1964) 25.
30. Walter Rodney, *How Europe Underdeveloped Africa* (1972 ; Washington, D.C.: Howard University P, 1982) 229.
31. Cheikh Anta Diop, *Precolonial Black Africa: A Comparative Study of the Political and Social Systems of Europe and Black Africa, from Antiquity to the Formation of Modern States, (African World Press Edition)*, trans. Harold J. Salemson (Westport: Lawrence Hill, 1987) 73.
32. Diop, *Pre-Colonial Black Africa* 74.
33. Akinnaso, "One Nation" 134.
34. Akinnaso, "One Nation" 135.
35. Akinnaso, "One Nation" 135.
36. *The Constitution of the Federal Republic of Nigeria (Promulgation) Decree, 1989* (Lagos, Nigeria: Federal Government of Nigeria, 1989): Sec. 53, 45.
37. The Constitution of the Federal Republic of Nigeria (Lagos, Nigeria: Federal Government of Nigeria, 1999): Sec. 55, 29.
38. Akinnaso, "One Nation" 137.
39. Akinnaso, "One Nation" 137
40. F. Niyi Akinnaso, "Towards the Development of a Multilingual Language Policy in Nigeria," *Applied Linguistics* 12.1 (1991): 35.
41. Akinnaso, "One Nation" 142.
42. Akinnaso, "One Nation" 142.
43. Kiswahili is originally the language of a people known as Waswahili, who inhabit the coast of Kenya, Tanganyika and the Island of Zanzibar (the latter two constitute what is now known as Tanzania). The language later spread to eventually become the most commonly used language in East Africa. Through commercial interactions between Africans and Arabs that date back to the 9th century A.D., the language absorbed elements of Arabic. This centuries-old trade, which was carried out in KiSwahili, was the major source of prosperity for an East African Civilization which

flourished around this time. Gold, among other commodities, was traded at the centers of this civilization—Kilwa, Mombasa, Sofola, Malinda and Zanzibar. The gold was derived from mines located in Southern Africa, including Southern Zimbabwe and Mozambique. The East African Civilization later fell victim to Portuguese invaders who were attracted by its wealth. (Sources: Basil Davidson, *African Civilization Revisited*. Trenton, N.J.: Africa World Press, 1990, p. 280 & Ngugi Wa Thiong'O, *Moving the Center: the Struggle for Cultural Freedoms*, Portmouth, N.H.: Heinemann, p. 170.).

44. Davidson, *Modern Africa* 164.
45. Ngugi Wa Thiong'O, *Moving the Center: the Struggle for Cultural Freedoms* (Portsmouth: Heinemann, 1993) 41.
46. Akinnaso, "One Nation" 142.
47. Wa Thiong'O 41.
48. Wa Thiong'O 170.
49. Ake 33.
50. Ake 52.
51. Olusegun Obasanjo, "Our Desperate Ways," *The Nigerian Times* March 1993: 4.
52. Ake 59.
53. Ake 61.
54. Ake 65–66.
55. Ake 66.
56. Ake 79.
57. Ake 85.
58. Ake 91.
59. Ake 85.
60. Ake 83.
61. Klevor Abo, "Defining Democracy." *West Africa* 23–29 Nov. 1992: 2015.
62. In like manner, I condemn categorically and in the strongest terms, the terrorism that stroke various targets (including the twin towers in New York city) in the United States on September 11, 2001 and killed nearly four thousand innocent men, women and children. This type of wanton destruction of the lives of innocent and defenseless civilians cannot be justified by any type of cause.
63. Abo 2015.
64. Abo 2015.
65. Ake 90.
66. Ake 94.
67. Ake 94.
68. Ake 98.
69. Ake 98.
70. Ake 101.
71. Ake 103.
72. Ake 103.
73. Ake 104.
74. Ake 104.

75. Nzongola Ntalaja, "The Crisis in Zaire," *Africa's Crisis* (London, Eng.: Institute for African Alternatives, 1987) 12.
76. Ake 106.
77. Ake 112.
78. Ake 106.
79. Ake 106.
80. Ake 107.
81. Ake 108.
82. Ake 108.
83. Ake 109.
84. Ake 110.
85. Ake 111.
86. Ake 111.
87. Ake 111.
88. Robert H. Jackson & Carl G. Rosberg, *Personal Rule in Black Africa: Prince, Autocrat, Prophet, Tyrant* (Berkeley: University of California P, 1982) ix.
89. Jackson & Rosberg 1.
90. Jackson & Rosberg 1.
91. Jackson & Rosberg 3.
92. Jackson & Rosberg 3.
93. Jackson & Rosberg 5.
94. Davidson, *Modern Africa* 172.
95. Jackson & Rosberg 5.
96. Benjamin Ewuku Oguah, "African & Western Philosophy: A Comparative Study," *African Philosophy* (Lanham: UP of America, 1984) 221.
97. Jackson & Rosberg 10.
98. Jackson & Rosberg 10.
99. Jackson & Rosberg 11.
100. Falola & Ihonvhere 217.
101. Nwabueze 73.
102. Nwabueze 73.
103. Jackson & Rosberg 17.
104. Jackson and Rosberg 16.
105. Jackson and Rosberg 19.
106. Jackson and Rosberg 20.
107. Nwabueze, *Nigeria's Presidential Constitution* 11.
108. Jackson & Rosberg 12.
109. Nwabueze, *Nigeria's Presidential Constitution* 11.
110. Nwabueze, *Nigeria's Presidential Constitution* 12.
111. Wa Thiong'O 83.
112. Wa Thiong'O 77.
113. Ntalaja 7.
114. Ntalaja 8.
115. Ntalaja 19.
116. Ntalaja 21.
117. Ntalaja 8.

118. Ntalaja p. 8.
119. Ntalaja 23.
120. Wa Thiong'O 49.
121. Ntalaja 10.
122. Ntalaja 10
123. Ntalaja 11.
124. Wa Thiong'O 65.
125. Ntalaja 12.
126. Ntalaja 17.
127. Ntalaja 13.
128. Ntalaja 13.
129. Ntalaja 17
130. Ntalaja 9.
131. Ntalaja 18.
132. Bode Onimode, "The African Crisis and Nigeria," *Africa's Crisis* (London, Eng.: Institute for African Alternatives, 1987) 27.
133. Onimode 30.
134. Onimode 30.
135. Wa Thiong'O 52–53.
136. Onimode 30.
137. Onimode 30.
138. Onimode 31.
139. Onimode 31.
140. Onimode 32.
141. Onimode 32.
142. *Africa Confidential*, 34.1, 8 Jan. 1993: 6.
143. Onimode 33.
144. Onimode 33.
145. Obasanjo, "Our Desperate Ways" 4.
146. Onimode 34.
147. Onimode 34.
148. Kempton Makamure, "Contradictions in the Socialist Transformation of Zimbabwe," *Africa's Crisis* (London, Eng.: Institute for African Alternatives, 1987) 74.
149. Makamure 76.
150. Abdoulaye Bathily, "Senegal's Fraudulent 'Democratic Opening,'" *Africa's Crisis* (London, Eng.: Institute for African Alternatives, 1987) 88.
151. Bathily 88.
152. Bathily 89.
153. Bathily 91.
154. Brian Moyo, "Nyerere Calls for Equality Between North and South: Economic Disparity Castigated," *West Africa* 23–29 Nov. 1992: 2016.
155. Bathily 92.
156. Bathily 92.
157. Bathily 93.
158. Bathily 93.
159. Bathily 88.

160. Bathily 93.
161. Bathily 94.
162. Wa Thiong'O 71.
163. Wa Thiong'O 173.
164. Wa Thiong'O 74.
165. Ntalaja 14.
166. Claude Welch, Jr. ed., *Civilian Control of the Military: Theory and Cases From Developing Countries* (Albany: State University of New York P, 1976) 2.
167. Welch 3.
168. Welch 6.
169. Welch 9.
170. Welch 17.
171. Welch 32.
172. Welch 33.
173. Welch 28.
174. "Togolese protest over new leader," BBC News, BBC, London, Gt. Brit., 8 February, 2005. (http://news.bbc.co.uk/go/pr/fr/-/1/hi/world/africa/4245861.stm).
175. "Freemensons Condemn Togo election," BBC News, BBC, London, Gt. Brit., 17 May, 2005. (http://news.bbc.co.uk/go/pr/fr/-/1/hi/world/africa/4555671.stm).
176. "Mauritania's ex-leader in Qatar," BBC News, BBC, London, Gt. Brit., 22 August, 2005. (http://news.bbc.co.uk/go/pr/fr/-/1/hi/world/africa/4172792.stm).
177. Samuel Decalo, *Coups and Army Rule in Africa: Motivations & Constraints* (New Haven: Yale University P, 1990) 2.
178. Decalo 2.
179. Decalo 4.
180. Decalo 5.
181. Decalo 5.
182. Decalo 5.
183. Decalo 5.
184. Decalo 5.
185. Decalo 6.
186. Decalo 6.
187. Decalo 6.
188. Decalo 7.
189. Decalo 7.
190. Decalo 7.
191. Decalo 14.
192. "Country profile: Ivory Coast." BBC News, BBC, Gt. Brit., 5 December, 2005. (http://news.bbc.co.uk/1/hi/world/africa/country_profiles/1043014.stm).
193. Decalo 7.
194. Decalo 7.
195. Decalo 8.

196. Decalo 11.
197. Decalo 11.
198. Decalo 8.
199. Decalo 9.
200. Decalo 11.
201. Decalo 13.
202. Basil Davidson, *African Nationalism and the Problems of Nation-Building* (Lagos, Nigeria: the Nigerian Institute of International Affairs, 1987) 13.
203. Decalo 13.
204. Decalo 17.
205. Decalo 19.
206. Decalo 20–21.
207. Decalo 23.
208. Decalo 23.
209. Decalo 23.
210. Decalo 23.
211. Decalo 24.
212. Decalo 30.
213. Decalo 31.
214. Decalo 26.
215. Decalo 26.
216. Decalo 26.
217. Decalo 26.
218. John W. Harbeson, "Military Rulers in African Politics," *The Military in African Politics*, ed. John W. Harbeson (Westport: Praeger, 1987) 2.
219. Harbeson 6.
220. Harbeson 5.
221. Harbeson 12.
222. Harbeson 12.
223. Decalo 13.
224. Harbeson 14.
225. Harbeson 18.
226. "Burundi, Hell in Bujumbura: An Account of A Coup Against Democracy," *West Africa* 1–7 Nov. 1993: 1974.
227. Richard A. Joseph, "Principles and Practices of Nigerian Military Governments," *Military Rule in African Politics* ed. John W. Harbeson (Westport: Praeger, 1987) 68.
228. Joseph 68.
229. Joseph 68.
230. Joseph 68.
231. National Intelligence Council, "Mapping Sub-Saharan Africa's future," March 2005. (http://www.cia.gov/nic/PDF_GIF_confreports/africa_future.pdf.).
232. Larry Diamond, *Class, Ethnicity and Democracy in Nigeria: the Failure of the First Republic* (Syracuse: Syracuse University P, 1988) 17.
233. Diamond 45.
234. Diamond 28.

235. Danjuma also served as Nigeria's defense minister during the first term of Olusegun Obasanjo's civilian presidency of Nigeria.
236. "Danjuma On Nigeria," *Newswatch*, 2 Nov. 1992: 13.
237. "Danjuma On Nigeria" 13.
238. Olusegun Obasanjo, *My Command: An Account of the Nigerian Civil War, 1967–70* (1980;Ibadan, Nigeria: Heinemann, 1981) 144.
239. Diamond 290.
240. Diamond 290.
241. Alaba Ogunsanwo, *The Transformation of Nigeria: Scenarios and Metaphors* (Lagos, Nigeria: University of Lagos P, 1991) 5–6.
242. Ogunsanwo 6–7.
243. Ogunsanwo 6.
244. Ogunsanwo 8.
245. Ogunsanwo 9.
246. Ogunsanwo 13.
247. Ogunsanwo 9.
248. Ogunsanwo 19.
249. Ogunsanwo 26.
250. Davidson, *African Nationalism* 13.
251. Davidson, *African Nationalism* 14.

NOTES TO CHAPTER FOUR

1. Ake 1.
2. Ake 1.
3. Diamond 26.
4. Ogunsanwo 7.
5. Diamond 34.
6. Diamond 23–24.
7. See Nnamdi Azikiwe,*Zik: A Selection From the Speeches of Nnamdi Azikiwe*. Cambridge, Britain: The Cambridge University Press, 1961, p. 100.
8. Diamond 41.
9. Diamond 16.
10. B.J. Oritsetsaninomi, ed., *Nigeria: 1965 Crisis & Criticism: Selections From Nigerian Opinion* (Ibadan, Nigeria: Ibadan University P, 1966) 47.
11. Diamond 28.
12. In the U.S. media's discourse of America's imperial occupation of Iraq and its consequences, there is a tendency to cast Iraqi national issues and challenges in terms of the sectarian lines of division separating the Shiites, the Sunnis and the Kurds. This type of divisive discourse is somewhat reminiscent of the nature of colonial divide and conquer tactics that Britain applied to its colonial administration of Nigeria.
13. Diamond 26.
14. Diamond 28.
15. Diamond 27.
16. Diamond 27.

17. Diamond 51.
18. Diamond 31.
19. Diamond 32.
20. Diamond 32.
21. Diamond 34.
22. Diamond 41.
23. Eme Ekekwe, *Class and State in Nigeria* (Lagos, Nigeria: Longman, 1986) 111.
24. Falola & Ihonvbere 217.
25. Nwabueze 423.
26. Nwabueze 424.
27. S. A. Aluko, "How Many Nigerians? An Analysis of Nigeria's Census Problems, 1901–63," *The Journal of Modern African Studies*, 3.3 (1965): 382–384.
28. Diamond 136.
29. Aluko 385.
30. This writer served as one of the enumerators for this exercise.
31. Arthur Nwankwo, *Nigeria: Political Danger Signals, the Politics of Federalism, Census, Blanket Ban and National Integration* (Enugu, Nigeria: Fourth Dimension Publishers, 1991) 55.
32. Aluko 385.
33. Nwankwo 54.
34. J.G. Ottong, "Population of Nigeria." 2 March, 2006. (http://www.online-nigeria.com/population/?blurb=13).
35. Aluko 375.
36. Aluko 376.
37. Aluko 376.
38. *Nigeria: 1965 Crisis and Criticism* 47.
39. Diamond 141.
40. Diamond 142.
41. Diamond 159.
42. Nwabueze 228.
43. Diamond 158.
44. Diamond 158.
45. Ekekwe 126–132.
46. Ekekwe 133.
47. Ekekwe 127 & 135.
48. Ekekwe 130.
49. Ekekwe 135.
50. *Nigeria: 1965 Crisis and Criticism* 47.
51. Diamond 204–206.
52. Diamond 203.
53. Diamond 219.
54. Eric Agume Opia, *Why Biafra? Aburi, Prelude to the Biafran Tragedy* (San Rafael: Leswing P, 1972) 57.
55. Diamond 223.
56. Diamond 238.

57. Diamond 238.
58. Ekekwe 130.
59. Cries of marginalization have extended to the contemporary national politics of Nigeria. Virtually every majority or minority group in Nigeria has, at one time or the other, claimed that it's being politically marginalized. Even the North that is viewed as the privileged region of the country, joined in cries of political marginalization after the shift of Nigeria's presidency to the South with the election of President Olusegun Obasanjo in 1999.
60. Diamond 155.
61. Opia 55.
62. Diamond 156.
63. Diamond 100.
64. Akintola was removed without a vote of no-confidence in the legislative house. The governor based his removal on the petition of AG's legislators.
65. Diamond 97.
66. Diamond 91.
67. The emergency lasted for six months.
68. Diamond 107.
69. Diamond 112.
70. Diamond 51.
71. Ake 149.
72. Obasanjo, *My Command* 11.
73. Opia 110.
74. John D. Clarke, *Yakubu Gowon: Faith in a United Nigeria* (London, Eng.: Frank, 1987) 95.
75. Clarke 95.
76. Obasanjo, *My Command* 6.
77. Opia 66.
78. Clarke 63.
79. Obasanjo, *My Command* 6.
80. Awa 25.
81. Awa 25.
82. For details, see pages 47 to 50 of Obasanjo, Olusegun. *My Command: An Account of the Nigerian Civil War, 1967–70.* London, England: Heinemann, 1980.
83. Ekekwe 137.
84. Oyeleye Oyediran ed., *Survey of Nigerian Affairs* (Ibadan, Nigeria: Oxford UP of Nigeria, 1978) 7.
85. *Survey of Nigerian Affairs* 7.
86. Harbeson 18.
87. Joseph 71.
88. Joseph 71.
89. Segun Gbadegesin charges that the politicians of the Second Republic saw the issue of new states merely as a political instrument for votes. This implies that national integration was not at issue. He notes that the ruling party at the center, the National Party of Nigeria (NPN), in particular,

promised new states despite the constitutional problems involved. See page 117 of Segun Gbadegesin, "The Politics of Ethnicity," *The Politicization of Society During Nigeria's Second Republic, 1979–1983*. Segun Gbadegesin (ed.). New York, N.Y: The Edwin Mellen Press, 1991.

90. Joseph 71.
91. Joseph 76.
92. Diamond 302.
93. Diamond 302.
94. Diamond 302.
95. Ekekwe 139.
96. Ogunsanwo 25.
97. Ekekwe 139.
98. Ekekwe 140.
99. Ekekwe 141.
100. Ekekwe 139.
101. Section 8 (1) of the 1979 Constitution of Nigeria sets out the criteria for the creation of new states as follows:
    "An Act of the National Assembly for the purpose of creating a new state shall only be passed if -
    (a) a request, supported by at least two-thirds majority of members (representing the area demanding the creation of the new State) in each of the following, namely -
        (i)   the Senate and the House of Representatives,
        (ii) the House of Assembly in respect of the area, and
        (iii) the local government councils in respect of the area, is received by the National Assembly;
    (b) a proposal for the creation of the State is thereafter approved in a referendum by at least two-thirds majority of the people of the area where the demand for creation of the state originated;
    (c) the result of the referendum is then approved by a simple majority of all the States of the Federation supported by a simple majority of members of the House of Assembly; and
    (d) the proposal is approved by a resolution passed by two-thirds majority of members of each House of the National Assembly."
102. Segun Gbadegesin, "Politics of Ethnicity," *The Politicization of Society During Nigeria's Second Republic, 1979–1983*, ed. Segun Gbadegesin (New York: The Edwin Mellen P, 1991) 117.
103. Ekekwe 143.
104. "Catalogue of Events," *West Africa* 34.13, 28 June–4 July 1993: 1081.
105. "Catalogue of Events" 3.
106. E. A. Ijagbemi, "Historical Development 2: Nigeria Since Independence," *Nigeria In Maps* (London, Eng.: Hodder, 1982) 38.
107. Margaret A. Novicki, "Interview: Adebayo Adedeji," *Africa Report* Nov./Dec. 1993: 59.

108. Adegboyega Somide, "Federalism, State Creation and Ethnic Management in Nigeria," *Problems and Prospects of Sustaining Democracy in Nigeria* ed. Bamidele A. Ojo (Huntington: Nova Science Publishers, 2001) 34.
109. "Interview: Adebayo Adedeji" 59.
110. "Catalogue of Events" 1081.
111. "Catalogue of Events" 1081.
112. This refers to "the Transition to Civil Rule (Political Program) (Amendment) (No. 3) Decree (No. 52) of 1992."
113. Victor Okafor, "Can Nigeria Survive Babangida's Scuttling of Democracy?" *The Philadelphia Tribune* 29 June 1993: 6A.
114. Nwabueze 374.
115. Nwabueze 374.
116. Diamond 19.

NOTES TO CHAPTER FIVE

1. This study uses the terms, "Afrocentric" and "Africa-centered" interchangeably.
2. The theory includes adapted elements of Claude Ake's Theory of Political Integration. See Ake, Claude. *A Theory of Political Integration*. Homewood, Illinois: the Dorsey Press, 1967. There are two reasons why I found aspects of Ake's theory applicable to my work. One, the book exhibits a thorough grasp of the problem of nation-building in the new states. Two, the work projects a sound knowledge of the specific case of Nigeria.

   But my theory derives essentially from the facts, findings and observations of my study of the twin problem of leadership and political integration in Nigeria in particular and Africa in general. My study benefited from the practical insights that I derived from my own first-hand experience of Nigerian politics. My coverage, as a journalist, of the politics of Nigeria, including a presidential campaign in 1979 and the proceedings of the national legislature of Nigeria from 1979 to 1983, gave me a deep understanding of the attitudes and behavior of Nigerian political leaders. That firsthand experience, along with my sixteen years of researching and teaching in Black Studies (Africology) in the United States imbued me with a vision and knowledge that made this book possible.
3. Ake 2.
4. Ake 2.
5. Asante, *Afrocentricity* 31.
6. Asante, *Kemet* 7–8.
7. Asante, *Kemet* 13.
8. Asante, *Kemet* 13.
9. Ogunsanwo 8.
10. Rodney 241.
11. Wa Thiong'O 51.
12. Diop, *The African Origin of Civilization* xiv.
13. Diop, *The African Origin of Civilization* xv.

14. Diop, *The African Origin of Civilization* xv.
15. Diop, *The African Origin of Civilization* xiv.
16. Daudi Ya Azibo, *Liberation Psychology* (Philadelphia: An Unpublished Manuscript, 1990) 20.
17. Lacinary Keita, "The African Philosophical Traditions," *African Philosophy* (Lanham: UP of America, 1984) 57.
18. Richard A. Wright, "Investigating African Philosophy," *African Philosophy* (Lanham: UP of America, 1984) 65.
19. Diop, *The African Origin of Civilization* 74.
20. Diop, *Precolonial Black Africa* 59.
21. Diop, *Precolonial Black Africa* 59.
22. Diop, *Pre-Colonial Black Africa* 61.
23. Diop, *Precolonial Black Africa* 61.
24. Diop, *Pre-Colonial Black Africa* 62.
25. Frank Willet, *African Art: An Introduction* (New York: Praeger, 1971) 111–112.
26. Willet 111–112.
27. Willet 111–112.
28. Willet 111–112.
29. Wright 59.
30. Diop, *The African Origin of Civilization* 45.
31. Keita 59.
32. Keita 69.
33. Keita 70.
34. Keita 70.
35. Keita 70.
36. Asante, *Kemet* 12.
37. Diamond 158.
38. Ogunsanwo 9.
39. Ogunsanwo 9.
40. Ogunsanwo 9.
41. Asante, *Afrocentricity* 49.
42. Azibo 20.
43. Wa Thiong'O 51.
44. Asante, *Afrocentricity* 5.
45. Asante, *Kemet* 8.
46. Asante, *Afrocentricity* 5.
47. Keto, *The Africa Centered Perspective of History* 33.
48. See Diop, Cheikh Anta. *The African Origin of Civilization: Myth or Reality.* Cook, Mercer, Trans. New York, N.Y.: Lawrence Hill Books, 1974. & Diop, Cheikh Anta. *Civilization or Barbarism: An Authentic Anthropology.* (Ngemi, Yaa-Lengi, Trans., Salemson, Harold J, ed.). Brooklyn, N.Y.: Lawrence Hill Books, 1991.
49. Ohaegbulam 22.
50. Ohaegbulam 22.
51. Ohaegbulam 22.
52. Ohaegbulam 22.

53. See Williams, Chancellor. *The Destruction of Black Civilization: Great Issues of A Race From 4500 B.C. To 2000 A.D.* Chicago, ILL.: Third World Press, 1974., Jackson, John G. *Introduction to African Civilizations.* New York: University Books, 1970., Van Sertima, Ivan. *Blacks In Science: Ancient & Modern.* New Brunswick, N.J.: Transaction Books, 1883., & Bernal, Martin. *Black Athena: The Afroasiatic Roots of Classical Civilization.* New Brunswick, N.J.: Rutgers University Press, 1991.

54. Keto, *The Africa Centered Perspective of History* 22.

55. Asante, *Afrocentricity* 53.

56. Ake 103.

57. Ake 103.

58. Ake 112.

59. Ake 106.

60. Ake 111.

61. Akinnaso 134.

62. Akinnaso 135.

63. Asante, *Kemet* 6–7.

64. "Aminian" is this writer's term for exploitative, anti-people politics which hinges on the belief that the end, no matter its diabolical nature, justifies the means. It is derived from Idi Amin's style of leadership in Uganda, which was one that did not hesitate to sacrifice the very people, whose welfare he was supposed to promote, whenever his need for self-preservation so dictated.

65. Awa 25.

66. See Asante, Molefi Kete (ed.). *African Culture: the Rhythms of Unity.* Westport, Conn.: Greenwood Press, 1985.

67. In other words, unlike the Western conception of religion, African "religion" is not a distinct phenomenon in African traditional life. Life itself is religious; thus, unlike in the West, you are not religious only when you worship in the church on Sundays or Saturdays as the case maybe. What is then described as African religion permeates the entire fabric of African life in traditional society. It is more correctly the spiritualistic marrow of the bone of African culture.

68. John S. Mbiti, *African Religions and Philosophy: Second Edition* (1969; London, G. Brit.: Heinemann, 1990) 15.

69. Mbiti 101.

70. That is, when it is interpreted from the Afrocentric or the Africa-centered perspective.

71. Ake 109.

72. Ake 110.

73. Ake 110.

74. Ake 112.

75. Ake 112.

76. "African Charter for Popular Participation in Development and Transformation (Arusha, 1990)," *African Contemporary Record: Annual Survey and Documents* ed. Marion E. Doro (New York: Africana, 1988–89) Vol. 21: c65.

77. "African Charter for Popular Participation" c66.

78. Diop, *Pre-Colonial Black Africa* 64.
79. Gertie Englund, ed., *The Religion of the Ancient Egyptians: Cognitive Structures and Popular Expressions (Proceedings of Symposia in Uppsala and Bergen 1987 and 1988)* (Stockholm, Sweden: Tryckeri Balder AB, 1989) 23.
80. Maulana Karenga, *Selections From the Husia* (Los Angeles: The University of Sankore P, 1984) 29.
81. Karenga 29.
82. Karenga 29.
83. Karenga 30.
84. *The Religion of the Ancient Egyptians* 23.
85. *The Religion of the Ancient Egyptians* 81.
86. Siegfried Morenz. *Egyptian Religion* (Ithaca: Cornell UP, 1973) 113.
87. *The Religion of the Ancient Egyptians* 81.
88. *The Religion of the Ancient Egyptians* 81.
89. *The Religion of the Ancient Egyptians* 82.
90. *The Religion of the Ancient Egyptians* 87.
91. Diop, *Pre-Colonial Black Africa* 65.
92. Basil Davidson. *African Civilization Revisited* (Trenton: Africa World P, 1991) 101.
93. Nwabueze 380.
94. Davidson, *Modern Africa* 82.
95. Victor Okafor, "AT&T Cannot Over-Apologize For Truly Racist Cartoon," *The Philadelphia Tribune* 15 Oct. 1993: 6A.
96. Okafor, "At&T" 6A.
97. Diop, *The African Origin of Civilization* xv.
98. Diop, *The African Origin of Civilization* xv.
99. General Ibrahim Gbadamosi Babangida was Nigeria's military leader from August 27, 1985 to August 27, 1993.
100. "Nigeria: Maradona Plays Into Extra Time," *Africa Confidential* 34.17, 27 Aug. 1993: 7.
101. Nwankwo 119.
102. Nwankwo 120.
103. Nwankwo 120.
104. Nwankwo 120.
105. Asante, *Afrocentricity* 2.
106. In the context of this book, the terms antebellum and postbellum refer respectively to the periods in Nigeria's political history prior to 1960 and the period after 1983.
107. Diamond 57.
108. Diamond 72.
109. Davidson, *Modern Africa* 171.
110. Davidson, *Modern Africa* 171.
111. Richard Drayton. The wealth of the west was built on Africa's exploitation. USA/Africa Dialogue, No. 1027. 21 August, 2005. (http://www.utexas.edu/conferences/Africa)
112. Drayton.

113. Ekwueme Felix Okoli, *Institutional Structure and Conflict in Nigeria* (Washington, D.C.: UP of America, 1980) 3.
114. Diamond 296.
115. Diamond 179.
116. Diamond 322.
117. Diamond 322.
118. The government of national unity was composed of ministers drawn from the victorious and defeated alliances in the 1964 election. The election gave Prime Minister Balewa's Nigerian National Alliance (NNA) more than a two-third majority in the federal legislature—198 of the 253 contested seats. Thus, strictly speaking, Balewa did not need the votes of the defeated parties in order to rule. But, in my view, the bitterness and distrust generated by that election made his "government of national unity" a political necessity. This government of national unity consisted of a 54-member cabinet made up of 22 members of the Northern Peoples Congress (NPC), 14 members of the Nigerian National Democratic Party (NNDP), 15 members of the National Convention of Nigerian Citizens (NCNC) and three "pro-NPC" independents. (Source: Larry Diamond, *Class, Ethnicity and Democracy in Nigeria: the Failure of the First Republic.* Syracuse, N.Y.: Syracuse University Press, 1988, p. 227.)
119. Ladipo Adamolekun, *Politics and Administration in Nigeria* (Ibadan, Nigeria: Spectrum, 1986) 82.
120. Diamond 159.
121. Diamond 121.
122. Okoli 41.
123. The 1979 Presidential Constitution of Nigeria (as does the 1999 Constitution) provides that federal appointments should reflect the ethnic diversity of the nation. See page 64 of Ben. O. Nwabueze's *Nigeria's Presidential Constitution: The Second Experiment in Constitutional Democracy.* Ikeja, Nigeria: Longman, 1985.
124. Dr. Nnamdi Azikiwe, Nigeria's Ceremonial President during the First Republic and member of the NCNC, offers a different reason for his party's alliance with the NPC. Azikiwe holds that the alliance was designed to save the nation from disintegration that would have resulted from an alliance by the two leading Southern political parties.
125. Diamond 57.
126. Okoli 35.
127. Okoli 35.
128. Okoli 4.
129. Diamond 293.
130. Julius O. Ihonvbere & Timothy M. Shaw, *Towards a Political Economy of Nigeria* (Brookfield: Gower, 1988) 76.
131. Ihonvbere & Shaw 76.
132. Ekekwe 97.
133. Ekekwe 97.
134. Ekekwe 115.
135. Awa 266.

136. In fact, in 1960, the Leader of the Opposition in the Nigerian House of Representatives had alleged that Britain had coerced Nigerian leaders at the London Constitutional Conference of 1958 to agree to a Mutual Defense Pact as a condition for granting independence. (Source: Eme O. Awa, *Federal Government in Nigeria*. Berkeley, California: University of California Press, 1964).

137. In 2002, the OAU renamed itself as the African Union (AU), but this African Union still falls short of Nkrumah's dream of a commonwealth of African states.

138. Davidson, *Modern Africa* 209–214.

139. Adamolekun 86.

140. Adamolekun 86.

141. *Nigeria, 1965: Crisis and Criticism* 69.

142. Ake 112.

143. Ake 106.

144. Diamond 11.

145. *Nigeria, 1965: Crisis and Criticism* 5.

146. *Nigeria, 1965: Crisis and Criticism* 69.

147. Adamolekun 87.

148. *The Religion of the Ancient Egyptians* 81.

149. *The Religion of the Ancient Egyptians* 81.

150. Diamond 58.

151. Diamond 112.

152. Diamond 190.

153. The January 15 coup was actually one of two coups that had been planned for that month. After the ill-fated and riotous 1965 regional election in the West, the Nigerian National Alliance (NNA), the ruling party at the center, had planned to precipitate a crisis in the East, which would justify the imposition of a state of emergency there. As part of this plan, Major General Ironsi, the Commanding Officer of the Nigerian Armed Forces, was asked by the Defense Minister, Alhaji Muhammadu Ribadu, to take his accumulated leave. The Inspector General of Police, Mr. Louis Edet, was also ordered to take a leave. A student of the University of Nigeria, Nsukka, Isaac Boro, was given arms and ammunition with which to start an insurrection in the Rivers area of the eastern region. This would have served as a justification for a Federal Government Declaration of a state of emergency in the East. On January 13, 1966, the Premier of the Northern Region, the Sarduana of Sokoto, held a secret meeting with Chief Akintola, the Premier of the Western Region and Brigadier S.O. Ademolegun, who was acting as the GOC of the Nigerian Armed Forces. But the coup of January 15 overtook all those schemes. (Eric Agume Opia, *Why Biafra? Aburi, Prelude to the Biafran Tragedy*. San Rafael, California: Leswing Press, 1972, pp. 61–62).

154. Opia 63.

155. Opia 65.

156. A new example of such a partnership is a political arrangement that was inaugurated in Nigeria on August 27, 1993. A civilian "interim" Head of

State, Ernest Shonekan, was appointed to replace General Ibrahim Babangida who retired from office as from that day. The original plan was for the armed forces to hand over political power to an elected civilian president on August 27, 1993. This did not materialize because ex-military President Babangida had nullified the June 12, 1993 presidential election which would have made the transition possible. Thus, what was put in effect in Nigeria on August 27, 1993 was a new form of military rulership which was led by an appointed civilian puppet. This was the first of its kind in Nigeria's political history.

157. Welch 5.
158. General Ibrahim Badamasi Babangida, "An Address By the President, Commander-in-Chief of the Armed Forces of the Federal Republic of Nigeria, General Ibrahim Badamasi Babangida, CFR, DSS, MSS, FSS mni, To the National Assembly," Abuja, Nigeria, 17 Aug. 1993: 25.
159. Obasanjo, *My Command* 6.
160. Opia 65.
161. Opia 66.
162. Joseph 70.
163. Opia 66.
164. Opia 67.
165. Joseph 70.
166. Clarke 66.
167. A. D. Yahaya, "The Struggle for Power in Nigeria," *Nigerian Government and Politics Under Military Rule, 1966–79*, ed. Oyeleye Oyediran (New York: St. Martin's P, 1979) 264.
168. A. D. Yahaya, "The Struggle for Power in Nigeria," *Nigerian Government and Politics Under Military Rule, 1966–79*, ed. Oyeleye Oyediran (New York: St. Martin's P, 1979) 264.
169. Opia 69.
170. Opia 67.
171. Decalo 21.
172. Nwankwo 41.
173. Currently, Nigeria has 774 local governments.
174. Nigeria now consists of thirty states. Nwankwo's book was published in 1991, and at that time, Nigeria had twenty states.
175. Nwankwo 42.
176. Clarke 61.
177. Clarke 70.
178. Obasanjo 146.
179. *Survey of Nigerian Affairs* 7.
180. Joseph 70.
181. Obasanjo, *My Command* 137.
182. Obasanjo, *My Command* 144.
183. Joseph 71.
184. Lateef Jakande, "The Press and Military Rule," *Nigerian Government & Politics Under Military Rule, 1966–79*, ed. Oyeleye Oyedira (New York: St. Martin's P, 1979) 117.

185. Decalo 21.
186. Joseph 72.
187. Joseph 72.
188. Bolaji A. Akinyemi, a noted Nigerian international studies scholar and one-time Nigerian Foreign Secretary, writes that Gowon "avoided taking decisions on controversial foreign issues until it was clear which way the African majority on that issue was." (Bolaji Akinyemi, "Muhammed/Obasanjo Foreign Policy," *Nigerian Government & Politics Under Military Rule, 1966–79*. Oyeleye Oyediran, ed. New York, N.Y.: St. Martin's Press, Inc., 1979, p. 152.
189. Bolaji A. Akinyemi, "Muhammed/Obasanjo Foreign Policy," *Nigerian Government & Politics Under Military Rule, 1966–79*, ed. Oyeleye Oyediran (New York: St. Martin's P, 1979) 153.
190. Joseph 72.
191. "Connections" is a code term by which Nigerians refer to "who you know." For those Nigerians who subscribe to this viewpoint, "who you know" rather than "what you know" determines access to jobs, contracts, etc. In my opinion, "connections," to the extent that it undermines merit, is anti-thetical to the Maatic philosophy of human existence. However, one recognizes that the perversion of "connections" is not a peculiarity of the Nigerian nation. Here in the United States, one hears the same whispers and even public outcries, from time to time, that "who you know," rather than "what you know" is what gets one access to public power and choicy public appointments.
192. Any one who seeks to bring about social change must exhibit exemplary conduct. Nothing could be as counter-productive as a perception that the men and women in leadership do not practice what they supposedly stand for. One of the factors that enabled Murtala Muhammed to win the loyalty and admiration of Nigerians was that he projected a sense of incorruptibility.
193. *Nigerian Government and Politics* 266.
194. Ogunsanwo 17.
195. Prior to Mohammed's administration, Nigeria had maintained a pro-Western policy of neutrality in Angola under which it sought to "reconcile" the three warring parties—MPLA, FNLA and UNITA. Of the three parties, MPLA was the most Africa-centered. (The policy of neutrality only had the effect of prolonging Portuguese colonial rule by letting "blacks kill blacks.") But Muhammed changed that policy to a pro-MPLA stance, which was in accordance with the wishes of Nigerians at home and abroad. Nigeria, consequently, donated the sum of 13.5 million naira to MPLA (in 1976, this amount would be equivalent to about $17 million dollars) and launched an international campaign which eventually enabled MPLA to obtain the recognition of the Organization of African Unity at an Extraordinary Summit in 1976. See Bolaji A. Akinyemi, "Muhammed/Obasanjo Foreign Policy," *Nigerian Government & Politics Under Military Rule, 1966–79*. Oyeleye Oyediran, ed. New York, N.Y.: St. Martin's Press, 1979, pp. 150–168.

196. Joseph 74.
197. Joseph 72.
198. A.D. Yahaya, "The Struggle for Power in Nigeria, 1966–79," *Nigerian Government & Politics Under Military Rule, 1966–79*, ed. Oyeleye Oyediran (New York: St. Martin's P, 1979) 266.
199. Joseph 72–73.
200. Joseph 75.
201. Lt. General Theophilus Y. Danjuma had played a key role in the assassination of General J.T.U. Aguiyi-Ironsi in 1966. In fact, in a 1992 interview, which was published in *Newswatch*, a Nigerian news magazine, Danjuma stated that he was the one who arrested General Ironsi during the counter-coup of July 1966—an operation which he described as "a revenge coup." By this, he meant that the July strike was designed to avenge the killings of Northern military and civilian leaders during the January 1966 coup. See "Danjuma: Frank to a Fault," *Newswatch*. Nov. 2, 1992, p. 10.
202. "Danjuma On Nigeria" 14.
203. "Danjuma On Nigeria" 14.
204. Joseph 74.
205. Joseph 74.
206. Joseph 74.
207. "Danjuma On Nigeria" 14.
208. Joseph 74.
209. But wide publicity for government actions against corruption can do much more than simply make the government in question "look good." It can help to instill fear in the minds of would-be perpetrators of public corruption.
210. Joseph 75.
211. Joseph 76.
212. Ogunsanwo 19.
213. Joseph 77.
214. Joseph 77.
215. Joseph 77.
216. Ray Ofoegbu, "Foreign Policy and Military Rule," *Nigerian Government & Politics Under Military Rule, 1966–79*, ed. Oyeleye Oyediran (New York: St. Martin's P, 1979) 145.
217. Ofoegbu 145–146.
218. Akinyemi 168.
219. Ogunsanwo 18.
220. Nwabueze 423.
221. Nwabueze 73.
222. Nwabueze 74.
223. It is wrong to suggest that the political parties of the Second Republic were replicas of their predecessors in the First Republic. Even though some parallels exist between the parties of the two political eras, there are notable differences indicative of a shift towards trans-ethnic politics. For instance, while it is true that the National Party of Nigeria (NPN) of the Second Republic (the party that produced the national president) was dominated

by the Hausa/Fulani group like the Northern Peoples Congress (NPC) of the First Republic (the party that produced the prime minister at that time), the NPN had a broader followership than the NPC. Besides those Northern states that it controlled, the NPN also won the governorships of two southern states. This was not the case in the First Republic when the NPC had control of only the Northern Region, in addition to the center. Similarly, the Nigerian Peoples Party (NPP) of the Second Republic (which drew the bulk of its followership from the Igbo ethnic group) was not necessarily a carbon copy of the National Council of Nigerian Citizens (NCNC) of the First Republic (whose membership was predominantly Igbo). The NPP not only controlled the governorships of the two Igbo states during the Second Republic, it also made an in-road into the North where it controlled a state government. The Unity Party of Nigeria (UPN) of the Second Republic also recorded an appreciable difference from the Action Group (AG) of the First Republic even though in both eras the UPN and AG were based largely on Yoruba followership. In the Second Republic, the UPN controlled the five Yoruba states of that time period and a northern state. Thus, in their reincarnations during the Second Republic, these three dominant parties achieved encouraging but not considerable in-roads into the traditional North-South polarity of Nigerian politics. The creation of states, among other factors, must have accounted for this tilt (though a miniscle one) toward trans-ethnic politics.

224. President Shagari had invited all the parties to join him in a government of national unity, but the UPN, the PRP, and the GNPP declined. Only the NPP agreed to form an accord with the president's party.
225. Nwabueze 306.
226. "Danjuma On Nigeria" 17.
227. I covered the national legislature of Nigeria from 1979 to 1983 for the Federal Radio Corporation of Nigeria (FRCN), Lagos, Nigeria.
228. Nwabueze 74.
229. Nwabueze 74.
230. Nwabueze 74–75.
231. Nwabueze 77.
232. Nwabueze 85.
233. Nwabueze 87.
234. During the First Republic, Nigeria had a decentralized police system consisting of the federal police and the local government police. This led to several problems, including charges and counter-charges by politicians about "police bias" during elections. Such was the perception held of the police at this time that the leader of a national party suggested that the army, instead of the police, should be asked to supervise elections in the country. See page 21 of *Nigeria 1965, Crisis and Criticism: Selections From Nigerian Opinion*. Ibadan, Nigeria: Ibadan University Press, 1966.
235. Nwabueze 204.
236. Nwabueze 288.
237. Ogunsanwo 19.

238. *African Alternative Framework to Structural Adjustment Programs for Socio-Economic Recovery and Transformation* (Addis Ababa, Ethiopia: United Nations Economic Commission for Africa, 1991) 34.
239. Nwabueze 423.
240. Nwabueze 377.
241. Nwabueze 325.
242. Nwabueze 374.

NOTES TO CHAPTER SIX

1. I have here and there, deliberately used the term, "tribalism," instead of "ethnicity" in this study because the latter does not adequately capture the gravity and crudity of this social malady.
2. Ekekwe 70.
3. Ekekwe 70.
4. Davidson, *Modern Africa* 198.
5. Davidson, *Modern Africa* 100.
6. "Interview: Adebayo Adedeji" 60.
7. "Interview: Adebayo Adedeji" 60.
8. Rodney 224.
9. Under the 1999 Constitution, this is in force at this time.
10. "Interview: Adebayo Adedeji" 59.
11. "Interview: Adebayo Adedeji" 59.
12. OBEMALA is a term that this writer coined from a sample of three names representing the A Roadmap for Understanding African Politicss of a cross-section of Nigerian traditional rulers. Those three A Roadmap for Understanding African Politicss are: Oba, Emir and Alafin, representing the Oba of Benin, the Emir of Kano and the Alafin of Oyo. OBEMALA was derived by taking the first two letters of Oba and Emir and the first three letters of Alafin.
13. Mbiti 183.
14. Under the present dispensation, the Chief Justice of Nigeria performs this function. This colonially-derived role of the Chief Justice does not and cannot carry the sacred significance and aura of a swearing-in ceremony performed by the Obemala of Nigeria who serves as an intermediary between God, or divinity and human beings. The Obemala, being an embodiment of the constellation of the nation's spiritual and traditional political forces, is better fitted to elicit from a new national leader a commitment to the unalloyed and honest service of the nation. The Obemala, in short, carries greater reverence than a chief justice who lacks a direct connection with the people.
15. Diop, *Pre-Colonial Black Africa* 66.
16. Ake 31.

NOTES TO CHAPTER SEVEN

1. *The Constitution of the Federal Republic of Nigeria (Promulgation Decree) 1989* (Lagos, Nigeria: Federal Government of Nigeria) 99.

2. "The BBC World Service," BBC, London, Gt. Brit., 23 June, 1993.
3. Oyeleye Oyediran, "The Politics of Transition Without End," *Transition Without End: Nigerian Politics and Civil Society Under Babangida*, eds. Larry Diamond, et al (Boulder: Lynne Rienner P, 1997) 1.
4. "The BBC World Service" 23 June 1993.
5. "The BBC World Service" 26 June 1993.
6. *The Constitution of the Federal Republic of Nigeria* Sec. 132(1,2,3&4).
7. "Nigeria: Army Arrangements," *Africa Confidential* 34.13, 2 July 1993: 3.
8. Babangida 25.
9. "The BBC World Service" 21 June 1993.
10. "The BBC World Service" 21 June 1993.
11. "The BBC World Service" 21 June 1993.
12. Obasanjo, "Our Desperate Ways" 4.
13. Babangida, "An Address" 15.
14. Falola & Ohonvbere 219.
15. "The BBC World Report" 10 July 1993.
16. Babangida, "An Address" 27.
17. "Nigeria: Army Arrangements" 1.
18. Abiola eventually died, under circumstances that still remain a mystery, while in political incarceration in Nigeria.
19. "The BBC World Service" 21 June 1993.
20. "The BBC World Service" 10 July 1993.
21. Babangida 29.
22. For details of the effects of SAP on the Nigerian economy, see Anyanwu, John C. "President Babangida's Structural Adjustment Program and Inflation in Nigeria." *Journal of Social Development in Africa.* 7. No. 1 (1992), pp. 5–24.
23. *Africa Research Bulletin* 30.1, 16 Jan.-15 Feb. 1993: 11150.
24. *Africa Research Bulletin* 11137.
25. *African Alternative Framework* 15.
26. African Alternative Framework 15.

NOTES TO CHAPTER EIGHT

1. "First Female President in Africa," *USA-Africa Dialogue, #1323* 10 November 2005. (http://www.utexas.edu/conference/Africa)
2. Ohaegbulam 166–67.
3. *African Alternative Framework* 1.
4. *The Atlas of Africa*, (Paris, France: Jeune Afrique, 1973) 66.

Bibliography

Abo, Klevor. "Defining Democracy." *West Africa* 23–29 Nov. 1992: 2015.

Achebe, Chinua. *The Trouble With Nigeria.* London, England: Heinemann, 1983.

Adedeji, Adebayo. "Ensuring a Successful Transition." *West Africa* 11–17 Nov. 1991: 1878–1880.

African Alternative Framework to Structural Adjustment Programs For Socio-Economic Recovery and Transformation. Addis Ababa, Ethiopia: United Nations Economic Commission For Africa, 1991.

Africa Research Bulletin. 30.1 (1993): 11137–11150.

Ahanotu, Austin M. "The Role of Ethnic Unions in the Development of Southern Nigeria: 1916–66." *Studies in Southern Nigerian History.* Ed. Boniface Obichere. London, Gt. Brit.: Frank, 1982. 155–174.

Aharoni, Yair. *The Foreign Investment Decision Process.* Boston: Harvard University Graduate School of Business, 1966.

Ajayi, J.F.A. *Milestones in Nigerian History.* Ibadan, Nigeria: Ibadan University P, 1962.

Adamokekun, Ladipo. *Politics and Administration in Nigeria.* Ibadan, Nigeria: Spectrum, 1986.

Ake, Claude. *A Theory of Political Integration.* Homewood: the Dorsey P, 1967.

Akinyemi, A. Bolaji. "Muhammed/Obasanjo Foreign Policy." *Nigerian Government and Politics Under Military Rule, 1966–79.* Ed. Oyeleye Oyediran. New York: St. Martin's P, 1979. 150–168.

Aluko, S.A. "How Many Nigerians? An Analysis of Nigeria's Census Problems, 1901–63." *The Journal of Modern African Studies.* 3.3 (1965): 371–92.

Akinnaso, F. Niyi. "One Nation, Four Hundred Languages: Unity and Diversity in Nigeria's Language Policy." *Language Problems and Language Planning.* 13.2 (Summer 1989): 133–146.

———."Toward the Development of a MultiLingual Lnaguage Policy in Nigeria." *Applied Linguistics.* 12.1 (1991): 29–61.

Anyanwu, John C. "President Babangida's Structural Adjustment Program and Inflation." *Journal of Social Development in Africa.* 7.1 (1992): 5–24.

Asante, Molefi K. A Six-State Continent? *African Concord.* 17 Sept., 1987: 16–18.

———. *Afrocentricity.* Trenton: Africa World P, 1989.

————. *Kemet, Afrocentricity and Knowledge.* Trenton: Africa World P, 1990.

Atlas of Africa. Paris, France: Jeune Afrique, 1973: 66.

Awa Eme, O. *Federal Government in Nigeria.* Berkeley: University of California P, 1964.

Awolowo, Obafemi. *The Strategy and Tactics of the Peoples Republic of Nigeria.* London, Eng.: Macmillan, 1970.

Ayeni, Olugbenga. "Transition Setback?" *West Africa.* 26 Oct.-1 Nov. 1992: 1819–1821.

Azikiwe, Nnamdi. *Zik: A Selection from the Speeches of Nnamdi Azikiwe.* Cambridge, Eng.: The Cambridge University P, 1961.

Babangida, Badamasi Ibrahim. "An Address by the President, Commander-in-Chief of the Armed Forces, of the Federal Republic of Nigeria, General Ibrahim Badamasi Babangida, CFR, DSS, MSS, FSSmni, to the National Assembly." Abuja, Nigeria, 17 Aug. 1993.

Babu, Abdur Rahman. "Africa Urged to Adopt Social Economies." *West Africa.* 11–17 Nov. 1991: 1992.

Barbour, K.M., J.S. Oguntoyinbo, J.O.C. Onyemlukwe, and J.C. Nwafor. *Nigeria In Maps.* London, Eng.: Hodder, 1982.

Barrett, Lindsay. "President Babangida Talks to the Soldiers: Back to Base." *West Africa.* 12–18 Feb. 1990: 213–214.

Basi, R.S. *Determinants of United States Private Direct Investment in Foreign Countries.* Kent: Kent State University, 1963.

Bathily, Abdoulaye. "Senegal's Fraudulent 'Democratic Opening.'" *Africa's Crisis.* London, Eng.: Institute for African Alternatives, 1987. 87–95.

"BBC World Reports." BBC. London, Gt. Brit. 21, 23, 26 June & 7 July 1993.

Blondel, Jean. *Political Leadership.* Beverly Hills: Sage, 1987.

Bryant, Coralie, and Louise G. White. *Managing Development in the Third World.* Boulder: Westview P, 1982.

"Burundi, Hell In Bujumbura: An Account of A Coup Against Democracy. *West Africa.* 1–7 Nov. 1993: 1974.

Chanainwa, D. "African Initiatives and Resistance In Southern Africa." *General History of Africa: Africa Under Colonial Domination 1880–1935, Vol. II.* Ed. A.A. Boahen. Berkeley: Heinemann, 1985. 194–220.

Cheru, Fantu. *African Renaissance: Roadmaps to the Challenge of Globalization.* London: Zed Books, 2002.

"Catalogue of Events." *West Africa.* 28 June-4 July 1993: 1080–1081.

Constitution of the Federal Republic of Nigeria (Promulgation Decree). Lagos, Nigeria: Federal Government of Nigeria, 1989.

Constitution of the Federal Republic of Nigeria. Lagos, Nigeria: Federal Government of Nigeria, 1999.

"Country profile: Ivory Coast." BBC News, BBC, Gt. Brit., 5 December, 2005.

"Danjuma On Nigeria." *Newswatch.* 2 Nov. 1992: 13–25.

Davidson, Basil. *Modern Africa.* New York: Longman, 1986.

Davidson, Basil. *African Nationalism and the Problems of Nation-Building.* Lagos, Nigeria: the Nigerian Institute of International Affairs, 1987.

Davidson, Basil. *African Civilization Revisited: from Antiquity to Modern Times.* Trenton: Africa World P, 1991.

Decalo, Samuel. *Coups and Army Rule in Africa: Motivations & Constraints.* New Haven: Yale UP, 1990.

Diamond, Larry. *Class, Ethnicity and Democracy in Nigeria: the Failure of the First Republic.* Syracuse: Syracuse UP, 1988.

Dodge, Dorothy. *African Politics in Perspective.* London, Gt. Brit.: D. Van Nostrand, 1966.

Diop, Cheikh Anta. *The African Origin of Civilization: Myth or Reality.* Trans. Mercer Cook. Westport: Lawrence, 1974.

Diop, Cheikh Anta. *PreColonial Black Africa: A Comparative Study of the Political and Social Systems of Europe and Black Africa, From Antiquity to the Formation of Modern States. (Africa World Press Edition).* Trans. Harold J. Salemson. Westport: Lawrence, 1987.

Drayton, Richard. The wealth of the west was built on Africa's exploitation. USA/ Africa Dialogue, No. 1027. 21 August, 2005.

Elaigwu, Isama J. "Cultural Diversity and the Federal Solution: An African Perspective." Lecture. Temple University, Philadelphia, Fall 1990.

England, Gertie. Ed. *The Religion of the Ancient Egyptians: Cognitive Structures and Popular Expressions (Proceedings of Symposia in Uppsala and Bergen 1987 and 1988).* Stockhold: Tryckeri Balder AB, 1989.

Fajana, M.A., and B.J. Biggs. *Nigeria in History.* Ibadan, Nigeria. Longmans, 1964.

Falola, Toyin, and Julius Ihonvbere. *The Rise and Fall of Nigeria's Second Republic, 1979–84.* Totowa: Ed Books, 1985.

"Freemasons condemn Togo election." BBC. London, Gt. Brit.17 May, 2005.

"First Female President in Africa." *USA-Africa Dialogue, #1323.* 10 November 2005.(http://www.utexas.edu/conference/Africa).

Gavshon, Arthur. *Crisis in Africa: Battleground of East and West.* Middlesex, Eng.: Penguin, 1981.

Gbadegesin, Segun. *The Politicization of Society During Nigeria's Second Republic, 1979–1983.* New York: The Edwin Mellen P, 1991.

Gould, David F. "Political Risk Assessment In the Corporate Planning Environment." *Global Risk Assessments: Issues, Concepts and Applications.* Ed. Jerry Rogers. Riverside: Global Risk Assessment, 1983: 15–25.

Green, Robert T. *Political Instability As a Determinant of U.S. Foreign Investment.* Austin: The University of Texas School of Business, 1972.

Harbeson, John W., ed. *The Military in African Politics.* Westport: Praeger, 1987.

Idowu, Paxton, et al. ""A Bloody Attempt." *West Africa.* 30 April-6 May 1990: 696–697.

Ijagbemi, E.A. "Historical Development 2: Nigeria Since Independence." *Nigeria In Maps.* London, Eng.: Hodder, 1982. 38.

Ihonvbere, Julius O, and Timothy M. Shaw. *Towards A Political Economy of Nigeria.* Brookfield, VT.: Gower Publishing Company, Ltd., 1988.

Jackson, John G. *Introduction to African Civilization.* New York: University Books, 1970.

Jackson, Robert H., and Carl G. Rosberg. *Personal Rule in Black Africa: Prince, Autocrat, Prophet, Tyrant.* Berkeley: University of California P, 1982.

Jakande, Lateef. "The Press and Military Rule." *Nigerian Government and Politics Under Military Rule, 1966–79.* Ed. Oyeleye Oyediran. New York: St. Martin's P, 1979. 110–123.

Joseph, Richard A. "Principles and Practices of Nigerian Military Government." *Military Rule in African Politics.* Ed. John W. Harbeson. Westport: Praeger, 1987. 67–91.

Khalid, Mansour., ed. *Africa Through the Eyes of a Patriot: A Tribute to General Olusegun Obasanjo.* London: Kegan Paul, 2001.

Karenga, Maulana. *Selections From the Husia.* 1984. Los Angeles: The University of Sankore P, 1989.

"Kenya: Failing the Democracy Test." *Africa Confidential.* 34.I (1993): 1–4.

Keita, Lacinary. "The African Philosophical Traditions." *African Philosophy.* Ed. Richard A. Wright. Lanham: UP of America, 1984. 57–76.

Keto, Tsehloane C. *The Africa-Centered Perspective of History.* Blackwood: K.A. Publications, 1989.

——. "The Implications of an Afrocentric World-view for Africa," a Presentation at an African Continental Caucus Lecture Series, Spring, 1991.

——. *Vision and Time: Historical Perspective of an Africa-centered Paradigm.* Lanham: UP of America, 2001.

Kotecha, Ken C. & Adams, Robert W. *African Politics.* Washington, D.C.: UP of America, 1981.

Liebenow, J. Gus. *African Politics: Crisis and Challenges.* Bloomington: Indiana UP, 1986.

Makamure, Kempton. "Contradictions in the Socialist Transformation of Zimbabwe." *Africa's Crisis.* London, Eng.: Institute for African Alternatives, 1987. 69–77.

"Mauritania's ex-leader in Qatar." BBC News. London, Gt. Brit. 22 August, 2005. (http://news.bbc.co.uk/go/pr/fr/-/1/hi/world/africa/4172792.stm).

Mazrui, Ali A. & Tidy, Michael. *Nationalism and New States in Africa.* Portsmouth: Heinemann, 1984.

Mbiti, John S. *African Religions and Philosophy.* 1969. Portsmouth: Heinemann, 1990.

Moyo, Brian. "Nyerere Calls for Equality Between North and South: Economic Disparity Castigated." *West Africa.* 23–29 Nov. 1992: 2016.

National Intelligence Council, "Mapping Sub-Saharan Africa's future." March 2005.

Ndukwu, E.C. "International Financial Organizations and the NIEO." *The Future of Africa and the New International Economic Order.* Eds. Ralp I. Onwuka, and Olajide Aluko. London, Eng.: McMillan, 1986. 132–149.

"Nigeria: Army Arrangments." *Africa Confidential.* 34.13 (1993): 1–3.

"Nigeria: Maradona Plays Into Extra Time." *Africa Confidential.* 34.17 (1993): 7.

Oritsetsaninomi, B.J. ed. *Nigeria: 1965 Crisis & Criticism: Selections From Nigerian Opinion.* Ibadan, Nigeria: Ibadan UP, 1966.

Ottong, J.G. "Population of Nigeria." 2 March, 2006.

"Nigeria Reports It Foiled a Coup By Army Rebels." *The New York Times.* 23 April 1990: A1.

Novicki, Margaret A. "Interview: Adebayo Adedeji." *Africa Report.* Nov./Dec. 1993: 58–60.

Ntalaja, Nzongola. "The Crisis in Zaire," *Africa's Crisis.* London, Eng.: Institute for African Alternatives, 1987. 7–26.

Nwabueze, Ben O. *Nigeria's Presidential Constitution: The Second Experiment in Constitutional Democracy.* Ikeja, Nigeria: Longman, 1985.

Nwankwo, Arthur. *Nigeria: Political Danger Signals, The Politics of Federalism, Census, Blanket Ban and National Integration.* Enugu, Nigeria: Fourth Dimension, 1991.

Obasanjo, Olusegun. *My Command: An Account of the Nigerian Civil War, 1967–70.* London, Eng.: Heinemann, 1980.

Obasanjo, Olusegun. "Our Desperate Ways." *The Nigerian Times.* March 1993: 4.

Ohaegbulam, Festus Ugboaja. *Towards An Understanding of the African Experience: From Historical and Contemporary Perspectives.* New York: UP of America, 1990.

Oguah, Eruku Benjamin. "African and Western Philosophy: A Comparative Study," *African Philosophy.* Ed. Richard A. Wright. Lanham, MD: UP of America, 1984. 213–226.

Ofoegbu, Ray. "Foreign Policy & Military Rule." *Nigerian Government and Politics Under Military Rule, 1966–79.* Ed. Oyeleye Oyediran. New York: St. Martin's P, 1979. 124–149.

Ogunsanwo, Alaba. *The Transformation of Nigeria: Scenarios and Metaphors.* Lagos, Nigeria: University of Lagos P, 1991.

Okafor, Victor. "Afrocentric Theory & Practice: Going Beyond Facades." *The Philadelphia Tribune.* 2 April 1993: 6A.

———. "At&T Cannot Over-Apologize For Truly Racist Cartoon." *The Philadelphia Tribune.* 15 Oct. 1993: 6A.

Okoli, Ekwueme Felix. *Institutional Structure and Conflict in Nigeria.* Washington, D.C.: UP of America, 1980.

Onimode, Bade. "The African Crisis In Nigeria." *Africa's Crisis.* London, Eng.: The Institute For African Alternatives, 1987. 27–35.

Onwudiwe, Ebere. "In Nigeria, Voiceless Victims of Debt." *The New York Times.* 20 April 1990: A33.

Opia, Eric Agume. *Why Biafra? Aburi, Prelude to the Biafran Tragedy.* San Rafael: Leswing P, 1972.

Organization For Economic Co-operation And Development. *International Direct Investment And The New Economic Environment.* Paris, France, OECD, 1989.

Oyediran, Oyeleye. ed. *Survey of Nigerian Affairs.* Ibadan, Nigeria: Oxford UP of Nigeria, 1978.

Oyediran, Oyeleye. "The Politics of Transition Without End," *Transition Without End: Nigerian Politics and Civil Society Under Babangida.* Eds. Larry Diamond, et al. Boulder: Lynne Rienner P, 1997. 1–30.

Rodney, Walter. *How Europe Underdeveloped Africa.* 1972. Washington, D.C.: Howard UP, 1982.

"Rwanda: How the Genocide Happened." BBC News. London, Gt. Brit. 1 April, 2004.

Somide, Adegboyega. "Federalism, State Creation and Ethnic Management in Nigeria." *Problems and Prospects of Sustaining Democracy in Nigeria*. Ed. Bamidele Ojo. Huntington: Nova Science Publishers, 2001. 19–36.

Thiong'O, Wa Ngugi. *Moving the Center: The Struggle for Cultural Freedoms*. Portsmouth: Heinemann, 1993.

"Togolese protest over new leader." BBC. London, Gt. Brit. (http://news.bbc.co.uk/go/pr/fr/-/1/hi/world/africa/4245861.stm).

Walton, Hanes., and Robert C. Smith. *American Politics and the African American Quest for Universal Freedom*. New York: Longman, 2000.

Welch, Jr., Claude E. ed. *Civilian Control of the Military: Theory and Cases From Developing Countries*. Albany: State University of New York P, 1976.

World Almanac and Book of Facts. Ed. Mark S. Hoffman. New York: World Almanac, 1993.

Wright, A. Richard. "Investigating African Philosophy." *African Philosophy*. Ed. Richard A. Wright. Lanham, MD.: UP of America, 1984. 41–55.

Yahaya, A.D. "The Struggle for Power in Nigeria, 1966–79." *Nigerian Government and Politics Under Military Rule, 1966–79*. Ed. Oyeleye Oyediran. New York: St. Martin's P, 1979. 259–275.

Index

Printed in the United States
114779LV00002B/169-174/P

9 780415 981064